The Opening
of the Eyes

The
Opening
of the Eyes

DAISAKU IKEDA

World Tribune
Press

Published by

World Tribune Press
606 Wilshire Blvd.
Santa Monica, CA 90401

Design by Lightbourne, Inc.
Source artwork: www.istockphoto.com

ISBN 978-1-935523-34-5

24 23 22 21 20   4 5 6 7 8

Contents

Editor's Note

This series of lectures by SGI President Ikeda were published in SGI-USA's *Living Buddhism* from the November 2004 issue to the April 2005 issue, the June 2005 issue to the December 2005 issue and the January–February 2006 issue to the July–August 2006 issue.

Please also see *The Writings of Nichiren Daishonin*, vol. 1, pp. 220–98, for "The Opening of the Eyes."

- GZ, page number(s)—refers to the *Gosho zenshu*, the Japanese-language compilation of letters, treatises, essays and oral teachings of Nichiren Daishonin.

- LSOC, page number(s)—refers to *The Lotus Sutra and Its Opening and Closing Sutras*, translated by Burton Watson (Tokyo: Soka Gakkai, 2009).

- OTT, page number(s)—refers to *The Record of the Orally Transmitted Teachings*, translated by Burton Watson (Soka Gakkai: Tokyo, 2004).

- WND, page number(s)—refers to *The Writings of Nichiren Daishonin*, vol. 1 (WND-1) (Tokyo: Soka Gakkai, 1999) and vol. 2 (WND-2) (Tokyo: Soka Gakkai, 2006).

Preface

"Opening of the Eyes"—A Call To Open Our Eyes to Nichiren, To Open Our Eyes to the People

Religion is the pillar of humanity. Philosophy is the backbone of life.

The Soka Gakkai has advanced based on the strength of its members' solid grounding in Buddhist study, a pursuit that can be likened to the rigorous training of a master swordsman. Opening the pages of Nichiren Daishonin's writings with the spirit of receiving direct instruction and guidance from the Daishonin himself, members everywhere have deepened their understanding of faith, practice and study; summoned forth courage; and emerged victorious in their struggles for kosen-rufu. When we advance with Nichiren's writings as our foundation, we will never be deadlocked.

The lectures I received in my youth from my mentor, second Soka Gakkai president Josei Toda, continue to resonate vibrantly in my heart even now. His lectures covered such topics as life, happiness, government, culture, peace, human integrity, the principles of organization and the mentor-disciple relationship. His free and far-reaching discourses truly revived Nichiren Buddhism in the present age—and, more specifically, in people's actual lives and in society.

Above all, based on Nichiren's writings, President Toda called on people to stand up as Bodhisattvas of the Earth and work for the genuine welfare and prosperity of their country. His compassionate guidance and encouragement awakened a sense of courage and mission in the depths of their lives. I am firmly convinced that in the seven hundred years following the Daishonin's death, no one had ever read his writings from the perspective that all people are Bodhisattvas of the Earth. President Toda, however, lectured on the Daishonin's teachings based on his own inner awareness and sense of mission as a Bodhisattva of the Earth, which he gained as a result of his spiritual awakening in prison during World War II.

It goes without saying that President Toda's lectures also played a pivotal and decisive role in my own life. In fact, my first fateful encounter with my mentor (on August 14, 1947) took place during one of his lectures on the Daishonin's treatise "On Establishing the

Correct Teaching for the Peace of the Land." After joining the Soka Gakkai, I attended his lectures on the Lotus Sutra, and later I was able to have early-morning study sessions with him, during which he discussed the profound philosophy and principles of Nichiren Buddhism. President Toda was truly a master in giving lectures. I was so impressed that I remember thinking, *There are three kinds of lectures: unskilled, skilled and artistic—Mr. Toda's belonged to the last category.* As President Toda's disciple, I also exerted myself on the front lines by giving lectures and striving to convey the greatness of Nichiren Buddhism to as many people as possible.

Like a lion's roar, the truth and justice of Nichiren Daishonin is a powerful force for defeating the devilish nature inherent in human life. The reverberations of his invincible life force that surmounted successive major persecutions impart courage, hope, confidence and joy to those challenging painful obstacles and hardships. His words of profound contemplation and introspection teach us the correct path of kosen-rufu and life. For that reason, making his writings our foundation is also the correct path leading to victory both in life and in our struggle for kosen-rufu.

We of the SGI aspire to make the twenty-first century an age of the victory of the people, the victory of youth and the victory of humanity. Now, more than ever before, people around the world are searching for a humanistic religion. Out of the hope that it may serve as a key for ushering in such an age and become a source of inspiration and growth for my fellow SGI members everywhere, I have decided to embark on a new series of lectures on "The Opening of the Eyes," an important writing embodying the great lion's roar of the Daishonin. Toward realizing a century of life and a century of humanity, I would like to discuss the essence of Nichiren Buddhism and the steadfast commitment of the SGI, an organization that has inherited the true spirit of the Daishonin. I would also like to leave behind a solid spiritual foundation for the SGI of the future.

Philosophy is what empowers our struggle to be victorious in life. All of you who are earnestly studying and internalizing Nichiren Buddhism, an extremely lofty and profound practical philosophy, are certain to become eternal "doctors of philosophy." I began this series of lectures with the ardent prayer that each of you will illuminate the deepening darkness of modern society with the brilliant light of the Daishonin's writings—the eternally treasured teachings of hope—and develop into courageous people of philosophy who will build a century of humanity.

DAISAKU IKEDA
November 18, 2006

Introduction

The central theme of Nichiren Daishonin's lengthy two-part treatise, "The Opening of the Eyes," can indeed be summed up in the short phrase *opening the eyes*.

While the Daishonin's original text of this writing is not extant, there is a record indicating that it consisted of a total of sixty-six pages: sixty-five sheets of paper for the body of the work and one sheet of paper on which the Daishonin himself had written "The Opening of the Eyes" as the title page.[1]

"Opening the eyes" means exactly that: "to open the eyes." It can also be read as the Daishonin's call: "Open your eyes!"

How can we open the closed eyes of people's hearts? With what light can we illuminate the darkness of ignorance?[2] It is Nichiren Daishonin, the Buddha of the Latter Day of the Law, who opened a path to answer these questions.

The flame of Nichiren's struggle as the votary of the Lotus Sutra—a struggle aimed at leading humanity to enlightenment and actualizing the principle of "establishing the correct teaching for the peace of the land" while battling against all manner of devilish functions—only burned even more brightly when he was exiled to snowbound Sado Island. We can discern his unyielding resolve

Nichiren Daishonin's Writing Paper

"The Opening of the Eyes" was written on sixty-five sheets of handmade Japanese paper. Unfortunately, because the original manuscript was lost when a great fire raged through Minobu in 1875, there is no way to confirm exactly which kind or size of paper it was written on.

Being exiled on Sado Island obviously made it difficult for the Daishonin to procure paper, as he confirms when he writes, "There is very little writing paper here in the province of Sado" ("Letter from Sado," WND-1, 306). How, then, did he obtain sufficient paper to write "The Opening of the Eyes" and other treatises and letters while in exile?

Historians speculate that, while he was staying at Echi* immediately after the Tatsunokuchi Persecution (in September 1271, which was followed by his exile to Sado at the end of October), his disciples may have prepared a supply of paper for him, or that paper may have been among the offerings made to him by his followers. It is also thought that the disciples who accompanied him to Sado may have brought a large quantity of paper along with them.

3

Using this paper, Nichiren continued writing at a furious pace even in the midst of great persecution. While in Echi, he sent numerous letters to those followers who were imprisoned in the aftermath of his arrest, as well as to Toki Jonin, Shijo Kingo, Ota Jomyo and others. And during the journey from Echi to Sado and immediately after his arrival at Sado, he not only wrote a steady stream of letters to his followers, but also composed the treatise "The Opening of the Eyes." The voluminous body of letters and treatises he produced during that period attests to his strenuous and unremitting effort to encourage his followers.

* Echi: A fief held by Homma Rokuro Saemon, the deputy constable of Sado Island. It was located in what is now Atsugi City in Kanagawa Prefecture, adjacent to Tokyo. After the Tatsunokuchi Persecution, which occurred on September 12, 1271, Nichiren was held in custody at Homma's residence at Echi before being taken to exile on Sado on October 10, arriving there on October 28.

from the following well-known passage of "The Opening of the Eyes": "This I will state. Let the gods forsake me. Let all persecutions assail me. Still I will give my life for the sake of the Law . . . Here I will make a great vow . . . I will be the pillar of Japan. I will be the eyes of Japan. I will be the great ship of Japan. This is my vow, and I will never forsake it!" (WND-1, 280–81).

From the standpoint of society, he was an exile. Though he was the victim of persecution by the powerful and was innocent of the charges brought against him, he found himself sentenced to exile, a penalty second in severity only to execution,[3] and placed in a veritable prison of nature. As was to be expected, however, no chains of any form could ever shackle his spirit.

Throughout the pages of human history, there are many wise people and sages who bravely endured attack and oppression. The Daishonin stands out among them for having declared his intent to save all humankind and secured the path to do so while exiled under the harshest of conditions. "I will be the pillar of Japan," he cried invincibly. No persecution or devilish force could hinder the Daishonin, who had stood up to fulfill his vow to lead all people to enlightenment.

A person awakened to the inherent Law of life can truly become a colossus of the noblest human spirit.

Nichiren Buddhism is a "religion for all human beings." It was Nichiren who firmly established the great path of the "human religion" elucidated in the Lotus Sutra, the essence of Mahayana Buddhism, and who left behind the means for all people to realize genuine happiness and lasting peace.

The Daishonin is truly the "pillar," the "eyes" and the "great ship" of all humankind. However, the befuddled rulers of Japan of his day, as well as perverse and fawning priests dwelling in the world of animals,[4] tried to topple this pillar.

Writing in the Midst of Extreme Conditions

In another writing, "The Actions of the Votary of the Lotus Sutra," Nichiren Daishonin gives a detailed account of how he came to compose "The Opening of the Eyes": "After everyone had gone [following the Tsukahara Debate,[5] held in January 1272, on Sado], I began to put into shape a work in two volumes called *The Opening of the Eyes*, which I had been working on since the eleventh month of the previous year.[6] I wanted to record the wonder of Nichiren, in case I should be beheaded. The essential message in this work is that the destiny of Japan depends solely upon Nichiren. A house without pillars collapses, and a person without a soul is dead. Nichiren is the soul of the people of this country. Hei no Saemon has already toppled the pillar of Japan, and the country grows turbulent as unfounded rumors and speculation rise up like phantoms to cause dissention in the ruling clan. Further, Japan is about to be attacked by a foreign country, as I described in my *On Establishing the Correct Teaching*. Having written to this effect [in *The Opening of the Eyes*], I entrusted the manuscript to Nakatsukasa Saburo Saemon-no-jo's [Shijo Kingo's] messenger" (WND-1, 772).

In this passage, the Daishonin recalls his sentiments in writing "The Opening of the Eyes," which he completed in February 1272. He begins by saying that he started planning the treatise in November 1271, immediately after arriving on Sado on October 28.

Nichiren reached Tsukahara on Sado on November 1, amid extremely frigid temperatures. The place where he initially stayed was a dilapidated shrine called the Sammai-do, in the middle of a graveyard. He writes that "it stood on some land where corpses were abandoned" ("The Actions of the Votary of the Lotus Sutra," WND-1, 769). It was a tiny structure consisting of a single room with four posts. No statues of the Buddha were enshrined there; the boards of the roof did not

Shijo Kingo

While "The Opening of the Eyes" was addressed to all of Nichiren Daishonin's followers, it was specifically sent to Shijo Kingo. This is also evident from such statements relating to this treatise as: "I entrusted the manuscript to Nakatsukasa Saburo Saemon-no-jo's [Shijo Kingo's] messenger" ("The Actions of the Votary of the Lotus Sutra," WND-1, 772), and "As for matters of doctrine, I have discussed them in the work that I sent earlier to Shijo Saburo Saemon-no-jo [Shijo Kingo]. You should read that work very, very carefully" ("Why No Protection from the Heavenly Gods?," WND-2, 432).

In fact, a messenger, dispatched with various offerings by Shijo Kingo out of concern for Nichiren's welfare, visited Sado Island in February 1272. Nichiren apparently had this messenger deliver the treatise to Shijo Kingo, with the understanding that the latter would ensure that it was read by all his followers in Kamakura.

The Daishonin held Shijo Kingo in the highest esteem for having accompanied him at the time of the Tatsunokuchi Persecution, ready to die at his side. He writes in famous praise of his disciple's action: "In what lifetime could I possibly forget it?" ("The Place of the Cluster of Blessings," WND-1, 1069), and "This can only be called wondrous" ("The Persecution at Tatsunokuchi," WND-1, 196). It is not difficult to imagine, therefore, that Shijo Kingo was chosen as the recipient of "The Opening of the Eyes," because he was not only one of the leading followers in Kamakura but also a disciple who embodied the spirit of not begrudging one's life for the sake of the Law.*

In "The Opening of the Eyes," Nichiren states that he is writing this treatise to send to his "close disciples" as a "keepsake" from him (see WND-1, 269), and stresses the importance of reading it based on faith that is infused with a spirit of selfless dedication to Buddhism.

*"Not begrudging one's life" means not sparing even our own lives in seeking to spread the Mystic Law and to pursue Buddhism. This phrase appears in "Encouraging Devotion," the 13th chapter, and elsewhere in the Lotus Sutra.

meet, and the walls were full of holes. It was little more than a deserted shack.

In an extreme environment where icy winds blew mercilessly and snow piled high, he placed fur skins on the floor to lie or sit on and spent his days and nights wrapped in a straw coat. In addition to the freezing northern winter to which he was unaccustomed, he also faced a shortage of food provisions. As a result, during November, he sent back some of the young disciples who had accompanied him.

"It is impossible to describe these matters in writing" ("Aspiration for the Buddha Land," WND-1, 214), the Daishonin says, referring to the deplorable conditions that confronted him on Sado. He admits to feeling as though he had passed through the realm of hungry spirits and fallen alive into one of the eight cold hells[7] (see "Letter to Horen," WND-1, 519). He also observes: "Exiles to this island seldom manage to survive. Even if they do, they never return home. So no one is going to be punished for killing an exile"

("The Actions of the Votary of the Lotus Sutra," WND-1, 771).

In such a perilous environment, Nichiren immersed himself deep in thought and composed an important work for the enlightenment of humankind. Over the course of approximately three months, he planned out and wrote this treatise, which, in terms of current Japanese standard, four hundred-character manuscript pages, comes to more than one hundred pages in length. After arriving on Sado, he set to work right away on this task to lead all people to Buddhahood.

Discussing the Daishonin's spiritual state while on Sado, President Toda once remarked: "Buddhahood is a state of absolute happiness. A state of being that at each moment is like a translucent ocean or a cloudless sky, utterly invincible and fearless—this is how I perceive the Daishonin's state of life during his exile on Sado.

"When the Daishonin says, 'Sacrificing your life for the Lotus Sutra is like exchanging rocks for gold or dung for rice' ("The Actions of the Votary of the Lotus Sutra," WND-1, 764), and 'For what I have done, I have been condemned to exile, but it is a small suffering to undergo in this present life and not one worth lamenting. In future lives I will enjoy immense happiness, a thought that gives me great joy' ("The Opening of the Eyes," WND-1, 287), I keenly feel that this portrays the state of life of the Buddha of the Latter Day."[8]

In fact, while living under conditions of indescribable hardship, Nichiren earnestly pondered the question of how he could enable all people to attain Buddhahood; and he clearly constructed the means for achieving this goal by writing "The Opening of the Eyes" and "The Object of Devotion for Observing the Mind." As I have said, what sets the Daishonin apart in greatness from countless other historic figures who have endured persecution is that he, amid extreme difficulties, laid a solid foundation to thoroughly secure the path for the enlightenment of all humanity.

"The Opening of the Eyes" Was Written After Nichiren Revealed His True Identity

In the passage from "The Actions of the Votary of the Lotus Sutra" that I cited earlier, Nichiren says that his purpose in writing "The Opening of the Eyes" was to leave a record for posterity of the "wonder of Nichiren." We can surmise that the greatest "wonder of Nichiren" that he seeks to record here is his casting off his transient status and revealing his true identity at the time of the Tatsunokuchi Persecution.

On the occasion of his near-execution at Tatsunokuchi, the Daishonin discarded his transient aspect as "an ordinary person at the stage of hearing the name and words of the truth" (that is, someone who has taken faith in the Lotus Sutra) and revealed his true state of life as "the Buddha of limitless joy enlightened from time without beginning," a state of complete freedom that is at one with the eternal Mystic Law.

As a result of the Daishonin casting off the transient and revealing the true, the path to attaining enlightenment in one's present form—whereby we can manifest Buddhahood

in our ordinary mortal lives, just as we are—was opened to all people.

As he describes in detail in "The Opening of the Eyes," he won this fundamental victory of life—the victory of casting off the transient and revealing the true—in the course of his relentless struggle to surmount persecution after persecution and triumph over all obstacles. In the same way, when we maintain courageous faith, unafraid of any obstacles, then, no matter what happens, we, too, can defeat the darkness of ignorance and establish a self that manifests our enlightened Dharma nature.[9] This is how we cast off our own transient aspect and reveal our true selves. Casting off the transient and revealing the true is essential to our attainment of Buddhahood in this lifetime.

As Nichiren indicates when he says, "Here a single individual has been used as an example, but the same thing applies equally to all living beings" ("The Unanimous Declaration by the Buddhas," WND-2, 844), his casting off the transient and revealing the true elucidates the basic principle for attaining Buddhahood that applies to all people of the Latter Day of the Law; it is also proof of this principle and an example for others.

All people, if they possess unwavering faith in the Mystic Law, can develop a state of being as vast as the universe in their flesh-and-blood lives as ordinary people. You could say that Nichiren Daishonin was the very first person to demonstrate the truth that all people of the Latter Day could cast off the transient and reveal the true. To verify his casting off the transient and revealing the true and to provide a "clear mirror" or means so that others could do the same, Nichiren manifested the Gohonzon in a concrete graphic form.

The Daishonin is truly the pillar of all humankind, because his example of discarding the transient and revealing the true makes it possible for all people to bring forth their own inherent Buddha nature. Herein lies the most profound significance of his assertions that "the destiny of Japan depends solely upon Nichiren," and "Nichiren is the soul of the people of this country" ("The Actions of the Votary of the Lotus Sutra," WND-1, 772).

Opening the eyes is thus also a call "to open your eyes to Nichiren."

Opening Our Eyes to the Spirit of "Not Begrudging One's Life"

Opening our eyes to Nichiren means opening our eyes to the votary of the Lotus Sutra and, therefore, also opening our eyes to the Lotus Sutra. In this way, multiple meanings apply to the phrase *opening the eyes*, as is evident in various passages in "The Opening of the Eyes." I would now like to cite a number of specific passages where the Daishonin in effect urges us: "Open your eyes to Nichiren."

First of all, there is the well-known passage I quoted earlier that alerts us to open our eyes to the Daishonin's casting off the transient and revealing the true: "On the twelfth day of the ninth month of last year [1271], between the hours of the rat and the ox (11:00 P.M. to 3:00 A.M.), this person named Nichiren was beheaded. It is his soul that has come to this island of Sado and, in the second month of the following year, snowbound, is writing this to send to his close disciples. [The

description of the evil age in the "Encouraging Devotion" chapter seems] terrible, but [one who cares nothing about oneself for the sake of the Law has] nothing to be frightened about" (WND-1, 269).

Indeed, in this passage he is saying, "Open your eyes to the 'soul' of Nichiren." He essentially declares: "The ordinary person Nichiren was beheaded at Tatsunokuchi. It is the 'soul' of Nichiren that is now writing 'The Opening of the Eyes' on Sado." "Soul," here, refers of course to the "Buddha of limitless joy enlightened since time without beginning" that is the true identity revealed by Nichiren when he cast off his transient status.

Here, I would like to focus on the fact that, in terms of the overall structure of "The Opening of the Eyes," this passage comes right at the start of the section where the Daishonin explains how he read the Lotus Sutra with his life, especially "Encouraging Devotion," the 13th chapter. In this passage, he declares that no matter how fearful the descriptions in the "Encouraging Devotion" chapter of the ways that the three powerful enemies will persecute the practitioners of the correct teaching, these things are not in the least frightening to the soul of Nichiren. In this way, he shows us a glimpse of the vast and fearless state of the Buddha of limitless joy enlightened since time without beginning.

The "Encouraging Devotion" chapter details the terrible persecutions that will befall the votaries of the Lotus Sutra in the evil age after the Buddha's passing, describing, for example, how the three powerful enemies will incite the secular authorities to repress the votaries. There is also a scene where a multitude of bodhisattvas numbering "eight hundred thousand million *nayutas*[10]" make a vow to struggle with the spirit of not begrudging their lives when encountering such life-threatening persecutions. The "Encouraging Devotion" chapter contains the lines, "We care nothing for our bodies or lives / but are anxious only for the unsurpassed way" (LSOC, 233). It expounds that the intrepid spirit of not begrudging one's life and seeking solely to enable all people to enter the unsurpassed way to Buddhahood is a fundamental requisite of bodhisattvas.

In "Letter from Sado," which was written around the same time as "The Opening of the Eyes," Nichiren asserts that when evil priests seeking fame or profit conspire with ignorant officials to unjustly attack the votary of the Lotus Sutra, those with the selfless "heart of a lion king" can attain Buddhahood (see WND-1, 302).

Accordingly, we can read the phrase *opening the eyes* as including the meaning: "Open your eyes to Nichiren's spirit of not begrudging his life."

The Teacher of the Latter Day Is a Person Who Thoroughly Battles All Obstacles and Devilish Forces

Next, I would like to read the passage in which Nichiren states his conclusion after discussing in detail how the persecutions he has encountered mirror the persecutions by the three powerful enemies described in the "Encouraging Devotion" chapter. In this passage, too, we can discern the meaning, "Open your eyes to Nichiren": "The Buddha and Devadatta[11] are like a form and its shadow—in lifetime after lifetime, they are never separated. Prince Shotoku and his archenemy Moriya[12] appeared at the same time, like the blossom and the calyx of the lotus.[13] If there exists a votary of the Lotus Sutra, then the three types of enemies are bound to exist as well. The three types of enemies have already appeared. Who, then, is the votary of the Lotus Sutra? Let us seek him out and make him our teacher. [As the Lotus Sutra says, to find such a person is as rare as for] a one eyed-turtle to chance upon a piece of driftwood [with a hole just the right size to hold him]"[14] (WND-1, 278).

"Let us seek him out and make him our teacher," Nichiren says. His conclusion is that the votary of the Lotus Sutra who struggles dauntlessly against the three powerful enemies is the correct teacher who will lead the people of the Latter Day to enlightenment. Only someone able to battle all obstacles and devilish forces can be regarded as the teacher of the Latter Day of the Law.

As the Daishonin indicates when he says, "If they [devils] did not [arise], there would be no way of knowing that this is the correct teaching" ("Letter to the Brothers," WND-1, 501), those who rigorously uphold and practice the correct teaching in this evil latter age will be assailed by storms of obstacles and devilish functions without fail.

The only way to liberate the people of the Latter Day of the Law from fundamental suffering is to firmly establish the means by which the Buddha nature inherent in all human beings can be manifested in each individual's life and in society. This great path can be opened only by those who are able to establish the deep, strong faith necessary to defeat the fundamental darkness[15] inherent in human life. That is because all obstacles and devilish functions are in essence manifestations of fundamental darkness. A teaching that does not indicate the importance of battling fundamental darkness cannot be called the correct teaching for the Latter Day of the Law, nor can a person espousing such a teaching be regarded as the teacher of the Latter Day of the Law.

Fundamental darkness originally referred to the fundamental delusion or doubt toward the Mystic Law that assails bodhisattvas who have advanced to the final stage of practice. Even bodhisattvas at the stage of near-perfect enlightenment could stray from the correct path on account of this illusion or doubt.

The Latter Day, during which the Buddha predicts "the pure Law will become obscured and lost,"[16] is indeed a time when the correct teaching is obscured and evil intensifies. Battling fundamental darkness is an indispensable part of practicing the correct teaching in this latter age. Hence in "The Opening of the Eyes," Nichiren emphasizes two points.

First of all, through the fivefold comparison,[17] he clarifies what is the correct teaching of the Latter Day of the Law. The correct teaching is the doctrine of "three thousand realms in a single moment of life" hidden in the depths of the Lotus Sutra and the doctrine of "the original cause and original effect" expounded in the "Life Span" chapter of the Lotus Sutra's essential teaching. Expressed more simply, it is the principle of the "true mutual possession of the Ten Worlds" (WND-1, 235), whereby in defeating our fundamental darkness through pure and strong faith, we can bring the eternal state of the world of Buddhahood to manifest in the other nine worlds within our lives. This is the teaching that enables us to reveal the world of Buddhahood within our other nine worlds and realize the "attainment of Buddhahood in our present form" and the "attainment of Buddhahood in this lifetime." This alone is the correct teaching of the Latter Day.

Secondly, he emphasizes the importance of making and maintaining a vow. The correct teaching of the Latter Day hidden in the depths of the "Life Span" chapter of the essential teaching of the Lotus Sutra is "difficult to believe and difficult to understand" ("The Object of Devotion for Observing the Mind," WND-1, 356). However, by making the Buddha's great wish for the enlightenment of all people our own and vowing to undertake the struggle for kosen-rufu with a steadfast, unremitting spirit, we can forge and strengthen our faith. And it is none other than Nichiren, who cast off his transient status and established the great teaching for the enlightenment of all people in this defiled age, who is the teacher of the Latter Day of the Law and the Buddha of the Latter Day of the Law.

While I already quoted the passage indicating the Daishonin's vow at the start of my lecture, I would like to cite it here again more fully: "This I will state. Let the gods forsake me. Let all persecutions assail me. Still I will give my life for the sake of the Law . . . Whatever obstacles I might encounter, so long as persons of wisdom do not prove my teachings to be false, I will never yield! All other troubles are no more to me than dust before the wind.

"I will be the pillar of Japan. I will be the eyes of Japan. I will be the great ship of Japan. This is my vow, and I will never forsake it!" (WND-1, 280–81).

The above two points—the clarification of the correct teaching and the importance of making a vow—comprise the backbone of "The Opening of the Eyes." I will discuss them in more detail later during the course of these lectures.

Opening Our Eyes to Nichiren's Perseverance and Compassion

I would like to quote another related passage: "When it comes to understanding the Lotus Sutra, I have only a minute fraction of the vast ability that T'ien-t'ai and Dengyo[18] possessed. But as regards my ability to endure persecution and the wealth of my compassion for others, I believe they would hold me in awe" (WND-1, 242).

We can also interpret this passage, which so many of us have engraved in our hearts, as the call "to open your eyes to Nichiren."

Here, Nichiren humbly states that his understanding of the Lotus Sutra is inferior to that of T'ien-t'ai and Dengyo, but in "The Opening of the Eyes," as I noted earlier, he reveals the supreme wisdom to grasp the essential Law that enables all people of the Latter Day to attain enlightenment. This essential Law is the ultimate teaching for actualizing the mutual possession of the Ten Worlds and manifesting the world of Buddhahood in one's own life. While explaining this teaching is itself difficult, sharing it with others and enabling them to demonstrate it in their own lives are even more so.

What we have, then, is a struggle that no one had ever undertaken before: an evil age, the difficult-to-believe essential Law, and

an ordinary person who was determined to propagate that Law. It was inevitable therefore that persecution would follow. Nichiren, while enduring one intense persecution after another, revealed the world of Buddhahood in his own life as an ordinary human being. He offered his own life and practice as an example, and established the means by which to spread this essential Law to all people.

The driving force that enabled him to carry through and complete this struggle was his vow and, on an even deeper level, his boundless compassion for all living beings. It is because of this immense compassion that we regard the Daishonin as the Buddha of the Latter Day.

Nichiren himself indicates that compassion lies at the very heart of *shakubuku*, the struggle to propagate the correct teaching in order to liberate people from fundamental suffering. He thus declares, "I, Nichiren, am sovereign, teacher, and father and mother to all the people of Japan" (WND-1, 287). This is the conclusion of "The Opening of the Eyes," and also a call urging us "to open your eyes to Nichiren's compassion."

Quoting one of the passages I have just cited, President Toda maintained that striving to help people attain enlightenment and to realize a fundamental inner transformation in the lives of all humankind represents the Buddha's work, and he called on his fellow members to devote themselves to this challenge: "Enabling all people to become Buddhas, elevating the character of all people to something of supreme value—this is what it means to carry out 'the Thus Come One's work' (see LSOC, 202).

"In 'The Opening of the Eyes,' the Daishonin writes: 'When it comes to understanding the Lotus Sutra, I have only a minute fraction of the vast ability that T'ien-t'ai and Dengyo possessed. But as regards my ability to endure persecution and the wealth of my compassion for others, I believe they would hold me in awe' (WND-1, 242). The profound meaning behind this passage is the Daishonin's commitment—to which he gave his entire life—to make it possible for all human beings to attain Buddhahood. This is a vivid example of 'the Thus Come One's work.' My fellow members of the Soka Gakkai, we, too, must carry out this work. How, then, should we strive to enable all people to obtain the state of Buddhahood?"[19]

With his vision of universal enlightenment and the inner transformation of all humankind, Nichiren brought forth the "power of endurance in the face of persecution" and the "power of compassion" in order to establish and propagate the entity of the Law. Inheriting Nichiren's spirit, the Soka Gakkai has—since the time of first president Tsunesaburo Makiguchi—embraced Nichiren Buddhism as the teaching for transforming reality and energetically advanced the struggle to lead humankind toward genuine happiness.

Compassion and Trust for the People Are the Foundation

We can thus identify a variety of meanings for the phrase *opening the eyes* of the writing's title, but "open your eyes to Nichiren" seems to be the key message. This call is based on a spirit of compassion and trust for the people. It could also be expressed as "open your eyes to the people."

Nichiren Buddhism is the "Buddhism of the oneness of mentor and disciple." Through his own life, Nichiren established the path by which ordinary people of the Latter Day could attain Buddhahood in their present form, and he taught that path to his disciples. He says: "Although I and my disciples may encounter various difficulties, if we do not harbor doubts in our hearts, we will as a matter of course attain Buddhahood. Do not have doubts simply because heaven does not lend you protection. Do not be discouraged because you do not enjoy an easy and secure existence in this life. This is what I have taught my disciples morning and evening, and yet they begin to harbor doubts and abandon their faith.

"Foolish men are likely to forget the promises they have made when the crucial moment comes" (WND-1, 283).

The implication here is that the path of the oneness of mentor and disciple of Nichiren and his followers comes into being when both have faith that is free of doubt[20] and infused with the spirit of not begrudging one's life. Faith as conceived by Nichiren precludes doubt [toward the power of the Mystic Law]. Therefore, it is only natural that our Buddhist practice includes actively battling the devilish nature inherent in life, as well as external obstacles and devilish functions that act as negative influences.

And he assures us that if we join him in this struggle, we will realize the fruit, or effect, of attaining Buddhahood without fail. This is because anyone can become one with the Daishonin in terms of his "practices and the virtues he consequently attained" ("The Object of Devotion for Observing the Mind," WND-1, 365)—that is, the cause and effect of his enlightenment. This means that the call "to open your eyes to Nichiren," which runs throughout this writing, is in fact based on a foundation of deep confidence in and respect for human beings.

I would like to clearly state, therefore, that the significance of opening the eyes in this treatise, in addition to its call "to open your eyes to Nichiren," lies in its fervent exhortations: "Open your eyes to the human being," and "Open your eyes to the people."

A Movement That Seeks To Enable All To Reveal Their Buddha Nature

Essentially, then, to correctly read "The Opening of the Eyes" is to recognize Nichiren Daishonin as our model for attaining Buddhahood in the Latter Day and as the lord of the teaching of the Latter Day of the Law who established the path for attaining Buddhahood. Also, from the perspective of the "Buddhism of the people" hidden in the depths of the Lotus Sutra, it could be said that to read "The Opening of the Eyes" is to base oneself on a profound respect and trust for human beings.

When viewed in this way, where can we find a person who has truly read this treatise correctly? I feel sure that President Toda's wisdom and perceptive insights will shine brightly once again in that regard. In concluding the first lecture in this series, I would like to introduce another quote by my mentor: "When reading the Daishonin's writings, even more than trying to understand the meaning of his words, I seek to come into contact with the Buddha's immense compassion, his towering conviction, his ardent spirit to protect and save the people, and his single-minded and solemn commitment to kosen-rufu.

"Whenever I read the Daishonin's writings, his brilliant spirit, like the midsummer sun at noon, floods my heart. My chest feels as if it is filled with a giant ball of molten steel. Sometimes I feel like a scalding hot spring is gushing forth inside me, or as if a great, earth-shaking waterfall is crashing over me."[21]

I firmly believe that the spirit described here by President Toda represents the Soka Gakkai's eternal guideline for reading the writings of Nichiren Daishonin. Reading his writings means coming into contact with the Daishonin's immense compassion and his philosophy for liberating all people from fundamental suffering, and is comparable to being irradiated by Nichiren's spirit for kosen-rufu.

As courageous Bodhisattvas of the Earth, let us build a network dedicated to opening the eyes of the people in order to bring light to the darkness and delusion that shrouds people's lives and enable all to reveal their Buddha nature. The world is yearning for the humanistic Buddhism of Nichiren Daishonin. Today, more and more people around the globe are turning their eyes to our great movement of peace, culture and education.

The Three Virtues—Sovereign, Teacher and Parent—Establishing the Buddhism of the People Through Compassion and Enduring Persecution

There are three categories of people that all human beings should respect. They are the sovereign, the teacher, and the parent. There are three types of doctrines that are to be studied. They are Confucianism, Brahmanism, and Buddhism. (WND-1, 220)

These [teachings set forth by sages and worthies in China] are theories that are cleverly argued, but that fail to take cognizance of either the past or the future. Mystery,[1] as we have seen, means darkness or obscurity, and it is for this reason that it is called mystery. It is a theory that deals with matters only in terms of the present. (WND-1, 221)

Confucius declared that there were no worthies or sages in his country, but that in the land to the west there was one named Buddha who was a sage.[2] This indicates that non-Buddhist texts [such as Confucianism] should be regarded as a first step toward Buddhist doctrine. Confucius first taught propriety and music[3] so that, when the Buddhist scriptures were brought to China, the [Buddhist] concepts of the precepts, meditation, and wisdom[4] could be more readily grasped. He taught the ideals of ruler and minister so that the distinction between superior and subordinate could be made clear, he taught the ideal of parenthood so that the importance of filial piety could be appreciated, and he explained the ideal of the teacher so that people might learn to follow. (WND-1, 221)

In their skill and depth of understanding, they [the six non-Buddhist teachers of India[5]] surpassed anything known in Confucianism. They were able to perceive two, three, or even seven existences, [or] a period of eighty thousand kalpas,[6] into the past, and they likewise knew what would happen eighty thousand kalpas in the future. As the fundamental principle of their doctrine, some of these schools taught that causes produce effects, others taught that causes do not produce effects, while still others taught that causes both do and do not produce effects. Such were the fundamental principles of these non-Buddhist schools. (WND-1, 222)

But not a single person who adheres to these ninety-five types[7] of higher or lower non-Buddhist teachings ever escapes from the cycle of birth and death. Those who follow teachers of the better sort will, after two or three rebirths, fall into the evil paths, while those who follow evil teachers will fall into the evil paths in their very next rebirth.

And yet the main point of these non-Buddhist teachings constitutes an important means of entry into Buddhism. (WND-1, 222)

Thirdly [following Confucianism and Brahmanism], we come to Buddhism. One should know that the World-Honored One of Great Enlightenment [Shakyamuni Buddha] is a great leader for all living beings, a great eye for them, a great bridge, a great helmsman, a great field of good fortune. The four sages[8] and three ascetics[9] of the Confucian and Brahmanical scriptures and teachings are referred to as sages, but in fact they are no more than ordinary people who have not yet been able to eradicate the three categories of illusion.[10] They are referred to as wise men, but in fact they are no more than infants who cannot understand the principles of cause and effect. With their teachings for a ship, could one ever cross over the sea of the sufferings of birth and death? With their teachings for a bridge, could one ever escape from the maze of the six paths?[11] But the Buddha, our great teacher, has advanced beyond even transmigration with change and advance,[12] let alone transmigration with differences and limitations.[13] He has wiped out even the very root of fundamental darkness, let alone the illusions of thought and desire that are as minor as branches and leaves. (WND-1, 223)

The True Sovereign, Teacher and Parent, and the True Causality of Attaining Buddhahood

The main theme running throughout "The Opening of the Eyes" is that of the three virtues.[14] This is clearly indicated in the Daishonin's opening lines: "There are three categories of people that all human beings should respect. They are the sovereign, the teacher, and the parent. There are three types of doctrines that are to be studied. They are Confucianism, Brahmanism, and Buddhism" (WND-1, 220). He thus identifies the three virtues—those of sovereign, teacher and parent—as qualities that all people should respect.

In addition, the Daishonin identifies Confucianism, Brahmanism and Buddhism as the philosophical and religious doctrines that people should study. By "Confucianism, Brahmanism, and Buddhism" in this passage, he means the various teachings of China, including Confucianism and Taoism; the various non-Buddhist teachings of India, including Brahmanism; and, of course, the various teachings of Buddhism. This covers all of the principal strains of thought that had been transmitted to Japan in the Daishonin's day.

The underlying focus of this treatise is to evaluate the world's major schools of thought and religion as known by Nichiren Daishonin and to clarify who should genuinely be revered by all humanity as the person possessing the three virtues—sovereign, teacher and parent.

The various gods, Buddhas, bodhisattvas, sages and worthies presented in these philosophies and religions are described as possessing one or more of the three virtues, and they have in fact been revered by many people. The Daishonin, however, focuses on the question of who possesses these three virtues, because only someone endowed with all three is suitable as an object of universal veneration and respect.

In "On Prayer," Nichiren writes: "Though one may be a parent, if of humble station, one cannot at the same time assume the role of sovereign. And though one may be a sovereign, if not also a parent, one may inspire fear. And though one may be both a parent and a sovereign, one cannot be a teacher as well.

"The various Buddhas [other than Shakyamuni], since they are known as World-Honored Ones, may be regarded as sovereigns. But since they do not make their appearance in this saha world,[15] they are not teachers. Nor do they declare that 'the living beings in it [the threefold world][16] are all my children.'[17] Thus Shakyamuni Buddha alone fulfills the three functions of sovereign, teacher, and parent" (WND-1, 343–44).

Here, the Daishonin explains that of all the various Buddhas expounded in the Buddhist scriptures, only Shakyamuni possesses the virtues of sovereign, teacher and parent. This assertion also holds true when we investigate teachings outside of Buddhism.

Nichiren Daishonin, discussing the philosophies and religions of ancient India and China in "The Opening of the Eyes," notes that the various central deities, such as the Hindu gods Shiva and Vishnu, as well as the ideal rulers and the sages and worthies who have left behind these teachings, were said to possess one or more of the three virtues. None of them, however, were considered endowed with all three.

In some cases, they may be endowed with traits such as nobility, dignity and strength, which correspond to the virtue of sovereign, but lack such qualities of the parent as compassion. Conversely, they may have compassion but lack nobility. Also, some, while having nobility and compassion, do not demonstrate the virtue of the teacher because they do not expound a teaching that leads people to happiness. For this reason especially, most sages and worthies are not endowed with all three virtues.

As his discussion of the virtues of sovereign, teacher and parent in terms of Confucianism, Brahmanism and Buddhism unfolds, the Daishonin examines the content of the respective teachings, as well as people's practice and conduct based on those teachings.

Because the three virtues are characteristics exhibited by Buddhas, bodhisattvas and various honored ones in relation to the people, it goes without saying that gauging who truly possesses these three virtues becomes extremely important in terms of what the people are taught and the type of practice they are urged to carry out.

Based on this analysis, Nichiren concludes that Shakyamuni alone embodies the three virtues—serving as sovereign, teacher and parent for all living beings. In contrast, he argues, the honored ones and teachers of Confucianism in China and Brahmanism in India were ignorant of the principles of cause and effect; therefore, they could not be regarded as genuinely possessing the virtues of sovereign, teacher and parent.

"The Opening of the Eyes" states: "One should know that the World-Honored One of Great Enlightenment [Shakyamuni Buddha] is a great leader for all living beings, a great eye for them, a great bridge, a great helmsman, a great field of good fortune. The four sages and three ascetics of the Confucian and Brahmanical scriptures and teachings are referred to as sages, but in fact they are no more than ordinary people who have not yet been able to eradicate the three categories of illusion. They are referred to as wise men, but in fact they are no more than infants who cannot understand the principles of cause and effect. With their teachings for a ship, could one ever cross over the sea of the sufferings of birth and death? With their teachings for a bridge, could one ever escape from the maze of the six paths? But the Buddha, our great teacher, has advanced beyond even transmigration with change and advance, let alone transmigration with differences and limitations. He has wiped out even the very root of fundamental darkness, let alone the illusions of thought and desire that are as minor as branches and leaves" (WND-1, 223).

By "the principles of cause and effect," the Daishonin is referring to the causality of life over the three existences—past, present and future—that determines human happiness. Later, based on the fivefold comparison, he further clarifies the doctrine of original cause and original effect,[18] which is the true causality of attaining Buddhahood. This is the doctrine of the true mutual possession of the Ten Worlds and the true three thousand realms in a single moment of life hidden in the depths of "Life Span," the 16th chapter of the essential teaching of the Lotus Sutra.

In the first half of "The Opening of the Eyes," the Daishonin concludes that, in terms of the teachings of Confucianism,

Brahmanism and Buddhism that have been transmitted to Japan thus far, only Shakyamuni appears to fully function as sovereign, teacher and parent to all living beings. And the Daishonin also clarifies, in terms of Shakyamuni's entire body of teachings, that the doctrine of three thousand realms in a single moment of life hidden in the depths of the Lotus Sutra is the true teaching for attaining Buddhahood and the great Law for liberating all people of the Latter Day from suffering. The reason he says Shakyamuni embodies all three virtues—sovereign, teacher and parent— is that Shakyamuni became enlightened to the true causality of attaining Buddhahood, manifested it in his own life, and then expounded it in the form of the Lotus Sutra.

The Practice of the Votary of the Lotus Sutra Embodies the Functions of Sovereign, Teacher and Parent

In the latter half of "The Opening of the Eyes," Nichiren details his struggles as the votary of the Lotus Sutra enlightened to this true causality of attaining Buddhahood and striving to make it accessible to all people of the Latter Day.

He alone has awakened to the great Law for attaining Buddhahood hidden in the depths of the Lotus Sutra, and he alone recognizes the deplorable prevalence throughout the land of erroneous teachings that hinder the propagation of this Law. He writes, "I, Nichiren, am the only person in all Japan who understands this" (WND-1, 239).

But no sooner does he expound the correct teaching and doctrines than he is assailed by unimaginable and unprecedented persecution. Describing his situation, he writes, "As mountains pile upon mountains and waves follow waves, so do persecutions add to persecutions and criticisms augment criticisms" (WND-1, 241).

In a time of conflict, in a polluted age, Nichiren nevertheless surmounts the daunting persecutions of exile and near execution and wages an unceasing spiritual struggle for the enlightenment of all people. He reveals his expansive state of life in the following passage: "When it comes to understanding the Lotus Sutra, I have only a minute fraction of the vast ability that T'ien-t'ai and Dengyo [the great teachers of Buddhism of China and Japan, respectively] possessed. But as regards my ability to endure persecution and the wealth of my compassion for others, I believe they would hold me in awe" (WND-1, 242).

Leaving a detailed explanation of this passage for another occasion, suffice it to say the Daishonin is here making a great declaration that no figure in the history of Buddhism since Shakyamuni surpasses him in terms of his compassion and forbearance in the face of persecution as he struggled to guide all people to enlightenment.

The latter half of "The Opening of the Eyes" delves into why the Daishonin, as the votary of the Lotus Sutra, fails to receive the protection of the Buddhist gods as the Lotus Sutra promises, and why those persecuting him fail to receive punishment. In fact, one reason the Daishonin wrote this treatise was to address these extremely important questions that invited both doubt and criticism. Indeed, these lingering questions formed the basis not only of the abuse the general popu-lace showered on the Daishonin but also the denunciations of erstwhile followers who had abandoned their faith and turned against him.

In this writing, the Daishonin directly addresses these questions and seeks to dispel people's doubts. He states: "This doubt lies at the heart of this piece I am writing . . . [I]t is the most important concern of my entire life" (WND-1, 243). As he sets about answer-ing these questions, what gradually becomes clear is that the Lotus Sutra's description of the votary's conduct in propagating the teach-ing and the persecutions he will encounter perfectly match the Daishonin's own conduct and the persecutions befalling him.

Specifically cited as proof that Nichiren Daishonin is the votary of the Lotus Sutra are: the Buddha's entreaties to the bodhisattvas to make a great vow to spread the sutra after his passing, as well as the description of the six difficult and nine easy acts[19] in "Treasure Tower," the 11th chapter; the demonstration that ordinary people can attain Buddhahood (the attainment of Buddhahood of evil people and women) in "Devadatta," the 12th chap-ter; and the intense persecution of the votary of the Lotus Sutra by the three powerful ene-mies[20] described in "Encouraging Devotion," the 13th chapter.

The fact that the Daishonin is the true votary of the Lotus Sutra who has awak-ened to the great Law hidden in the sutra's depths and is striving to propagate it for the enlightenment of all people of the Latter Day becomes gradually more incontrovertible as we see how his conduct matches the words of the Lotus Sutra.

After minutely examining his con-duct based on the Lotus Sutra passages, the Daishonin then makes his own powerful vow to free people from suffering. This is none other than the great lion's roar that begins: "This I will state. Let the gods forsake me. Let all persecutions assail me. Still I will give my life for the sake of the Law" (WND-1, 280).

Here, the Daishonin, from an unsur-passed spiritual height, gazes down calmly on the meaningless maneuvers of his persecu-tors and hostile ex-followers in league with them. This immortal passage resonates with Nichiren's pure, unadulterated spirit and his determination to fight on and break through people's ignorance, disbelief and delusion.

His state of life resembles a vast, glori-ous sun of compassion shining down on all, urging us to bring forth the brilliance of the treasure tower in our lives.

In this writing, the Daishonin further tells his disciples that practicing the cor-rect Buddhist teaching to lead all people to enlightenment is itself the direct path to less-ening karmic retribution[21] and transforming our karma, and it is the great path of attaining Buddhahood in this lifetime.

Lastly, the Daishonin indicates that the essence of propagation is compassion. Because of the immense compassion he feels for all people, he can unflinchingly battle evil, endure persecution and spread the Law.

Based on this compassion, Nichiren Daishonin unequivocally declares that he is the person who embodies the three virtues in the Latter Day of the Law. He says, "I, Nichiren, am sovereign, teacher, and father and mother to all the people of Japan" (WND-1, 287).

The Japan of Nichiren Daishonin's day is a land where the Law is about to perish. Who-ever can save the people of such a country can save all humankind. This statement, therefore, is none other than the Daishonin's declaration that he represents the object of devotion in terms of the Person—embodying the functions of sovereign, teacher and parent, not only for the people of Japan but for all humankind over the ten thousand years and more of the Latter Day of the Law.

Thus, the opening section of this treatise presents the three virtues as the main topic, while the concluding section proclaims that Nichiren Daishonin, as the votary of the Lotus Sutra, is the person who embodies them.

The Sovereign, Teacher and Parent of the Buddhism of Sowing of the Latter Day

In the foregoing, I have given an outline of "The Opening of the Eyes" as a treatise on the three virtues. Based on this, let's further consider the three virtues as embodied by Nichiren Daishonin—namely, the sovereign, teacher and parent of the Buddhism of sowing of the Latter Day of the Law.

The Daishonin did not merely awaken to Myoho-renge-kyo, the seed for attaining Buddhahood; he steadfastly upheld this great Law while taking on the shared sufferings of all living beings of the Latter Day as his own personal sufferings.[22] And, without begrudging his life, he also expounded and spread the Law for their sake. Evident in his selfless dedication are the virtues of sovereign, teacher and parent of the Buddhism of sowing of the Latter Day for awakening all

people of this evil age and enabling them to attain Buddhahood.

First, Myoho-renge-kyo is the fundamental Law of the universe. Not only did Nichiren awaken to this Law, but he also persevered in upholding it while overcoming relentless persecutions. This conduct proves that his life was completely one with Myoho-renge-kyo, and that he manifested a state of being in which he was one with the universe itself.

We can view this vast and noble state of life as the virtue of sovereign. The virtue of sovereign in terms of Shakyamuni is expressed by the phrase in "Simile and Parable," the 3rd chapter of the Lotus Sutra: "This threefold world is / all my domain" (LSOC, 105). The virtue of sovereign in terms of the Daishonin, meanwhile, could perhaps be expressed as follows: "The entire universe is my domain."

In his unceasing efforts to advance kosen-rufu in accord with his vow, summoning the heart of the lion king and remaining undaunted in the face of the direst persecution, we can see a majesty and dignity resembling that of the Lotus Sutra's gigantic Treasure Tower that rises magnificently in the air.

Next, the Daishonin developed a form of practice to make the Law of Myoho-renge-kyo, which he had revealed in his own life, accessible to all people. He guided people to the path of Buddhahood with the clear mirror of the Gohonzon and with the *daimoku* of faith and practice.[23] This can be viewed as a manifestation of the virtue of teacher.

And in order to free people from suffering, the Daishonin tirelessly continued teaching that ordinary people of the Latter Day could reveal the world of Buddhahood in their own lives. At the same time, he warned of the ills that arose from a mind of slander characterized by disbelief in the existence of the Buddha nature in oneself and others, and he denounced teachings that exerted a negative influence on people and drew them into slandering the Law. And though the Daishonin's castigation of slander provoked wave upon wave of persecution, he endured every onslaught. This is entirely due to his immense compassion.

Again, in "Simile and Parable," Shakyamuni's virtue of parent is indicated by the passage: "All living beings [in the threefold world] are my children" (LSOC, 105). Similarly, in Nichiren's conduct of spreading the teaching while enduring all hardship, we can discern the virtue of parent, characterized by a spirit of caring and concern for the well-being of the people of the Latter Day as if they were his own children.

A Pioneer and Example of Ordinary People Attaining Buddhahood

As the initiator and pioneer of kosen-rufu in the Latter Day, the Daishonin spread the great Law for the enlightenment of all people. And through that struggle, he naturally became endowed with the virtues of sovereign, teacher and parent.

From the standpoint of the disciples who follow in his footsteps, Nichiren's pioneering struggle can be regarded as the model of an ordinary person attaining Buddhahood in the Latter Day of the Law.

He writes, "Here, a single individual has been used as an example, but the same thing applies equally to all living beings" ("The Unanimous Declaration by the Buddhas," WND-2, 844). The Daishonin serves as our first example of an ordinary person attaining Buddhahood. As such, we regard him as the object of devotion in terms of the Person.

Related to this point, I recall that Tsunesaburo Makiguchi, the Soka Gakkai's first president, drew a distinction between the position of a sage or worthy who discovers the truth and teaches it to others and that of us ordinary people who create value by believing in and practicing that truth. He felt it was perfectly reasonable that only one sage or worthy might discover the ultimate truth and that others would have the mission of practicing that truth and proving its validity. He explains it this way: "The process of revealing the teaching (in other words, the teaching system) employed by the pioneering sage or worthy so that we will place our faith in that teaching, and the process of ordinary people adopting it in their daily lives—that is, the process by which we come to believe in, be guided by and strive for lives of supreme happiness based on that teaching—ought to be completely different."[24]

In other words, he is saying that after a sage or worthy appears and establishes a fundamental truth or teaching that all people should believe and practice, it is up to us ordinary people to put the conclusions of that sage or worthy into practice and experience the results for ourselves, thereby gaining an understanding of the truth with our own lives. He notes, however, that there are those who seek to transmit the teaching of the sage or worthy by demanding that people go through the same process by which the sage or worthy reached his conclusion. But doing so, he declares, is a great mistake and a pointless waste of time, and he criticizes such individuals for mistakenly thinking that truth is the same as value.[25]

President Makiguchi regarded the realization of happiness for oneself and others as the ultimate purpose or goal of human life. For him, therefore, actually eliminating suffering and creating happiness was the end, while theory was nothing more than a means for achieving it. Moreover, he felt it desirable that an ordinary person serve as the model in those efforts.

That is, if the role model offering the highest concrete example is a person who is complete and perfect, then those seeking to emulate that example will find it a goal inspiring reverence but also personally unapproachable and unattainable. Instead, President Makiguchi regarded someone who carries out the beneficial practice of sowing seeds [of enlightenment] while remaining an ordinary person of the lowest standing in society as a person of unsurpassed character.[26]

Most respectworthy is a person who can serve as a model for those whose lives are steeped in suffering.

Nichiren Daishonin was born as an ordinary person in an age rife with suffering, and he dedicated his life to the humanistic practice of enabling struggling, ordinary people to bring forth their inherent Buddhahood. As a result, he encountered all manner of persecution. Through those ordeals, he read the Lotus Sutra with his life, thereby proving the validity of its teachings, and he showed through his example the incredible strength and potential within all human beings.

With regard to this point, President Makiguchi said, "If this (Shakyamuni's Buddhism, and the Lotus Sutra in particular) becomes relevant to the actual world as a result of Nichiren Daishonin's appearance, and, moreover, if the universal principle of causality is proven by the persecutions for the Law that he underwent in his lifetime, then won't the abstract ideals of the Lotus Sutra have become a reality in our lives?"[27]

He continued: "This is not simply limited to the one person Nichiren Daishonin. As he indicates when he says that it applies to all people, this is something that we who carry out faith and practice for ourselves and others can easily prove."[28] The Daishonin thus stressed that he, who propagated the teaching while enduring immense hardship and persecution, is the Buddha of the Latter Day of the Law whom we should look to as our model.

President Makiguchi's insightful comments illustrate how he always approached Buddhism from the standpoint of a person of faith and practice. They also reveal his humanistic spirit to view all people as being equally precious and worthy of respect.

A Revolutionary New View of Religion

Finally, let's look at the revolutionary view of religion found in the Daishonin's conception of sovereign, teacher and parent.

In "The True Aspect of All Phenomena," he writes: "A common mortal is an entity of the three bodies, and a true Buddha. A Buddha [such as Shakyamuni or Many Treasures] is a function of the three bodies, and a provisional Buddha. In that case, though it is thought that Shakyamuni Buddha possesses the three virtues of sovereign, teacher, and parent for the sake of all of us living beings, that is not so. On the contrary, it is common mortals who endow him with the three virtues" (WND-1, 384).

According to traditional thinking, Shakyamuni was a great Buddha possessing the three virtues for the sake of living beings; but this view is in fact incorrect. It is because people possess the Buddha nature and are endowed with the potential to manifest Buddhahood that Shakyamuni could demonstrate the virtues of sovereign, teacher and parent for all living beings. That's why the Daishonin proclaims that it is living beings who endow Shakyamuni with the three virtues.

Here we see a radical new approach to the three virtues, and to the very nature of religion. In the conventional view, sovereigns rule and reign over their subjects, teachers instruct and educate their students, and parents give birth to and are honored by their children. Seen strictly in terms of such relationships, sovereign, teacher and parent are authority figures. Thus, when the Buddha is likened to sovereign, teacher and parent based on

that model, what will inevitably result is an authoritarian Buddhism.

But genuine sovereigns help their subjects become happy; genuine teachers enable their students to grow and develop; and genuine parents raise children into fine adults. Based on this model, sovereigns can manifest their power as sovereigns only because their subjects have the potential to become happy, teachers can function as teachers only because their students have the potential for wonderful development, and parents can fulfill their role as parents only because their children have the potential to grow into capable men and women.

The same principle applies to Buddhism. Buddhas can be endowed with the three virtues only because living beings have the potential to attain Buddhahood.

This statement by the Daishonin indicates a dramatic move away from an authoritarian religion characterized by obedient worship of Buddhas and deities and a reliance on priestly prayers for good fortune and protection to a humanistic, people-centered religion that exists for the happiness of all human beings.

2

The "Teaching Hidden in the Depths of the Sutra"—The Supreme Law That Opens the Path to Buddhahood for All People

The Lotus Sutra contains two important teachings.[1] The Dharma Analysis Treasury, Establishment of Truth, Precepts, Dharma Characteristics, and Three Treatises schools have never heard even so much as the name of these teachings. The Flower Garland and True Word schools, on the other hand, have surreptitiously stolen these doctrines and made them the heart of their own teachings. The doctrine of three thousand realms in a single moment of life is found in only one place, hidden in the depths of the "Life Span" chapter of the essential teaching of the Lotus Sutra. Nagarjuna and Vasubandhu were aware of it but did not bring it forth into the light. T'ien-t'ai Chih-che alone embraced it and kept it ever in mind. (WND-1, 224)

The Crucial Importance of the Doctrine of "Three Thousand Realms in a Single Moment of Life"

In this passage, Nichiren Daishonin calls the fundamental Law that serves as the key for the enlightenment of ordinary people "the doctrine of three thousand realms in a single moment of life," and states that it is "found in only one place, hidden in the depths of the 'Life Span' chapter of the essential teaching of the Lotus Sutra."

This three thousand realms doctrine implicit in "The Life Span of the Thus Come One," the 16th chapter, could be called the very heart of the Lotus Sutra, which was expounded to enable all people to reveal their Buddhahood. In short, it represents the "mutual possession of the Ten Worlds" and the "three thousand realms in a single moment of life" viewed as the supreme teaching for ordinary people to attain Buddhahood.

By explicitly expounding the Buddhist teaching implicit in the "Life Span" chapter, the Daishonin opened the way for fundamentally liberating people from suffering in the evil age of the Latter Day of the Law.

Nichikan, the twenty-sixth high priest of the Nikko lineage, known as a leading restorer of Nichiren Buddhism, interpreted the word *only* in the above passage as indicating three levels: (1) only in the Lotus Sutra; (2) only in the "Life Span" chapter; and (3) only hidden in the depths [of that chapter]. On that basis, he developed the system of comparison known as the "threefold secret teaching," which can be explained as follows:

First, in the context of Shakyamuni's lifetime teachings—comparing the true teaching (the Lotus Sutra) and the provisional teachings (all preceding sutras)—the three thousand realms doctrine is found only in the Lotus Sutra, the true teaching. Specifically, it is found in the theoretical teaching (first half) of the Lotus Sutra, in "Expedient Means," the 2nd chapter. Here, the theoretical three thousand realms teaching is revealed.

Second, in the context of the Lotus Sutra—comparing the essential teaching (latter half) and the theoretical teaching (first half) of the sutra—the doctrine is found only in the "Life Span" chapter of the essential teaching. Here, the actual three thousand realms doctrine explicit in the essential teaching is revealed.

Third, in the context of the "Life Span" chapter—comparing its implicit meaning with its explicit meaning, the former indicating the Buddhism of sowing and the latter, the Buddhism of the harvest—the doctrine is found only hidden in the depths or implicit in the text of the chapter, that is, in the Buddhism of sowing. Here, the actual practice of

the three thousand realms teaching implicit in the "Life Span" chapter is revealed.

In discussing the three thousand realms teaching, there is a tendency for people to become fixated on the number three thousand,[2] but the heart of this principle in fact lies in the mutual possession of the Ten Worlds—that is, the one hundred worlds.

After referring to the teaching hidden in the depths in the above passage, Nichiren writes, "The doctrine of three thousand realms in a single moment of life begins with the concept of the mutual possession of the Ten Worlds" (WND-1, 224). In subsequent passages, he explains at length the principles "original cause and original effect" and "true mutual possession of the Ten Worlds," stressing that they are the essential principles for the attainment of Buddhahood.

Further, when it comes to the mutual possession of the Ten Worlds in the actual practice of the three thousand realms teaching implicit in the "Life Span" chapter, it is specifically the principles "inclusion of Buddhahood in the nine worlds" and "inclusion of the nine worlds in Buddhahood" that hold great importance. This is as the Daishonin indicates when he writes, "[Shakyamuni Buddha] expounded the doctrine of three thousand realms in a single moment of life, explaining that the nine worlds have the potential for Buddhahood and that Buddhahood retains the nine worlds" ("The Selection of the Time," WND-1, 539).

The reason for focusing on this mutually inherent aspect of the nine worlds and Buddhahood is that it lays the groundwork for the idea of ordinary people attaining enlightenment. It clarifies that the pure and limitless life force of eternal Buddhahood can function dynamically within the lives of ordinary people wracked by earthly desires, karma and suffering.[3] Given that in the pre-Lotus Sutra teachings the lives of beings of the lower nine worlds were depicted as impermanent, this represents a dramatic transformation of the Buddhist view of life, which is analogous to "changing poison into medicine."[4]

The "Life Span" chapter of the Lotus Sutra refers to Shakyamuni's original attainment of enlightenment in the remote past. In this teaching, Nichiren discerned the means for attaining Buddhahood without having to discard one's body as an ordinary person of the nine worlds—in other words, the means for actualizing the principle of the mutual possession of the Ten Worlds.

Faith in the Mystic Law of Nam-myoho-renge-kyo, as well as prayer and action based on that faith, are key to transforming a life state in the nine worlds—steeped in earthly desires, karma and suffering—into Buddhahood. The Lotus Sutra describes how Bodhisattva Never Disparaging, while remaining an ordinary person, could transform his karma, attain the benefit of purifying his six sense organs,[5] and finally attain Buddhahood, as a result of dauntlessly maintaining his belief in the Buddha nature inherent in his own life and others and continuing to treat everyone with respect based on that belief (see LSOC, 308–13).

With pure, strong faith in our own Buddha nature and that of others, we can break through fundamental ignorance and illusion. With deep, earnest prayer, we can tap the life force of Buddhahood that is one with the Mystic Law. And through continuing to chant Nam-myoho-renge-kyo, we can ceaselessly manifest the power of Buddhahood in our lives and set ourselves on a course toward attaining enlightenment in this lifetime. In this way, the Daishonin secured the means for actualizing the mutual possession of the Ten Worlds by establishing the "actual practice of Nam-myoho-renge-kyo." This actual practice, encompassing faith from our hearts, prayer through our voices and the action of continuously chanting, spans the three categories of action—thoughts, words and deeds.

The Daishonin inscribed the Gohonzon, the embodiment of the Law of Nam-myoho-renge-kyo inherent in his own life, as a means to help us cultivate our own faith and belief in the Buddha nature in ourselves and others, which is indiscernible to the eye.

The Teaching "Hidden in the Depths" Reveals the True Intent

Next, let's consider the meaning of the teaching "hidden in the depths" of the "Life Span" chapter in terms of the three aspects of "text, principle and intent."[6]

Through various textual passages, including "as an expedient means I appear to enter nirvana,"[7] and such principles as "opening the near and revealing the distant"[8] and "the Buddha's original attainment of Buddhahood in the remote past," the "Life Span" chapter reveals Shakyamuni's true identity as the eternal Buddha who continuously—from the beginningless past into the eternal future—leads all people in all worlds, including this strife-filled saha world, to enlightenment. And it teaches that the Buddha's eternal life was acquired through bodhisattva practice in the remote past. This is clarified in the passage, "Originally I practiced the bodhisattva way" (LSOC, 268). The key to the attainment of Buddhahood of ordinary people lies in this bodhisattva practice in the remote past.

But when people become caught up with "text" and "principle"—words and their literal meaning—they inevitably become attached to the image of Shakyamuni as the lord of the teachings who reveals the aspect of "original effect"[9]—that is, as a Buddha adorned with superhuman features and characteristics. They then succumb to the mistaken belief of seeking to be saved from without by this Buddha. This quickly devolves into faith characterized by an abject reliance on an absolute being. Adherents to such a belief cannot attain true enlightenment, which is achieved by manifesting the world of Buddhahood from within.

Hence, the Shakyamuni that is presented in terms of the literal meaning of the "Life Span" chapter reveals the power of the eternal Mystic Law as the "Buddha of original effect." In contrast, the teaching hidden in the depths of the chapter (the Buddhism of sowing) focuses on the ordinary person Shakyamuni who carried out bodhisattva practice in the remote past, and it clearly establishes the "teaching and practice of original cause"[10] for ordinary people.

In terms of its text, or literal meaning, the "Life Span" chapter gives no explicit explanation of the enlightenment of ordinary people and the mutual possession of the Ten Worlds. But in terms of its intent, the essential teaching for ordinary people to attain enlightenment can be clearly discerned hidden in the depths of the chapter.

The Environment in Which the Daishonin Composed "The Opening of the Eyes"

Nichiren Daishonin composed "The Opening of the Eyes" in an extremely harsh environment. Cold and hunger were his constant companions. He writes: "There [in Sado], true to the nature of that northern land, I found the wind particularly strong in winter, the snows deep, the clothing thin, and the food scarce . . . I felt as though I had passed through the realm of hungry spirits and fallen alive into one of the cold hells" ("Letter to Horen," WND-1, 519).

Based on the Daishonin's various writings, we learn the following:

His initial residence at Tsukahara on Sado, the Sammai-do, was a crude structure. Though it was called a shrine, it was little more than a dilapidated hut; there was no Buddha image or a mat of any kind. To try to stay warm, the Daishonin spread a fur skin on the floor, wrapped himself in a straw coat and wore a bamboo hat.

There were gaps in the roof boards and holes in the walls. The wind blew in mercilessly and, on rainy days, the roof leaked terribly, affording no more protection from the elements than if he had been out in the open. In the winter, snow piled up inside.

Located in a field where corpses were buried or simply abandoned, the Sammai-do was isolated and remote from other inhabitants or passersby. All day long, the only sound was that of the wind. At night, there was a continuous onslaught of snow, hail and lightning. In the morning, everything was blanketed in white. For two months after the

Daishonin's arrival, a bitterly cold wind blew without cease even when it was not snowing, and the sky was always overcast.

Officials kept a sharp watch over the Daishonin's visitors day and night. At great personal risk, Abutsu-bo, one of the Daishonin's sincere local followers, carried food supplies to the Daishonin under cover of darkness.

Undaunted by the inhospitable environment in which he found himself exiled, the Daishonin wrote "The Opening of the Eyes" for the sake of the people of his day and of later generations.

Maintaining the All-Important Religious Spirit

It could be said that the enlightenment of ordinary people by means of the true mutual possession of the Ten Worlds and the true three thousand realms teaching implicit in "Life Span" represents the heart of the Lotus Sutra and the essence of Buddhism, and at the same time, the quintessential aim of religion.

In dialogues with noted thinkers and in lectures given around the world, I have frequently emphasized the importance of "the religious spirit" and of "the religious."[11] The religious spirit refers to the inner spiritual power to create courage from nihilism, hope from despair; it is a spirit to look for this spiritual power in oneself and others and in all universal phenomena. The religious spirit is to believe that the power to overcome any hardship or deadlock lies within us, and to

take positive action to create new value. All religions, one might say, were born from this innate human spirit. The religious spirit of humanity could be described as the starting point and wellspring of religion.

The Latter Day of the Law, the current era, is an age when people become attached to the fleeting and ephemeral; are at the mercy of greed, anger and foolishness; and are divided by mistrust and hatred. Nichiren also saw it as a time when religions would lose sight of their essential religious spirit and become alienated from people, an age when clerics would spend all their time quarreling among themselves about the superiority of their teachings—which had in reality become ossified, empty of meaning—and be ever more obsessed with doctrinal minutiae. The Great Collection Sutra describes the Latter Day as "an age of conflict when the pure Law will become obscured and lost."

Nichiren Daishonin clearly felt that unless this fundamental religious spirit was revived, neither the people nor the age could be saved. This led him to delve into the depths of the Lotus Sutra and therein find the true mutual possession and the true three thousand realms teachings, which make it possible for us to open the world of Buddhahood in our own lives. And that is why he could ultimately establish the three thousand realms doctrine implicit in the "Life Span" chapter as an actual practice whereby people could grasp the eternity of their own lives and, through their actions, bring their lives to shine with everlasting brilliance.

In the opening passage I have cited, the Daishonin says that such Buddhist schools of his day as the Dharma Analysis Treasury, Establishment of Truth, Precepts, Dharma

Characteristics, and Three Treatises "have never heard even so much as the name" of the principle of three thousand realms in a single moment of life. And he condemns the Flower Garland and True Word schools for having "surreptitiously stolen these doctrines and made them the heart of their own teachings" (WND-1, 224).

Viewed in the context of text, principle and intent, which I mentioned earlier, these various schools appropriated and incorporated into their own teachings merely the words of the "text" of the Lotus Sutra. Although they carried on as if they possessed the same "principle" or teaching as the sutra, they utterly failed to grasp its true "intent." Their erroneous and confused interpretations of the three thousand realms doctrine eloquently demonstrate the extent to which the existing schools of Buddhism in Nichiren's day had lost the vital religious spirit.

The religious spirit is to see the eternal and absolute in human beings and to wish to make people's lives shine. Nichiren's Buddhism of sowing, based on the supreme Law hidden in the depths of the Lotus Sutra, is a teaching directly founded on this religious spirit.

Josei Toda, the second Soka Gakkai president, said: "When all people manifest the life state of Buddhahood, that is to say, when they reveal the supreme value of their character, there will be neither war nor hunger in the world. There will be neither illness nor poverty. Enabling all people to become Buddhas, elevating the character of all people to something of supreme value—this is what it means to carry out 'the Thus Come One's work' (LSOC, 200)."[12]

Just as President Toda urged, we of the SGI, directly connected to Nichiren

Daishonin and giving free expression to the religious spirit, have spread our humanistic religion, the Buddhism of the people, throughout the world.

The Supreme Teaching To Be Propagated in the Latter Day of the Law

At the end of the passage I have cited, the Daishonin says that such leading Buddhist teachers as Nagarjuna and Vasubandhu of India "were aware of it [the doctrine of three thousand realms in a single moment of life] but did not bring it forth into the light," and that only the Great Teacher T'ien-t'ai of China "embraced it and kept it ever in mind" (WND-1, 224).

That "Nagarjuna and Vasubandhu were aware of it" indicates that these two teachers, who carried on the lineage of the correct Buddhist teaching after Shakyamuni's passing in the Former Day of the Law, understood the Lotus Sutra's ultimate principle but did not preach it. This is referred to as the concept of "clearly perceiving the truth in one's heart but not teaching it to others."

Nagarjuna, for example, recognized that the Lotus Sutra opened the way for people of the two vehicles, who were denied the attainment of enlightenment in other sutras, to become Buddhas. He praised the power of the Lotus Sutra to change poison into medicine, which was found in no other sutra, and called the Lotus Sutra the true secret teaching. This means he was aware of the Lotus Sutra's ultimate principle, which makes it possible for ordinary people of the nine worlds to manifest the state of Buddhahood in their lives and attain enlightenment.

As the Daishonin indicates, however, when he says that Nagarjuna and Vasubandhu "were aware of it but did not bring it forth into the light," they did not propagate the three thousand realms doctrine because the time had not yet arrived.

The statement, "T'ien-t'ai Chih-che alone embraced it and kept it ever in mind," refers to the fact that, during the Middle Day of the Law, only T'ien-t'ai carried out the practice of contemplation of and meditation on the three thousand realms teaching. But T'ien-t'ai's three thousand realms teaching was essentially limited to practice for oneself; he did not spread it widely as a teaching so that ordinary people could attain Buddhahood themselves and help others do the same.

Nichiren's real intent in talking about these correct teachers of the Former and Middle Days of the Law—who either "were aware of three thousand realms in a single moment of life but did not bring it forth" or who "embraced it and kept it ever in mind"—is to implicitly indicate that he is the one who will propagate this teaching in the Latter Day of the Law. The second half of "The Opening of the Eyes" details the Daishonin's propagation efforts as the votary of the Lotus Sutra.

The three thousand realms doctrine implicit in the "Life Span" chapter is a teaching of actual practice. The Law is not something that just exists; it must be spread. The value of the Law is only revealed when we teach it to others and thereby not only awaken them to the inner brilliance of their Buddha nature but bring our own lives to shine, as

well. It could even be said that unless spreading the Law creates value, there would be no point to the Law's existence.

In that sense, the crucial question is: Who will propagate the doctrine of three thousand realms in a single moment of life—specifically, the doctrine implicit in the "Life Span" chapter—and when? If the teaching implicit in the "Life Span" chapter is explained without mention of this important point, it will serve no real purpose.

The person who actually propagates the true three thousand realms in a single moment of life doctrine during the Latter Day of the Law is one who possesses the three virtues—sovereign, teacher and parent—in this age. And the lord of that teaching is none other than Nichiren Daishonin. To clarify this, the Daishonin wrote this passage about the doctrine hidden in the depths of the "Life Span" chapter.

3

Original Cause and Original Effect—Eternal Buddhahood and the Unending Bodhisattva Way Are Opened Through Faith

All the other sutras such as the Flower Garland, Wisdom, and Mahavairochana not only conceal the fact that people of the two vehicles can attain Buddhahood, but they also fail to make clear that the Buddha attained enlightenment countless kalpas in the past. These sutras have two flaws. First, because they teach that the Ten Worlds are separate from one another, they fail to move beyond the provisional doctrines and to reveal the doctrine of three thousand realms in a single moment of life as it is expounded in the theoretical teaching of the Lotus Sutra. Second, because they teach that Shakyamuni Buddha attained enlightenment for the first time in this world, referring only to his provisional aspect, they fail to reveal the fact stressed in the essential teaching that the Buddha attained enlightenment countless kalpas ago.[1] These two great doctrines are the core of the Buddha's lifetime of teachings, and the very heart and marrow of all the sutras.

The "Expedient Means" chapter, which belongs to the theoretical teaching, expounds the doctrine of three thousand realms in a single moment of life, making clear that persons of the two vehicles can achieve Buddhahood. It thus eliminates one of the two errors found in the earlier sutras. But it nevertheless retains the provisional aspect, and fails to reveal the eternal aspect, of the Buddha's enlightenment. Thus the true doctrine of three thousand realms in a single moment of life remains unclear, and the attainment of Buddhahood by persons of the two vehicles is not properly affirmed. Such teachings are like the moon seen in the water, or rootless plants that drift on the waves.

When we come to the essential teaching of the Lotus Sutra, then the belief that Shakyamuni first obtained Buddhahood during his present lifetime is demolished, and the effects of the four teachings are likewise demolished. When the effects of the four teachings are demolished, the causes of the four teachings are likewise demolished. Thus the cause and effect of the Ten Worlds as expounded in the earlier sutras and the theoretical teaching of the Lotus Sutra are wiped out, and the cause and effect of the Ten Worlds in the essential teaching are revealed. This is the doctrine of original cause and original effect. It reveals that the nine worlds are all present in beginningless Buddhahood and that Buddhahood is inherent in the beginningless nine worlds. This is the true mutual possession of the Ten Worlds, the true hundred worlds and thousand factors, the true three thousand realms in a single moment of life. (WND-1, 235)

In this passage, Nichiren Daishonin clarifies the doctrine of original cause and original effect, the principle of attaining Buddhahood expounded in "Life Span," the 16th chapter of the Lotus Sutra. Specifically, "original cause" and "original effect" refer to the causality of Shakyamuni's attainment of enlightenment in the remote past as described in this chapter. Here, Shakyamuni reveals that his actual enlightenment dates back to a time in the immeasurably distant past, numberless major world system dust particle *kalpas*[2] ago. Thus, the cause that made it possible for him to attain Buddhahood at that time is called "original cause," while the effect or result of his attaining Buddhahood is called "original effect."

In terms of the literal teaching of the "Life Span" chapter, the principle of attaining Buddhahood based on this original cause and original effect is explained in the context of Shakyamuni. But when viewed from the standpoint of the teaching implicit in the depths of the chapter, it is not limited solely to Shakyamuni. This doctrine also reveals the most fundamental and universal causality for attaining Buddhahood, and, as such, it constitutes the cause and effect of enlightenment for all people.

The Two Flaws of the Pre-Lotus Sutra Teachings

In the above passage, Nichiren paraphrases the writings of the Great Teacher Miao-lo of China and takes up the subject of the two doctrinal flaws evident in the pre-Lotus Sutra teachings.

The first flaw is that they do not reveal the "three thousand realms in a single moment of life" doctrine found in the theoretical teaching, or first half, of the Lotus Sutra. Their presentation of the Ten Worlds as separate from one another means that they divide Buddhist practice into stages and discriminate among certain types of people in terms of their capacity to attain Buddhahood. This discriminatory view is based on the belief that the Ten Worlds are separate and that the differences between them are fixed and unchanging.

Because the position of the pre-Lotus Sutra teachings is that of a virtually insurmountable chasm existing between the nine worlds and Buddhahood, they stress the need for countless kalpas of practice or insist that persons of the two vehicles (voice-hearers and cause-awakened ones) could never achieve enlightenment. These earlier sutras set forth provisional teachings as an expedient means, maintaining a rigid distinction or separation of each of the various Ten Worlds from one another, and as a result do not reveal the true teaching. That is why Nichiren says, "They fail to move beyond the provisional doctrines" (WND-1, 235).

In the theoretical teaching of the Lotus Sutra, this view of separation is invalidated. The theoretical teaching emphasizes the attainment of Buddhahood by persons of the two vehicles, sets forth the principle of the true aspect of all phenomena,[3] and clarifies the three thousand realms doctrine, which teaches that all living beings in the nine worlds are endowed with Buddhahood and therefore have the potential to realize enlightenment.

The second flaw of the pre-Lotus Sutra teachings is that they conceal Shakyamuni's original attainment of Buddhahood in the remote past, which is described in the essential teaching, or latter half, of the Lotus Sutra. The earlier sutras teach that Shakyamuni attained enlightenment for the first time in this world and only after having carried out arduous practice over an immeasurably long series of previous existences. His enlightenment in his present

lifetime is thus premised on the view that attaining Buddhahood necessitates countless kalpas of practice. At the heart of this perspective is the belief that the nine worlds and Buddhahood are separate.

The theoretical teaching of the Lotus Sutra elucidates that all people have the potential to achieve enlightenment. It therefore avoids one of the two flaws of the earlier sutras. But it still presumes that Shakyamuni attained enlightenment for the first time in his present life. Regarding this failure to disclose the truth of Shakyamuni's enlightenment in the remote past, Nichiren says: "[The theoretical teaching] nevertheless retains the provisional aspect, and fails to reveal the eternal aspect, of the Buddha's enlightenment. Thus the true doctrine of three thousand realms in a single moment of life remains unclear, and the attainment of Buddhahood by persons of the two vehicles is not properly affirmed" (WND-1, 235).

Discarding the provisional, or transient, aspect and revealing the true, or eternal, aspect means refuting the assumption that Shakyamuni first attained enlightenment in this world (his provisional identity as described in the earlier sutras and the theoretical teaching), and illuminating his original enlightenment in the remote past (his true identity as described in the "Life Span" chapter of the essential teaching).

Nichiren is saying that, without revealing the Buddha's true identity, it is meaningless to expound the attainment of Buddhahood by persons of the two vehicles, or the three thousand realms doctrine, which elucidates that all living beings in the nine worlds are endowed with Buddhahood. Because the theoretical teaching retains a provisional aspect, it does not fully establish the former nor does it elucidate the latter. Because the three thousand realms doctrine sketched in the theoretical teaching lacks a solid basis and remains indefinite, Nichiren compares it to "the moon seen in the water, or rootless plants that drift on the waves" (WND-1, 235).

"Casting Off the Transient and Revealing the True" and "Original Cause and Original Effect"

Let's expand on Nichiren's implication that the three thousand realms doctrine remains unclear without the explanation of the true, eternal aspect of the Buddha's enlightenment in the "Life Span" chapter—that is, without Shakyamuni's discarding his transient and revealing his true identity.

The "Life Span" chapter's disclosure that Shakyamuni actually attained enlightenment in the remote past both refutes the Buddha's provisional aspect and elucidates the original cause and original effect of his actual enlightenment.

Nichiren says that by shattering the assumption that Shakyamuni first achieved enlightenment in his present lifetime, the various effects of attaining Buddhahood described in the four teachings—that is, in the pre-Lotus Sutra teachings and the theoretical teaching of the Lotus Sutra—are also demolished. He further states that when these effects are annulled, the causes (or practices) for attaining Buddhahood described in the four teachings are likewise invalidated. One

purpose in casting off the transient and revealing the true is to completely refute the cause and effect of the Ten Worlds set forth in earlier sutras and the theoretical teaching. The cause and effect of the Ten Worlds are the cause and effect of attaining Buddhahood, while the nine worlds constitute the cause, and the world of Buddhahood, the effect.

The "Life Span" chapter thus clarifies the original cause and original effect, which represent the cause and effect of the Ten Worlds of the essential teaching—that is, the true cause and effect of attaining Buddhahood. This is another reason why Shakyamuni cast off the transient and revealed the true.

How are the original cause and original effect presented in terms of the literal teaching of the "Life Span" chapter? First, Shakyamuni proclaims, "It has been immeasurable, boundless hundreds, thousands, ten thousands, millions of nayutas of kalpas since I in fact attained Buddhahood" (LSOC, 265–66). In this passage, the Buddha indicates that he actually gained enlightenment in the incalculably remote past.

He also states: "Since I attained Buddhahood, an extremely long period of time has passed. My life span is an immeasurable number of asamkhya kalpas, and during that time I have constantly abided here without ever entering extinction" (LSOC, 267–68). Shakyamuni explains that as the Buddha enlightened since the distant past, his life is ever abiding and eternal. This ever-abiding and eternal state of life of Buddhahood is the effect of attaining enlightenment in the remote past—namely, the original effect.

Next, with regard to the original cause, Shakyamuni says, "Originally I practiced the bodhisattva way, and the life span that I acquired then has yet to come to an end but will last twice the number of years that have already passed" (LSOC, 268). In other words, he says that the life state of Buddhahood he obtained (the original effect) and the life state of the nine worlds in which he practiced the bodhisattva way to do so (the original cause) have endured endlessly throughout the numberless major world system dust particle kalpas in the past since he obtained enlightenment. And he adds that they will continue to exist for a duration twice as long again.

The life state of Buddhahood (original effect) is ever-abiding and eternal, and the life state of the nine worlds in which one practices the bodhisattva way (the original cause) is inexhaustible and never ending, too. In this way, the causality of enlightenment described in the essential teaching—that is, the doctrine of original cause and original effect—is dramatically different from the view in pre-Lotus Sutra teachings, which asserts that Buddhahood can only be realized by eliminating the life states of the nine worlds.

In fact, the "Life Span" chapter explains that the Buddha, even after becoming enlightened in the remote past, has ceaselessly pursued the bodhisattva way out of a desire to liberate from suffering those who dwell in the reality of the nine worlds. Here, the true aspect of the Buddha becomes clear through Shakyamuni, in the "Life Span" chapter, casting off the transient and revealing the true. This true identity, if you will, is that of the eternal Buddha who embodies a way of life dedicated to never-ending bodhisattva practice.

The life state of unceasing devotion to bodhisattva practice amid the reality of the nine worlds is a life state of the nine worlds; at the same time, the eternal life state

of Buddhahood provides the fundamental energy for manifesting this commitment to unending bodhisattva practice.

In earlier sutras, it was assumed that Shakyamuni—who attained enlightenment for the first time in his present existence—would, upon death, be reborn in a pure land in some other world and cease carrying out bodhisattva practice in this mundane world. But for the Buddha who originally attained enlightenment in the remote past, the mundane world is itself a pure land and a land of Tranquil Light.

From the perspective of this Buddha of the "Life Span" chapter, the reality of the nine worlds represents an opportunity to bring forth the eternal inner life force of Buddhahood; it also constitutes the arena for actualizing and expressing the wisdom and compassion of Buddhahood. In addition, this Buddha regards those suffering amid the reality of the nine worlds as children to be taken care of and led to happiness, and as friends with whom to share the limitless freedom of the state of Buddhahood.

The Buddha, who has realized this true, absolute freedom, exercises mastery over his body and mind through the power of Buddhahood and self-reliantly conquers all negativity and other devilish forces. At the same time, the Buddha recognizes that the power of Buddhahood also lies dormant within the lives of others and within the mundane world itself. Thus, in order to unlock and activate this latent power, he continually strives to awaken people to their Buddha nature. He does this by tirelessly pursuing courageous action, manifesting unlimited wisdom and engaging in sincere dialogue.

In this way, Shakyamuni's casting off the transient and revealing the true in the "Life

Span" chapter radically transforms earlier assumptions about the Buddha and about attaining Buddhahood.

It is to be pointed out, however, that the literal teaching of the "Life Span" chapter speaks primarily about the "original effect" of the Buddha who attained enlightenment in the remote past. Its only reference to the "original cause" is found in the passage, "Originally I practiced the bodhisattva way" (LSOC, 268).

The Beginningless World of Buddhahood and the Beginningless Nine Worlds

It was Nichiren who discerned that the essential Law for the attainment of Buddhahood by ordinary people was hidden in the depths of "Life Span." With regard to the doctrine of original cause and original effect, he writes: "It reveals that the nine worlds are all present in beginningless Buddhahood and that Buddhahood is inherent in the beginningless nine worlds. This is the true mutual possession of the Ten Worlds, the true hundred worlds and thousand factors, the true three thousand realms in a single moment of life" (WND-1, 235).

In terms of the literal meaning of the text, "beginningless Buddhahood" is the eternal and ever-abiding life state of Buddhahood gained by the Buddha of original attainment in the remote past. As indicated earlier, this Buddha is also endowed with the life states of the nine worlds. Therefore, Nichiren says, "The nine worlds are all present in

beginningless Buddhahood" (WND-1, 235).

This Buddha, though having secured the life state of Buddhahood, continues to struggle steadfastly in the reality of the nine worlds to lead living beings to enlightenment. For this Buddha, life states of the nine worlds that are steeped in suffering and sorrow function to help others attain Buddhahood. Ordinarily, suffering and sorrow tend to lead people to withdraw, to sap their vitality and strength. But when these are experienced in a life state of the nine worlds endowed with beginningless Buddhahood, they can function as empathy and great compassion to lead others to enlightenment. They can become powerful motivating emotions that arise because the power of Buddhahood is continuously active in our lives and because our lives are open to the world and those around us.

Next, Nichiren says, "Buddhahood is inherent in the beginningless nine worlds" (WND-1, 235). Let us first look at this passage based on the literal meaning of the text.

In his treatise *The Words and Phrases of the Lotus Sutra*, the Great Teacher T'ien-t'ai of China writes, "When the Buddha reached the first stage of security,[4] he had already acquired eternal life." In other words, by pursuing the bodhisattva way in the remote past, Shakyamuni had already acquired the ever-abiding life state of the world of Bodhisattva when he ascended to the first stage of security, the stage of nonregression.

All bodhisattvas initially make four universal vows,[5] including the vow to save innumerable living beings. We could say that people gain the ever-abiding life state of the world of bodhisattva when they have confidence that the bodhisattva way of life is correct and reaffirm their vow never to regress in bodhisattva practice. Because Shakyamuni possessed this unshakable vow, he pursued the path of bodhisattva practice without end even after he attained Buddhahood.

Nichikan, the twenty-sixth high priest of the Nikko lineage, known as a leading restorer of Nichiren Buddhism, commented on this passage from T'ien-t'ai just cited. In *The Six-Volume Writings*, he writes: "[From this principle it is very clear that] original cause is ever present. That is why it is called the beginningless nine worlds." Nichiren calls the ceaseless dedication to unending bodhisattva practice the "beginningless nine worlds."

The pre-Lotus Sutra teachings view the nine worlds as being impermanent and the world of Buddhahood as eternal and ever abiding. Consequently, to bridge the seemingly insurmountable gulf between them, they set forth the concept of working gradually toward enlightenment by carrying out Buddhist practice over countless lifetimes across an incalculably long period of time. But because these teachings are based on having to discard the nine worlds before one can reach the world of Buddhahood, they ultimately put forth a view that abhors and seeks to eliminate the earthly desires innate in the nine worlds.

In contrast, the essential teaching of the Lotus Sutra expounds both the eternal life state of Buddhahood and the eternal bodhisattva way that represents its actual practice, and reveals the principles of "the inclusion of the nine worlds in Buddhahood" and "the inclusion of Buddhahood in the nine worlds." Further, by clarifying the original cause and original effect of Shakyamuni's enlightenment, it indicates that the Ten Worlds exist eternally in the life of each person and invalidates all previously described causes and effects of attaining Buddhahood in earlier sutras.

By elucidating the original cause and original effect and the principle that Buddhahood and the nine worlds are originally inherent and eternally present in life, the essential teaching of the Lotus Sutra firmly establishes that life is endowed with the Ten Worlds. That is why Nichiren says that revelation of the doctrine of original cause and original effect in the essential teaching of the Lotus Sutra establishes the "true mutual possession of the Ten Worlds, the true hundred worlds and thousand factors, the true three thousand realms in a single moment of life" (WND-1, 235). It is to be remembered, however, that this explanation is based solely on the literal meaning of the sutra.

On a deeper level, we can view these principles as not only applying to the one person Shakyamuni but to all living beings. In other words, they demonstrate that all living beings are entities that originally seek to manifest their eternal Buddhahood and undertake unceasing bodhisattva practice and that, at their very core, all without exception yearn for the happiness of both themselves and others.

In Nichiren's statement about the original cause and original effect in the above passage, we can discern the intent hidden in the depths of the sutra: to reveal the original cause and original effect of enlightenment for all people.

Nichikan further comments on the teaching implicit in the "Life Span" chapter: "The Mystic Law of hearing the name and words of the truth in the remote past,[6] the actual three thousand realms in a single moment of life,[7] is hidden in the depths of the passage relating to [Shakyamuni's] original cause for attaining the first stage of security."

"First stage of security" means a state of mind in which the ultimate purpose of life is fixed on realizing enlightenment for oneself and actualizing the enlightenment of all people. It refers to a state of life in which one is firmly resolved to pursue the bodhisattva way eternally, no matter the difficulties, without ever regressing in practice. The moment in the distant past when Shakyamuni determined to forever practice the eternal bodhisattva way comprises the "original cause" of his enlightenment. Nichikan, however, goes a step further by saying that it is "the Mystic Law of hearing the name and words of the truth in the remote past, the actual three thousand realms in a single moment of life"—the fundamental Law for attaining Buddhahood (Nam-myoho-renge-kyo)—that was the driving force behind the practice that enabled him to achieve the first stage of security.

"Hearing the name and words of the truth" here means "the stage of hearing the name and words of the truth." This is the stage of practice of someone who hears about the Mystic Law for the first time and embraces faith in it. "The Mystic Law of hearing the name and words of the truth in the remote past," meanwhile, is the fundamental Law through which, by practicing, an ordinary person can realize Buddhahood, and Nichiren Daishonin directly revealed this Law as Nam-myoho-renge-kyo.

The literal teaching of the "Life Span" chapter emphasizes the original effect of Buddhahood attained by Shakyamuni, while the teaching hidden in the depths of the chapter emphasizes the one who practices the bodhisattva way, which is the original cause. The latter clarifies the original cause and original effect that represent the true causality for ordinary people in the nine worlds to become Buddhas in their present form. This is the original cause and original effect hidden in the depths of the sutra as taught in Nichiren Buddhism.

In other words, original cause is when an ordinary person hears about the Mystic Law for the first time, embraces faith and resolves to practice the unending bodhisattva way. And original effect is when the eternal life state of Buddhahood appears in the life of that ordinary person.

So what is meant by "beginningless nine worlds" in Nichiren Buddhism? We can interpret it to be the state of life at the moment when ordinary people in the nine worlds break through the ignorance and illusion that has previously controlled their lives. Because this state of life gives rise to the function of Buddhahood, Nichiren says, "Buddhahood is inherent in the beginningless nine worlds" (WND-1, 235).

It is faith that eradicates fundamental ignorance and illusion—faith in the eternal Mystic Law. Nichiren established Nam-myoho-renge-kyo and the Gohonzon to enable all people to base their lives on this faith.

In "Letter to Gijo-bo,"[8] commenting on the "Life Span" chapter passage "single-mindedly desiring to see the Buddha, not hesitating even if it costs them their lives," Nichiren writes, "As a result of this passage, I have revealed the Buddhahood in my own life" (WND-1, 389). After stating that faith in the Mystic Law (Myoho-renge-kyo) is characterized by the spirit of not begrudging one's life, he offers three interpretations of the line "single-mindedly desiring to see the Buddha" to explain his own attainment of

Buddhahood: (1) single-mindedly observing the Buddha, (2) concentrating one's mind on seeing the Buddha, and (3) when looking at one's own mind, perceiving that it is the Buddha (see WND-1, 390).

We can regard the first two interpretations as signifying the cause, indicating single-minded faith; and the third "when looking at one's own mind, perceiving that it is the Buddha," as signifying the effect, indicating the single-minded attainment of Buddhahood. The original cause and the original effect are actualized through single-minded faith.

Revealing the "beginningless world of Buddhahood" and the "beginningless nine worlds" in this manner closes the seeming divide between the impermanent life states of the nine worlds and the eternal life state of the world of Buddhahood and brings the two to exist together simultaneously. As a result, the mutual possession of the Ten Worlds is established in the true sense. When the mutual possession of the Ten Worlds is established, the doctrine of three thousand realms in a single moment of life is also established.

Therefore, Nichiren says, "This is the true mutual possession of the Ten Worlds, the true hundred worlds and thousand factors, the true three thousand realms in a single moment of life" (WND-1, 235).

The Fivefold Comparison—Clarifying the Causality of Life and the Fundamental Direction for Human Existence

In the first half of "The Opening of the Eyes," Nichiren Daishonin outlines the teaching that later [when it was systematized by the twenty-sixth high priest, Nichikan] came to be known as the fivefold comparison. Now, let's examine the significance of this comparison, while summarizing what we have covered so far.

We have already looked at how the three virtues—sovereign, teacher and parent—form the theme of "The Opening of the Eyes." Nichiren looks at the various individuals and beings widely respected as sovereign, teacher or parent in the main philosophies and religions of his time. He specifically investigates: (1) Confucianism and other philosophies and religious traditions of China, which are grouped together under the heading of Confucianism or non-Buddhist scriptures and referred to as the "external scriptures"; (2) the pre- and non-Buddhist teachings of India, including Brahmanism, which are together referred to as non-Buddhist teachings, or the "external way"; and (3) the teachings of Buddhism, which are referred to as the "internal

way." Nichiren also inquires into what people are actually taught and the attitude toward life they cultivate through revering one or another of these esteemed beings. He does so because the touchstone for a figure who embodies the truly outstanding qualities of sovereign, teacher and parent is whether the particular teaching that figure represents enables people to lead secure lives.

Thus, in "The Opening of the Eyes," taking up the theme of sovereign, teacher and parent, Nichiren delves incisively into the teachings and approaches to life that these different philosophies and religions propound. And the fundamental focus of his inquiry is the causal law of life.

The Heart of Philosophy or Religion Lies in Clarifying Cause and Effect

The purpose of the fivefold comparison is to clarify which religion or philosophy can actually enable people to overcome their sufferings and attain a state of unshakable happiness. This comparison involves evaluating the different teachings in terms of how they explain the workings of cause and effect in life—in other words, the causality of life, which refers to the causality behind happiness or unhappiness. Ultimately, it is the same as the causality of the Ten Worlds—and, therefore, importantly, of attaining Buddhahood—which we discussed last time.

Stated another way, the fivefold comparison examines the relative superiority and depth of each teaching, assessing how much each pursues and fundamentally recognizes the causality behind happiness or unhappiness.

For example, when a physician treats an illness, unless that treatment is based on a thorough understanding of the cause, it may only intensify the patient's condition. Similarly, unless the fundamental causes are thoroughly understood, efforts to solve human suffering and misery will end up only worsening the situation.

The heart of a religion or philosophy lies in clarifying cause and effect.

The Great Teacher T'ien-t'ai of China cites five outstanding characteristics of the Lotus Sutra, which he sums up as the five major principles—name, essence, quality, function and teaching.[1] Of these, "quality" means the central doctrine or teaching of a sutra, its heart or core. More specifically, T'ien-t'ai states that it is none other than the principle of cause and effect.[2]

The principle of cause and effect to which T'ien-t'ai refers is in fact the causality of life wherein individuals who are steeped in misery (cause) reveal their most sublime inner potential, overcome their sufferings and establish a life state of indestructible happiness (effect).

T'ien-t'ai defined the ultimate Law of enlightenment as the "true aspect." This "true aspect" (corresponding to "essence" in the five major principles), he says, can only be described as unfathomable, beyond the power of words to describe, beyond the mind's power to comprehend. He indicates, however, that the true aspect is inextricably related to the causality of attaining Buddhahood.

To borrow an analogy from T'ien-t'ai, the true aspect can be likened to a vast and unbounded space, while cause and effect can be likened to pillars and beams. With the pillars and beams, the space takes on the shape of a room. At the same time, the pillars and beams could not be called such if they did not shape the space into a room.[3]

In other words, the depth of the doctrine of causality expounded by a particular teaching correlates to the depth of the law of enlightenment that forms the teaching's basic premise.

The teaching of Nam-myoho-renge-kyo propagated by Nichiren consists of the ultimate Mystic Law (*myoho*) and the cause and effect that it is based on (*renge*). We can regard this single phrase, *Nam-myoho-renge-kyo*, as expressing the ultimate law of cause and effect for attaining Buddhahood. Therefore, by chanting Nam-myoho-renge-kyo even one time, we can realize the cause and effect of enlightenment in our lives at that very moment.

Looking at the religious and philosophical traditions discussed by Nichiren, we see many differences in how they explain the causality of life. In this treatise, Nichiren evaluates the relative depth of each teaching through the fivefold comparison, thereby clarifying the ultimate causality for attaining Buddhahood (Nam-myoho-renge-kyo) as the essential teaching for leading all people of the Latter Day of the Law to enlightenment.

Let us now discuss the content of the fivefold comparison based on Nichiren's statements.

Carving Out Our Destiny Through Our Own Will and Action

1. Buddhism is superior to non-Buddhist teachings.

The first comparison is between Buddhism, the "internal way," and the non-Buddhist teachings of China and India, the "external way."

Buddhism teaches that the principal cause determining our happiness or unhappiness lies within our own lives and that we are the protagonists with the power to decide our own destiny. This is why Buddhism is called the "internal way."

By contrast, a closer look at the non-Buddhist religions and philosophies reveals, first, that some do not recognize the principle of causality as it concerns individual fortune or misfortune. While some expound doctrines of accidentalism or indeterminism, according to which everything is coincidence or chance, others expound doctrines of determinism or fatalism, which hold that regardless of one's own efforts or actions everything is predetermined or predestined. There are also those who strike a middle ground between these

two perspectives. This refers to the teachings of the three ascetics, who are regarded as the founders of the non-Buddhist philosophies of India. Similar doctrines can also be found in various philosophies and currents of thought prevalent today.

Among the philosophies scrutinized by Nichiren are also those that, while recognizing the principle of causality within the parameters of the present existence, fail to pursue it into the periods before birth and after death, asserting that what happens in those periods is unknowable. These are represented by such schools of thought as Confucianism and Taoism,[4] and would also include Western rationalism, which is based on the development of modern science.

These kinds of philosophies cannot satisfyingly answer such questions as "Why are people born into different circumstances?" and "Why are there cases where the effects of good or evil actions do not appear in this lifetime?" Accordingly, they also cannot fully answer existential questions like "Why was I born?" or "What is the purpose of my life?"

Indian Brahmanism,[5] the six schools of philosophy[6] and other teachings in ancient India do expound the causality of life operating throughout past, present and future, but it is a causality colored by determinism or fatalism and subject to external forces such as nature or a deity that controls human destiny. As a result, these teachings seriously limit human will and autonomy.

In short, the ancient teachings of India and China other than Buddhism either fail to explain causality, or, if they do explain it, offer only a partial and biased doctrine. This is Nichiren's conclusion. Therefore, in "The Opening of the Eyes," he says with regard to the founders of these religions and philosophies, "They are no more than infants who cannot understand the principles of cause and effect" (WND-1, 223).

Buddhism, the "internal way," however, teaches that individuals are responsible for everything that happens to them; simply put, the idea that one reaps what one sows.

The reason we can calmly accept the concept of the strict law of cause and effect operating in our lives is that we apprehend the truth that we inherently possess within us the boundless transformative power and potential that is the Buddha nature. For us to keep making efforts to become happy, we need to know that the possibility for happiness exists within our lives.

Buddhism, the "internal way," enables us to awaken to our personal autonomy and responsibility—that is, to recognize that we have the power to carve out our destiny through our own will and actions in the present.

Mahayana Buddhism Seeks To Clarify the Cause for Attaining Happiness

2. Mahayana Buddhism is superior to Hinayana Buddhism.

The next level of the fivefold comparison is the comparison between Mahayana and Hinayana Buddhism. In "The Opening of the Eyes," however, Nichiren hardly touches on this particular comparison. He mentions it in passing in his comparison of true Mahayana and provisional Mahayana, or more specifically his comparison of the theoretical teaching of the Lotus Sutra and the provisional pre-Lotus Sutra teachings, when he refers to censuring people of the two vehicles (voice-hearers and cause-awakened ones), who were practitioners of the Hinayana teachings.[7] So although it is not discussed separately, we can view the comparison of Mahayana and Hinayana Buddhism as being included in this particular comparison.

Buddhism is referred to as the "internal way"; nevertheless, it encompasses a wide variety of teachings. Among these, the Hinayana teachings aim to enable people to free themselves from earthly desires, which are the cause of suffering, and attain nirvana—a state of supreme peace and tranquillity—through carrying out practices such as upholding precepts and engaging in meditation. But the happiness to which the Hinayana teachings aspire is passive, as they merely focus on eliminating the cause of unhappiness rather than actively seeking to enable people to open the path to their own happiness, much less open the way to happiness for others.

Moreover, since Hinayana posits the cause of unhappiness as earthly desires of the nine worlds that are inherent in our lives, the only way to completely eliminate these desires is to extinguish our lives altogether. The Hinayana approach to enlightenment has accordingly been referred to as "reducing the body to ashes and annihilating consciousness." Herein lies the limitation of the Hinayana teachings.

In contrast, the Mahayana teachings, instead of urging the elimination of earthly desires, state that by opening up and manifesting the wisdom of enlightenment in our lives, which are filled with earthly desires, we can properly control those desires and construct a pure, strong, self-motivated life. This is the principle of "earthly desires are enlightenment." Rather than merely helping people eliminate the causes of their unhappiness, the Mahayana teachings actively focus on enabling people to transform those causes into the causes for happiness, as well as to lead others to enlightenment.

True Mahayana Reveals That All People Are Endowed With Buddhahood

3. **True Mahayana is superior to provisional Mahayana.**

The Mahayana teachings can also be divided into two further categories: true Mahayana and provisional Mahayana.

The Lotus Sutra, which constitutes true Mahayana, elucidates that the lives of all people are originally endowed with the world of Buddhahood, the fundamental cause of happiness. ("All living beings alike possess the Buddha nature.") The Lotus Sutra also clarifies the truth of life that all people can tap and reveal that Buddha nature. (In "Expedient Means," the 2nd chapter, it sets forth the four aspects of Buddha wisdom—opening, showing, awakening and helping people enter the path of Buddha wisdom.[8])

The pre-Lotus Sutra Mahayana teachings, which make up the provisional Mahayana, insist that the people of the two vehicles, who are despised because they only seek their own enlightenment, as well as evil people and women, who are believed incapable of becoming happy, are not originally endowed with the Buddha nature. In this way, these teachings limit the causes of happiness. They are not true Mahayana but rather teachings expounded as an expedient means to accommodate the popular beliefs of the time. They are merely provisional teachings.

On the other hand, the Lotus Sutra, the true teaching, elucidates the Buddha's actual enlightenment to how all people—including people of the two vehicles, evil people and women—can equally attain Buddhahood. It also clarifies the doctrine (of "three thousand realms in a single moment of life") on which this teaching is based.

The Buddha's real intention is for all people to become happy. And it is in the Lotus Sutra, which expounds the principles that make this possible, that the Buddha's true enlightenment is directly revealed.

The Essential Teaching Overcomes the Fault of the Earlier Teachings

4. **The essential teaching of the Lotus Sutra is superior to the theoretical teaching of the Lotus Sutra.**

Even though all people possess within them the world of Buddhahood—the fundamental cause of happiness—whether they can actually bring it forth is another matter.

Viewed in terms of the eternity of life and the principle of cause and effect operating over past, present and future, the life state we experience in the present is due to our actions (karma) from countless former existences. The earlier sutras, including the theoretical teaching (first half) of the Lotus Sutra, teach that in order to change that karma, we need to steadfastly carry out good actions over an extremely long period of time and accumulate the positive benefits of those actions in our lives. According to this view, attaining enlightenment requires countless *kalpas* of Buddhist practice.

Furthermore, these sutras teach that Shakyamuni Buddha achieved enlightenment for the first time in his contemporaneous lifetime in India as a result of practice over an incalculably long period of time. This conception of attaining Buddhahood derives from the flawed approach of "abhorring and seeking to eliminate the earthly desires innate in the nine worlds," insisting that only by extinguishing our lives of the nine worlds (cause) can we bring forth the life of Buddhahood (effect).

By contrast, the essential teaching (latter half) of the Lotus Sutra explains that Shakyamuni actually attained Buddhahood in the remote past, numberless major world system dust particle kalpas ago and, because his life as a bodhisattva has endured unceasingly ever since, he has continually appeared in various forms to teach living beings. This reveals the true image of the Buddha. In other words, the nine worlds and the world of Buddhahood are also inherent and ever abiding in the life of the Buddha, Shakyamuni.

By explaining this fact, the essential teaching reveals that we can manifest the world of Buddhahood in our lives of the nine worlds, just as we are, thereby opening the way to attaining Buddhahood in our present form.

Making the Gohonzon Our Mirror and Nichiren Our Model

5. The Buddhism of sowing is superior to the Buddhism of the harvest.

The essential Lotus Sutra teaching opens the way to attaining Buddhahood in our present form. But when viewed in the context of its literal, surface meaning, we see that Shakyamuni could only acquire eternal life as a result of practicing the bodhisattva way prior to his enlightenment in the remote past. Achieving such ever-lasting life necessitated him reaching the first stage of security, which is the stage of nonregression. Then, having reached that stage, he could, with resolute faith, break through all fundamental darkness or illusion, attain wisdom and perceive that the nine worlds and the world of Buddhahood are innate and ever abiding in his own life.

The practice required to reach the first stage of security is extremely difficult, however, as is attaining the wisdom to actually perceive the world of Buddhahood in one's life. It is far beyond the ability of ordinary people. Accordingly, from the standpoint of its literal meaning, the essential teaching does not directly open the way for ordinary people to attain Buddhahood in their present form and achieve enlightenment in this lifetime.

But the teaching implicit in the Lotus Sutra's depths—namely, Nichiren Buddhism—directly reveals Nam-myoho-renge-kyo, which is both the driving force behind Shakyamuni's bodhisattva practice in attaining the first stage of security in the remote past, as well as the fundamental Law he perceived at that time. By seeking and faithfully embracing this Law, an ordinary person can immediately gain the fruit of Buddhahood.

Nichiren left us the Gohonzon, in which he faithfully depicts the world of Buddhahood he realized in his own life through Nam-myoho-renge-kyo while remaining an ordinary person. With the Gohonzon as our mirror and Nichiren as our model, we can instantly bring forth that enlightened state from within our own lives, through our deep faith and confidence that we, too, possess Buddhahood.

The Teaching of Cause and Effect in a Single Life Moment

Accordingly, the ultimate causality is contained in the ordinary person's strong, deep mind of faith. If we have the strength of faith to break through fundamental darkness and illusion, then our lives in the nine worlds will manifest their eternal nature (the beginning-less nine worlds), and we can attain the life state of Buddhahood.

In "On the Mystic Principle of the True Cause" (GZ, 870–77), Nichiren succinctly clarifies the relative superiority and depth of the various Buddhist teachings based on the principle of cause and effect. He describes four views of causality in which the highest is the "teaching of cause and effect in a single life moment."[9]

The provisional, pre-Lotus Sutra teachings taught as temporary expedients set forth a view of enlightenment that abhors and seeks to eliminate the earthly desires of the nine worlds. They maintain that only by freeing oneself of the nine worlds (cause) can one attain the world of Buddhahood (effect). As a result, Nichiren says, they embody a "teaching of cause and effect of disparate nature."

The theoretical Lotus Sutra teaching, meanwhile, because it explains that the nine worlds and the world of Buddhahood are both inherent in our lives, represents a "teaching of cause and effect of identical nature."

And the essential teaching of the Lotus Sutra, because it clarifies that the true body of the Buddha is characterized by both the nine worlds and the world of Buddhahood abiding eternally over past, present and future, constitutes a "teaching of cause and effect of eternal coexistence."

In contrast to these, Nichiren's unique essential teaching (that is, Nam-myoho-renge-kyo of the Three Great Secret Laws) hidden in the depths of "Life Span," the 16th chapter of the Lotus Sutra, elucidates that both the nine worlds and the world of Buddhahood are contained in the ordinary person's mind of faith. It also expounds that, through faith, one can manifest the world of Buddhahood at any time and attain enlightenment in his or her present form. That is why it is called a "teaching of cause and effect in a single moment of life."

In Nichiren Buddhism, one's mind or heart is certainly key. As Nichiren says, "It is the heart that is important" ("The Strategy of the Lotus Sutra," WND-1, 1000).

A Self That Embodies the Fundamental Purpose of Life

As the view of causality deepens with each progression through the fivefold comparison, the significance of the sovereign, teacher and parent whom all people should revere also deepens.

Even though figures deemed worthy of being respected as sovereign, teacher and parent may appear in the non-Buddhist scriptures and the religions and philosophies of ancient India and China, their teachings failed to view causality clearly. Consequently, no matter how widely those who embodied the virtues of sovereign, teacher and parent were venerated, or how much their supremacy was stressed, they could not provide people with a clear purpose in life. As a result people either led lives of blind searching or of passive obedience to authority.

Next, even within Buddhism, the Hinayana and provisional Mahayana teachings espouse a view of attaining Buddhahood and of causality that abhor and seek to eliminate the earthly desires of the nine worlds. In these teachings, the Buddha is revered as a special being. Adherents either lead lives satisfied with the small goal of simply eliminating their own earthly desires (in the case of Hinayana) or lives of empty illusion, waiting to be saved by some great fictional Buddha of universal salvation (in provisional Mahayana). In either case, a passive way of life is unavoidable.

But the Lotus Sutra, which is true Mahayana, reveals the true mutual possession of the Ten Worlds. It elucidates that living beings in the nine worlds are also endowed with the world of Buddhahood (revealed in the theoretical teaching), and that the Buddha who actually attained enlightenment in the remote past also possesses the nine worlds (revealed in the essential teaching). Therefore, it opens the way for people to live with profound hope, realizing that they can manifest from within the supreme life state of Buddhahood.

But the description of the Buddha who realized enlightenment in the remote past centers primarily on his having attained the effect of Buddhahood in its complete and perfect form. As a result, he remains merely an object for people to worship and idolize and does not become an example they can emulate in seeking to actualize the causality of attaining Buddhahood for themselves.

By contrast, in Nichiren Buddhism, Nichiren himself serves as the example of an ordinary person becoming a Buddha through the power of faith or strong inner resolve. Nichiren's struggles, his selfless practice, his vows, his heart of a lion king, as detailed in his writings, all show us the single-minded determination or spirit necessary for an ordinary person to attain Buddhahood. This is clear from such statements as: "Like Nichiren, for example" ("Letter from Sado," WND-1, 302), or "You need not seek far for an example" ("The Supremacy of the Law," WND-1, 614).

The fivefold comparison, by clarifying the ultimate principle of cause and effect, sets forth the highest goal or direction for continually improving our lives. Ultimately, it is a teaching that reveals the supreme sovereign, teacher and parent functioning as the ultimate example for ordinary people of the Latter Day of attaining Buddhahood in this lifetime.

"The Opening of the Eyes" is a writing that proclaims to all people of the Latter Day that Nichiren Daishonin is the votary of the Lotus Sutra, and he serves as the supreme model of an ordinary person attaining enlightenment. That is why it is called the writing that clarifies the object of devotion in terms of the Person.

5

A Vow for the Enlightenment of All People—The Power Deep Within Our Lives That Can Overcome All Obstacles

I, Nichiren, am the only person in all Japan who understands this [that the other Buddhist schools proffer slanderous teachings and cause people to fall into the evil paths of existence]. But if I utter so much as a word concerning it, then parents, brothers, and teachers will surely censure me, and the ruler of the nation will take steps against me. On the other hand, I am fully aware that if I do not speak out I will be lacking in compassion. I have considered which course to take in the light of the teachings of the Lotus and Nirvana sutras. If I remain silent, I may escape persecutions in this lifetime, but in my next life I will most certainly fall into the hell of incessant suffering. If I speak out, I am fully aware that I will have to contend with the three obstacles and four devils. But of these two courses, surely the latter is the one to choose.

If I were to falter in my determination in the face of persecutions by the sovereign, however, it would be better not to speak out. While thinking this over, I recalled the teachings of the "Treasure Tower" chapter on the six difficult and nine easy acts. Persons like myself who are of paltry strength might still be able to lift Mount Sumeru and toss it about; persons like myself who are lacking in supernatural powers might still shoulder a load of dry grass and yet remain unburned in the fire at the end of the kalpa of decline; and persons like myself who are without wisdom might still read and memorize as many sutras as there are sands in the Ganges. But such acts are not difficult, we are told, when compared to the difficulty of embracing even one phrase or verse of the Lotus Sutra in the Latter Day of the Law. Nevertheless, I vowed to summon up

a powerful and unconquerable desire for the salvation of all beings and never to falter in my efforts. (WND-1, 239–40)

The power of the spirit forges and strengthens human beings and builds rich character. A solid philosophy and firm commitment give rise to the distinctive qualities of an outstanding individual. "The Opening of the Eyes" is a treatise that contains the profoundest philosophy and the strongest commitment.

It contains the profoundest philosophy because it sets forth the great teaching for ordinary people's attainment of Buddhahood. This is an embodiment of the ultimate compassion, the opening of the way for the salvation of all humankind. Nichiren Daishonin recognized the existence of the eternal Mystic Law in the seemingly transient lives of human beings, and he established a path whereby each person could bring forth the power of that Law. Here we find the profoundest philosophy genuinely capable of giving hope and courage to all people.

By "strongest commitment," I mean the powerful commitment to kosen-rufu, with which we vow to propagate the great teaching that can free humankind from misery, no matter what obstacles or devilish forces arise. It goes without saying that underlying this commitment is a spirit of selfless dedication to the Law and an immense compassion to empathize with people's sufferings and to cherish their infinite potential.

In "The Opening of the Eyes," the Daishonin first reveals that the doctrine of

"actual three thousand realms in a single moment of life" hidden in the Lotus Sutra's depths is the teaching to be propagated in the Latter Day of the Law for the enlightenment of all humankind. We have already discussed this subject in detail.

Next, he identifies the true votary of the Lotus Sutra who will spread this great teaching. In other words, after revealing the fundamental Law for attaining Buddhahood, he turns to focus on the person who will propagate it.

At the beginning of this section of the treatise, the Daishonin discusses his own vow to stand up and spread the Mystic Law in the Latter Day—the vow he made when he first proclaimed the establishment of his teaching. This demonstrates the profound importance of a personal vow or pledge when taking on the challenge to propagate the Law in the latter age.

The Fundamental Darkness That Denies Human Potential for Buddhahood

Touching on how difficult it is to carry out kosen-rufu in this latter age, the Daishonin writes: "The Buddha predicted in the Nirvana Sutra that in the Latter Day of the Law those who abide by the correct teaching will be as few as the specks of dirt that can be placed on a fingernail, while those who slander the correct teaching will be as numerous as the specks of dirt in all the lands of the ten directions . . .

"Those who fall into the evil paths because of secular crimes will be as insignificant in number as the specks of dirt placed on a fingernail, but those who do so because of violations of the Buddhist teachings will be equal in number to the specks of dirt in all the lands of the ten directions. More monks than laymen, and more nuns than laywomen, will fall into the evil paths" (WND-1, 238).

The Latter Day of the Law is described as a defiled age, a time when people are said to have inferior capacity to understand Buddhism, and when monks and nuns of various Buddhist schools become increasingly decadent. While these are obviously important factors, the true essence of why propagation in the Latter Day is far more difficult than during the Former or Middle Days of the Law[1] cannot be fully understood without addressing the subject of slander of the Law.

Slander of the Law means denigrating the correct teaching, and it arises from disbelief in that teaching. "Correct teaching" indicates the Lotus Sutra, which expounds the enlightenment of all people. The sutra teaches that each of us, without exception, can attain Buddhahood. But this is difficult for many people to accept because they think of Buddhas as transcendent, otherworldly beings, somehow separate or different from mere mortals. This long-standing belief, derived from an authoritarian view of Buddhist faith and religion in general, had so influenced people that they could not believe in the Lotus Sutra or its teaching of universal enlightenment.

People's actual life experience has also made it difficult to believe in their potential for Buddhahood. Amid trying circumstances, they can scarcely imagine that anyone suffering as much as they are could possibly become a Buddha. When things are going smoothly, however, and people seem already happy, they tend to think there's no need to seek enlightenment or attain Buddhahood. Either way, it is rare for people to actually embrace faith in the correct teaching.

Consequently, because the idea of universal enlightenment is so difficult to believe, many lean toward authoritarian religions that promote the concept of transcendent, otherworldly gods or Buddhas. These religions often interpose a clergy as a necessary intermediary between the practitioners and these distant, transcendent beings.

When a practitioner of the Lotus Sutra striving to enable all people to attain enlightenment appears in a society where such religious views predominate, many who are stubbornly attached to their existing beliefs will resent and persecute that person—the very one actually practicing the correct teaching.

For example, illustrating the persecution that arises from disbelief in and slander of the correct teaching that expounds the enlightenment of all people, "Encouraging Devotion," the 13th chapter of the Lotus Sutra, describes the three powerful enemies taunting the sutra's practitioners with sarcastic contempt, "You are all no doubt Buddhas!" (LSOC, 233).

The Hinayana and provisional Mahayana teachings either make Shakyamuni out to be a special being possessing a state of life that human beings cannot attain, or they only discuss transcendent Buddhas far removed from the mortal realm, such as Amida or Mahavairochana.[2] Buddhist schools based on such teachings emerged during the Former and Middle Days of the Law, and the more they focused on otherworldly Buddhas, the more authoritarian they eventually became.

In the Latter Day of the Law, people fail to grasp the Lotus Sutra's true meaning and insist even more rigidly that authoritarian religion is correct; the prevailing religious attitude is one of submissive dependence on the power or beneficence of transcendent gods or Buddhas. As a result, people's attachment to faith in the teachings of their existing Buddhist schools grows even stronger, and mistaken views grow more rampant, as evidenced by the Daishonin's words, "Those who espouse Hinayana reject Mahayana, and those who espouse provisional teachings attack the true teaching" ("On the Buddha's Prophecy," WND-1, 400). That is, there is a prevalence of Buddhist schools that slander the Lotus Sutra.

In the end, these schools serve as negative influences producing many disbelievers and slanderers of the Lotus Sutra. They give rise to the lamentable situation in which "those who do so [fall into the evil paths] because of violations of the Buddhist teachings will be equal in number to the specks of dirt in all the lands of the ten directions" (WND-1, 238). Buddhism is originally a teaching for enabling people to attain enlightenment. As a result of believing in the erroneous doctrines of various Buddhist schools, however, people fall into the evil paths. This is what happens in the Latter Day, when the Law is about to perish.

The Daishonin stood up alone to lead the people of this dark age to enlightenment, and toward that end, he exposed in detail the hidden devilish nature of the various Buddhist schools of his day. In "The Opening of the Eyes," before sharing his vow in taking his solitary stand as the votary of the Lotus Sutra, the Daishonin exposes and harshly denounces the true nature of these schools that have degenerated into purveyors of slanderous teachings and cause people to fall into

the evil paths of existence. He identifies this devilish nature as a manifestation of the principle of "evil demons entering the body" (see LSOC, 233).[3]

The Root Cause of Slander of the Law

In "The Opening of the Eyes," the Daishonin points out that devils possess high-ranking priests who seem thoroughly conversant with the teachings of Buddhism, and through these priests they work to mislead many people (see WND-1, 239). In other words, devilish functions take over those who command a great deal of spiritual influence in society, aiming to confuse large numbers and cause them to fall into the evil paths.

It is not that the teachings Shakyamuni expounded prior to the Lotus Sutra are slanderous in and of themselves. The problem lies with aberrant priests who become attached to these teachings, misuse them and denigrate the Lotus Sutra; this is the root cause of slander of the Law. Furthermore, propagating the correct teaching in the Latter Day starts with overcoming the ignorance and delusion of those who support such slanderous priests.

As the Daishonin indicates when he says, "Fundamental darkness manifests itself as the devil king of the sixth heaven" ("The Treatment of Illness," WND-1, 1113), the true nature of the devil king is the fundamental darkness or illusion in the lives of all people. Dispelling the innate ignorance in people's hearts requires us to resolutely stand against and defeat evil influences and what Buddhism calls "bad friends." That is why correct Buddhist teaching has always stressed the importance of remaining constantly on guard against such negative influences, recognizing them for what they are and battling against them.

Some two hundred years into the Latter Day of the Law, only Nichiren Daishonin could see these priests' true inner reality of being "possessed by evil demons."

If a votary of the Lotus Sutra loudly proclaims the truth when everyone else has lost sight of the correct teaching, evil priests who have been deceiving the people will fear exposure and therefore attack that person. Meanwhile, those in the thrall of priestly deception, not willing to recognize their own folly in being deceived, will shun the practitioner of the correct teaching. They will regard him with hatred and jealousy, speak ill of him and ultimately persecute him.

A society where slander of the Law is rife will inevitably become one that represses the votary of the Lotus Sutra who proclaims the truth.

Nichiren Daishonin was well aware of this. Even so, he resolved to stand up alone for the sake of the people. His awareness of the obstacles ahead of him is evident from the unflinching consideration he gave this matter and the momentous struggle he waged in his heart before declaring the establishment of his teaching.

He describes some of that deep introspection in "The Opening of the Eyes." I am confident that the Daishonin's sublime inner struggle, which these words reveal, will be recognized for all time as an important page in the spiritual history of humankind.

Standing Up Alone Based on a Vow

Saying, "I, Nichiren, am the only person in all Japan who understands this" (WND-1, 239), the Daishonin indicates he alone realizes that evil influences causing people to slander the Law are rampant in the land.

In light of the Lotus and Nirvana sutras and other Buddhist scriptures, it is clear that if one tries to alert people to the fact that the country is filled with such slander, then the three obstacles and four devils are certain to arise. It is equally evident, however, that not speaking out constitutes a lack of compassion and as such destines one to the hell of incessant suffering in the next life. Consequently, based on the sutras, the Daishonin concludes that he should speak out.

As if choosing whether to take on the difficulty of sailing into stormy seas or accept the suffering of sinking in a dark abyss, the Daishonin clearly indicates that the correct course is to bravely venture into the storms of difficulty.

Of course, spreading the correct teaching in the Latter Day is by no means easy. The relentless onslaught of devilish forces, when the powerful wield their authority and commit persecution, can take an unimaginable mental and physical toll. The Daishonin, with his thorough grasp of the correct teaching of universal enlightenment, possessed deep insight into the Buddha nature inherent in human life. Perhaps this is why he could keenly apprehend the fearfulness of the devilish nature that seeks to obstruct the propagation of the correct teaching. Hence he says: "If I were to falter in my determination in the face of persecutions by the sovereign, however, it would be better not to speak out. While thinking this over . . ." (WND-1, 239).

So fierce and relentless is the struggle against devilish forces that one may well think: *If I'm going to turn back once I sail into tempestuous seas, then perhaps it would be better not to set out in the first place. If being battered by a storm of devilish functions might cause me to falter in my determination, then perhaps I should refrain from speaking out altogether.*

Similarly, the Daishonin deeply reflected on the challenges ahead before translating his conviction into courageous action. When he says it would be better not to speak out if it meant that he would falter in his determination, he is certainly not speaking from cowardice or weakness. The Daishonin understood the true nature of the devilish functions he would be up against. His earnest reflection on which course to take was that of a person with the genuine courage to ponder the incredibly difficult challenge of vanquishing the devilish forces that pervade the universe.

Although writing "while thinking this over" may give the impression of restful contemplation, an intense battle was raging in his heart, during which the Daishonin, then still in his early thirties, recalled the six difficult and nine easy acts described in "Treasure Tower," the 11th chapter of the Lotus Sutra.

Shakyamuni Buddha outlined the six difficult and nine easy acts to the assembly of bodhisattvas to encourage them to make a vow to spread the Lotus Sutra after his passing. The nine "easy" acts include such feats as lifting Mount Sumeru and hurling it across countless Buddha lands or walking into a great fire with a bundle of dry grass on one's back and remaining unburned. Even more

difficult than these are the six difficult acts—the most difficult of feats possible—which involve upholding and propagating the Lotus Sutra in the age after Shakyamuni's passing.

After explaining all this, Shakyamuni urges the bodhisattvas present to vow to exert themselves to propagate the Lotus Sutra after his death, regardless of the hardships it may entail. Later, in "The Opening of the Eyes," the Daishonin cites this exhortation by Shakyamuni as one of the "three pronouncements"[4] of the "Treasure Tower" chapter (see WND-1, 262).

The propagation of the Lotus Sutra after the Buddha's passing is the wish of all Buddhas throughout past, present and future. The Buddha, while thoroughly recognizing the difficulty of this undertaking, urges the bodhisattvas who will succeed him to boldly take on this challenge.

The six difficult and nine easy acts express the Buddha's intent. The Buddha, while plainly indicating the immense difficulty of spreading the Lotus Sutra after his passing, solemnly urges his disciples to make a vow. This can be regarded as a clear message to the practitioners of the Lotus Sutra in the Latter Day that, if they make a vow and establish solid faith in the Lotus Sutra, there is no hardship or obstacle that they cannot overcome.

Let us look at the three examples of the nine easy acts the Daishonin uses in weighing his own chances of success. He stresses that he is an ordinary mortal, describing himself as a person "of paltry strength," "lacking in supernatural powers" and "without wisdom" (WND-1, 239). What he wishes to communicate is that even if one should lack physical strength, supernatural powers or wisdom, a person who cherishes a strong vow or commitment to propagate the Law and advances together with the Buddha will be filled with infinite strength, courage and wisdom and can overcome even the most daunting obstacles. That is the message of boundless hope implicit in his words.

If they persevere in faith based on an unwavering commitment in an evil age, even ordinary people lacking in strength can summon the power of Buddhahood from within to overcome hardships and transform their lives.

Conversely, though some may boast of phenomenal strength, supernatural powers or wisdom, they may still find it exceedingly difficult to transform their individual lives.

What It Means To Make a Vow in Buddhism

After carefully considering the matter, the Daishonin at last makes his pledge: "I vowed to summon up a powerful and unconquerable desire for the salvation of all beings [literally, a desire for enlightenment] and never to falter in my efforts" (WND-1, 240). A powerful and unconquerable desire for enlightenment means the spirit to aspire for the attainment of Buddhahood, no matter what. This is the vow of a bodhisattva.

In fact, in the Mahayana teachings, all bodhisattvas are known to make four great vows: (1) to save innumerable living beings, (2) to eradicate countless earthly desires, (3) to master immeasurable Buddhist teachings and (4) to attain supreme enlightenment.

Words that constitute what could be described as the original form of these bodhisattva vows appear as a vow the Buddha makes in "The Parable of the Medicinal Herbs," the 5th chapter of the Lotus Sutra, "Those who have not yet crossed over I will cause to cross over, those not yet understood I will cause to understand, those not yet at rest I will put at rest, those not yet in nirvana I will cause to attain nirvana" (LSOC, 135). This wholly expresses the first vow to save innumerable living beings. It clearly conveys that the Buddha's actions are based on his resolute vow to lead all people to enlightenment. In this passage, we can also find expressions corresponding to the other three vows.

A vow in Buddhism can be likened to the power with which to sever the chains of karma, to free oneself from the fetters of the past and to forge a self that can look with hope to a new future. In other words, the power of a vow enables us to develop ourselves through the Buddha's teachings, to take charge of our own future direction based on a solid sense of self and to keep on making efforts toward that end.

Making a vow, then, is the fundamental principle of change. While it naturally entails trying to change oneself, it is also the impetus for transforming the lives of all people, as seen in the Buddha's vow in the "Medicinal Herbs" chapter.

In fulfilling the vow for the enlightenment of all people in the Latter Day, the Daishonin above all emphasizes the power of faith.

Believing in the boundless potential of human beings as entities of the Mystic Law may be considered the essence of the Lotus Sutra. Not only is this an expression of deep faith in the Mystic Law but also of profound trust and respect for human beings.

Bodhisattva Never Disparaging,[5] who is described in the Lotus Sutra and serves as a model for propagation in the Latter Day, was motivated by the same spirit. Although repeatedly attacked with "sticks of wood or tiles and stones" by the four kinds of believers—monks, nuns, laymen and laywomen—he persevered in the practice of venerating others. Sometimes he would retreat to a safe distance and shout words to the effect: "Even so, I respect you. You will all become Buddhas." He continued to venerate even those who showered him with criticism or who physically assaulted him. Bodhisattva Never Disparaging's practice is based on the philosophy that all human beings without exception possess the Buddha nature. Above all, he himself appears to have had an unwavering belief in the existence of the Buddha nature within the lives of all people.

In dramatic contrast, there is the case of Shariputra[6] who, in a past life, allowed himself to be defeated over his ordeal with the eye-begging Brahman[7] and as a result returned to the Hinayana teachings. When his good intentions were literally trampled on, Shariputra reflexively cried out: "This person is impossible to save!" Ultimately, he lost faith in the existence of the Buddha nature in all people.

The Brahman in this story was the devil king of the sixth heaven in disguise. It is the essential character of devils to strive to prevent one and all from manifesting their inherent Buddha nature. At heart, these dark functions seek to destroy people's belief in the tenet that all people are Buddhas.

Understandably, we might feel upset at being hated and attacked by the very individuals we are trying to lead to happiness. But, remaining true to one's profound conviction, like Bodhisattva Never Disparaging who continued to declare, "Even so, I respect you," is the hallmark of genuine Buddhist practitioners in the Latter Day of the Law. In a sense, the power of the vow or commitment to lead all people to enlightenment sustains an unswerving belief in the innate goodness of human beings, as well as the deep optimism that arises from that belief.

Nichiren Daishonin, through his profound vow, boldly stood up alone as the votary of the Lotus Sutra. He steadfastly persevered out of a desire to save all people who were being led by evil influences to commit slander of the Law. Consequently, as the Daishonin himself foresaw, he incurred the hatred of people throughout the land and brought a great storm of persecution upon himself.

Nevertheless, with the spirit, "I rejoiced, saying that I had long expected it to come to this" ("The Actions of the Votary of the Lotus Sutra," WND-1, 764), he struggled on with the resolute spirit expressed by the lines: "But still I am not discouraged" ("The Essentials for Attaining Buddhahood," WND-1, 748), "Not once have I thought of retreat" ("The Great Battle," WND-2, 465) and "So the battle goes on even today" ("On Practicing the Buddha's Teachings," WND-1, 392).

We can take it that the sole driving force that sustained the Daishonin's momentous lifelong struggle was the power of his vow. His example teaches us how, by maintaining our own vow, we can become one with the heart of the Buddha and bring forth the limitless power of Buddhahood from our lives.

In a defiled age, it is only through the power of a vow for the enlightenment of all people that we can defeat the evil functions that seek to incite distrust and doubt.

6

The Votary of the Lotus Sutra—One Who Practices the Correct Teaching With Outstanding Perseverance and Compassion

When he established his teaching in 1253, Nichiren Daishonin foresaw that great difficulties and obstacles would inevitably lie ahead of him. Nevertheless, he stood up as the votary of the Lotus Sutra, vowing to summon up "a powerful and unconquerable desire for the salvation of all beings and never to falter in [his] efforts" (WND-1, 240). His ensuing struggle was—just as he predicted and as corroborated by passages in the Lotus Sutra—a battle against an unending series of persecutions. He writes: "It is already over twenty years since I began proclaiming my doctrines. Day after day, month after month, year after year I have been subjected to repeated persecutions. Minor persecutions and annoyances are too numerous even to be counted, but the major persecutions number four" (WND-1, 240).

Fierce and Relentless Persecutions Arise From Hatred and Jealousy

"The major persecutions number four," says the Daishonin. In the two decades following the establishment of his teaching, he had encountered four great persecutions that threatened not only his own life but also the continued existence of his community of believers. Needless to say, these were the Matsubagayatsu Persecution (1260), the Izu Exile (1261), the Komatsubara Persecution (1264), and the Tatsunokuchi Persecution and Sado Exile (1271).

The Tatsunokuchi Persecution and subsequent Sado Exile constituted the authorities' greatest crackdown yet. Nichiren was dragged to the execution grounds and nearly beheaded. His followers were treated as if they were traitors. The government repression was so harsh that even those who had merely listened to his teaching were subjected to severe punishment (see WND-1, 240).

The four major persecutions clearly revealed the malice and brutality of those who schemed to do away with the Daishonin and destroy his community of believers.

With regard to the many other attacks and obstacles he encountered, Nichiren writes, "Minor persecutions and annoyances are too numerous even to be counted" (WND-1, 240). These included slander and abuse, false accusations, and harassment, as well as his followers being subjected to fines or banishment. Persecutions of this kind, which the Daishonin describes as "too numerous even to be counted," continued without cease, showing the relentlessness of his tormentors.

After the overview of his hardships to that point, the Daishonin goes on to cite various sutras and commentaries that clarify the true nature of those persecuting him.

These people are essentially driven by hatred and jealousy, a deep hostility arising from a swirling cauldron of complex negative emotions. The priests and lay followers of other Buddhist schools of the time bore strong feelings of resentment and jealousy because of Nichiren's pure and unswerving commitment to practicing the correct teaching as the votary of the Lotus Sutra. They also openly hated him for having refuted the errors of their schools.

The Daishonin here quotes passages from the Lotus Sutra indicating that hatred and jealousy toward the sutra's votary lie at the root of the persecution that confronts those who uphold the Law in the Latter Day (see WND-1, 240). These passages include the following:

Since hatred and jealousy toward this sutra abound even when the Thus Come One is in the world, how much more will this be so after his passing? (LSOC, 203)

On seeing those who read, recite, / copy, and uphold this sutra, / [a person who slanders the correct teaching will] should despise, hate, envy, / or bear grudges against them. (LSOC, 110)

It [the Lotus Sutra] will face much hostility in the world and be difficult to believe. (LSOC, 246)

He also refers to other Lotus Sutra and Nirvana Sutra passages detailing how insidious persecution arises from hatred and jealousy; and it manifests as slander and abuse, false accusations, banishment and exile, and other forms of direct and indirect violence aimed at alienating people from the correct teaching. To stress this point further, he quotes commentaries by T'ien-t'ai, Miao-lo, Dengyo, Chih-tu (the author of the *Tung-ch'un*) and others.[1]

Fierce and relentless persecutions befall the votary of the Lotus Sutra in the Latter Day of the Law because of the raging hatred and jealousy seething in the lives of the attackers.

An Age When Fundamental Darkness Reigns

When a little boy is given moxibustion treatment, he will invariably resent his mother; when a seriously ill person is given good medicine, he will complain without fail about its bitterness. And we meet with similar complaints about

the Lotus Sutra, even in the lifetime of the Buddha. How much more severe is the opposition after his passing, especially in the Middle and Latter Days of the Law and in a far-off country like Japan? As mountains pile upon mountains and waves follow waves, so do persecutions add to persecutions and criticisms augment criticisms . . .

It is now over two hundred years since the Latter Day of the Law began. The Buddha predicted that conditions would be much worse after his passing, and we see the portents of this in the quarrels and wranglings that go on today because unreasonable doctrines are prevalent. And as proof of the fact that we are living in a muddied age, I was not summoned for a doctrinal debate with my opponents, but instead I was sent into exile and my very life imperiled. (WND-1, 241–42)

The essence of this hatred and jealousy is fundamental darkness—an ignorance of and disbelief in the Mystic Law.

The Latter Day is characterized by a world rampant with disbelief in the correct teaching and with slander of the Law. When the votary of the Lotus Sutra expounds the correct teaching, the fundamental darkness in people's lives functions as a devilish force. Society in this defiled age mirrors the description in the Lotus Sutra of evil demons entering people's lives to persecute the sutra's practitioners.

It is just as the Daishonin says when he writes, "The fundamental darkness manifests itself as the devil king of the sixth heaven" ("The Treatment of Illness," WND-1, 1113). Likewise, in accord with his observation, "Evil demons hate good people" (WND-1, 1113), those whose lives have been possessed by demons, or devilish functions, harass the practitioners of the correct teaching.

The Daishonin also states: "The entire country of Japan hates me, Nichiren . . . Everyone from the ruler on down to the common people seethes in anger against me such as the world has never seen. This is the first time that the fundamental darkness has erupted in the lives of ordinary people caught in the illusions of thought and desire"[2] (WND-1, 1114).

In the Latter Day, when society abounds with slander of the Law, the three obstacles and four devils appear with even greater intensity than in the Middle Day of the Law during which T'ien-t'ai and Dengyo lived. This is because the prevalence of such slander stimulates the function of fundamental darkness and intensifies the three poisons—greed, anger and foolishness. Consequently, there is great hatred and jealousy toward the votary of the Lotus Sutra who expounds and spreads the correct teaching.

The Daishonin explains this in "The Opening of the Eyes," using the following allegory: "When a little boy is given moxibustion treatment, he will invariably resent his mother; when a seriously ill person is given good medicine, he will complain without fail about its bitterness" (WND-1, 241).

The fact that one is a practitioner of the Lotus Sutra unerringly spreading the Mystic Law stirs fierce resentment in those filled with disbelief toward it. As the Daishonin asserts, "[If devils did not arise], there would be no way of knowing that this is the correct teaching" ("Letter to the Brothers," WND-1, 501).

Though Having Committed No Wrong, the Votary Is Assailed by Repeated Persecution

Defamatory attacks are the means by which people of great arrogance try to discredit the just. Wishing to avoid dialogue or debate, and also seeking to preserve their own prestige, such people resort to the base means of spreading slander and lies about their enemies. They malign the just by branding them as villains.

"Encouraging Devotion," the 13th chapter of the Lotus Sutra, describes how arrogant priests revered as sages—the third of the three powerful enemies—will make defamatory allegations against the votary of the Lotus Sutra to the ruler, ministers and other influential people in society. Also, the Nirvana Sutra depicts numerous non-Buddhists going to King Ajatashatru[3] and falsely accusing Shakyamuni—asserting, for example, that he was greedy for profit and that he employed spells and magic. Making claims that were the total opposite of the truth, they denounced the Buddha as "a man of incomparable wickedness" (WND-1, 240).

In a sound society, there will naturally be leaders who can see through such lies. The Daishonin notes that T'ien-t'ai and Dengyo initially encountered various persecutions

in the Middle Day of the Law but that their rulers ultimately discerned and clarified what was true, thus putting an end to their harassment.

In the Latter Day of the Law, however, when priests of evil intent distort the Buddhist teachings, society's leaders lose both the ability and the will to distinguish between good and evil. Hence, Nichiren writes: "Unreasonable doctrines are prevalent. And as proof of the fact that we are living in a muddied age, I was not summoned for a doctrinal debate with my opponents" (WND-1, 241–42). Here, he refers to the government's outrageous conduct in its judicial affairs, as was evidenced by his summary sentencing to exile—which was tantamount to a death sentence—without being given a fair opportunity to defend himself against the charges brought against him.

"Rulers who cannot discern the truth" are comparable, in today's democratic age, to societies in which people accept lies and stand by silently while others are unjustly maligned.

If lies and misrepresentations are allowed to go unchecked, people will store them in their minds as facts. A society that fails to combat such distortions is sure to suffer spiritual corruption and decline. Therefore, in advancing kosen-rufu in the Latter Day, it is absolutely vital for us to engage in energetic and insightful debate and discourse in order to ward off the fundamental darkness in people's lives and confront slander of the Law, which is so spiritually destructive. This is the only way we can restore society's spiritual health.

While I have been focusing specifically on false accusations and lies used to attack the votary of the Lotus Sutra, it is no simple matter in any circumstance to speak out and proclaim the truth in a corrupt society where right and wrong, good and evil, are confused. Rather, the more one champions the truth, the fiercer the storms of persecution will grow. It is like one person standing up in olden times to explain that earth revolves around the sun, while everyone is firmly convinced of the opposite. Those who champion the truth will encounter persistent and incomprehensible persecution. This, indeed, is a mark of their veracity and integrity.

Discussing the qualifications of a votary of the Lotus Sutra in the Latter Day of the Law, the Daishonin writes, "If persecutions greater than those that arose during the Buddha's lifetime keep occurring again and again to someone who is not guilty of the slightest fault, then one should realize that that person is a true votary of the Lotus Sutra in the age after the Buddha's passing" ("On Repaying Debts of Gratitude," WND-1, 696).

Although the votary has committed no offense, he is continuously assailed by momentous persecutions. The Daishonin vividly describes this, "As mountains pile upon mountains and waves follow waves, so do persecutions add to persecutions and criticisms augment criticisms" (WND-1, 241).

Aware from the outset of the inevitability of meeting persecution, the Daishonin courageously stood up alone as the Lotus Sutra's votary. Having already waged an unceasing twenty-year struggle, he continued expounding the correct teaching with the impassioned roar of a lion in his place of exile on Sado Island.

Upholding the Law Through Perseverance and Compassion

When it comes to understanding the Lotus Sutra, I have only a minute fraction of the vast ability that T'ien-t'ai and Dengyo possessed. But as regards my ability to endure persecution and the wealth of my compassion for others, I believe they would hold me in awe. (WND-1, 242)

In the above passage, the Daishonin describes his own identity as the votary of the Lotus Sutra.

Even supposing that T'ien-t'ai and Dengyo surpassed him in depth of understanding the Lotus Sutra, the Daishonin asserts that he exceeds them in perseverance and compassion.

Naturally, to spread the Mystic Law in the Latter Day, it is important to talk to others based on a profound understanding of the Lotus Sutra—in other words, to present the sutra's teaching and doctrines logically and coherently. So while the Daishonin may concede the higher ground to T'ien-t'ai and Dengyo in providing lucid and rational theoretical explanations, he by no means diminishes the need for such explanations.

More important, however, are perseverance (that is, the ability to endure persecution) and compassion, which are indispensable to actually spreading the Law in the evil Latter Day and to helping even those experiencing the greatest suffering attain genuine happiness.

Perseverance and compassion are like two sides of the same coin. Profound compassion based on a wish to free all people from suffering gives one incomparable strength to endure persecution and spread the Law.

To endure persecution, to persevere amid obstacles, does not mean passive acceptance. The Latter Day is an age when evil is rampant. Those aware of their mission to defeat this evil and awaken others to life's ultimate truth must be prepared to fight continually through any obstacle or difficulty. Their actions are essentially motivated by a solemn, rigorous compassion not to let anyone in the Latter Day fall into the unfortunate trap of slandering the Law. This unwavering compassion leads directly to all people's enlightenment in the Latter Day.

The Joy of Faith Based on the Principle of "Voluntarily Assuming the Appropriate Karma"

With this body of mine, I have fulfilled the prophecies of the sutra. The more the government authorities rage against me, the greater is my joy. For instance, there are certain Hinayana bodhisattvas, not yet freed from delusion, who draw evil karma to themselves by their own compassionate vow. If they see that their father and mother have fallen into hell and are suffering greatly, they will deliberately create the appropriate karma in hopes
that they too may fall into hell and share in and take their suffering upon themselves. Thus suffering is a joy to them. It is the same with me [in fulfilling the prophecies]. Though at present I must face trials that I can scarcely endure, I rejoice when I think that in the future I will escape being born into the evil paths. (WND-1, 243)

Compassion is the driving force behind perseverance, while perseverance is proof of deep compassion. To explain this, the Daishonin discusses the principle of "voluntarily assuming the appropriate karma."[4]

Here, the Daishonin states that his experiencing great persecutions corresponds with the principle of bodhisattvas voluntarily assuming karma and choosing to take on suffering out of a desire to lead living beings to enlightenment. And just as bodhisattvas regard undergoing suffering on behalf of living beings as a source of joy, Nichiren says he also views experiencing pain and hardship as a result of these present persecutions as a cause for rejoicing, because it will enable him to escape falling into the evil paths in future existences.

The Daishonin's assertion that voluntarily assuming the appropriate karma is a source of joy echoes the final lines of "The Opening of the Eyes," where he states: "For what I have done, I have been condemned to exile, but it is a small suffering to undergo in this present life and not one worth lamenting. In future lives I will enjoy immense happiness, a thought that gives me great joy" (WND-1, 287).

The principle of "voluntarily assuming the appropriate karma" is the logical conclusion of the Buddhist concept of transforming one's karma. Simply put, it represents a way of life in which we change karma into mission.

Everything that happens in our lives has meaning. Moreover, the Buddhist way of life is to find and discover meaning in all things. Nothing is futile or meaningless. Whatever a person's karma may be, it definitely has some profound significance.

This is not just a matter of mere outlook. Changing the world starts by changing our fundamental state of mind, which is a key Buddhist principle. A powerful determination to transform even negative karma into mission can dramatically transform the real world. By changing our inner state of mind, we can change any suffering or hardship into a source of joy, regarding it as a means for forging and developing our lives. To turn even sorrow into a source of creativity—that is the way of life of a Buddhist.

Nichiren Daishonin teaches us this essential path through his own life and actions as the votary of the Lotus Sutra.

Having a fighting spirit is itself the direct path to happiness. Only through struggles and challenges can we develop inner strength and construct truly creative lives. Also, by maintaining unwavering faith in the correct teaching no matter what obstacles or hardships arise, we can enter the orbit of happiness for all eternity. Attaining Buddhahood in this lifetime means securing this orbit in our daily lives during our present existence.

The practitioner of the correct teaching who ceaselessly struggles to spread the Law may be interpreted as the ultimate paragon of humanity that Nichiren sets forth based on the Lotus Sutra.

Viewed from such a lofty state of life, all difficulties become the genuine foundation for our personal development and growth. Practitioners of the correct teaching who endure obstacles with the awareness, "[If devils did not arise], there would be no way of knowing that this is the correct teaching" ("Letter to the Brothers," WND-1, 501), come to embody the Mystic Law without fail. They attain the expansive state of life in which they can regard all difficulties as "peace and comfort" (OTT, 115), and rejoice at them with the spirit conveyed when Nichiren writes, "The greater the hardships befalling him, the greater the delight he feels, because of his strong faith" ("A Ship to Cross the Sea of Sufferings," WND-1, 33).

By clearly revealing this state of life to his followers and everyone throughout the land in "The Opening of the Eyes," Nichiren Daishonin sought to open the eyes of all people shrouded in fundamental darkness. He also strove to convey the quintessential joy experienced by the votary of the Lotus Sutra.

7

The Profound Debt Owed to the Lotus Sutra and the Protection Received by Those Who Spread the Supreme Law of Universal Enlightenment

The Requirements of a Votary of the Lotus Sutra

Nichiren Daishonin cites making a vow as the first and most essential requirement of a votary of the Lotus Sutra in the Latter Day of the Law—that is, the vow to maintain steadfast faith in the Lotus Sutra, the teaching of enlightenment, and to share it with others, irrespective of the difficulties one may encounter along the way.

Next, he stresses the importance of having perseverance, specifically in terms of enduring persecution. The hallmark of a votary of the Lotus Sutra is to remain true to one's vow and to persevere even amid the most overwhelming obstacles. However, this is not simply a matter of passive forbearance; rather, it means waging a ceaseless struggle to surmount every trial and emerge victorious.

Also, along with perseverance, Nichiren lists compassion as a vital requirement. This is because the strength to endure hardships derives from compassion for others. Nothing can daunt the compassion of a votary of the Lotus Sutra determined to lead all people of the Latter Day to enlightenment. In the face of such compassion, even the greatest obstacles are, says the Daishonin, "no more . . . than dust before the wind" (WND-1, 280).

Lastly, by explaining the Buddhist principle of "voluntarily assuming the appropriate karma," the Daishonin teaches that a votary who practices exactly as the sutra teaches calmly surmounts all sufferings and hardships that are part of life in the evil age of the Latter Day and possesses a state of life of boundless joy.

The Doubts of Others and the Daishonin's Own Doubts

And yet the people doubt me, and I too have doubts about myself. Why do the gods not assist me? Heavenly gods and other guardian deities made their vow before the Buddha. Even if

the votary of the Lotus Sutra were an ape rather than a man, they should address him as the votary of the Lotus Sutra and rush forward to fulfill the vow they made before the Buddha. Does their failure to do so mean that I am in fact not a votary of the Lotus Sutra? This doubt lies at the heart of this piece I am writing. And because it is the most important concern of my entire life, I will raise it again and again here, and emphasize it more than ever, before I attempt to answer it. (WND-1, 243)

Nichiren had made a vow, and he possessed perseverance, compassion and joy. He had a towering state of life. It goes without saying, therefore, that he had stood up with the conviction that he was the votary of the Lotus Sutra of the Latter Day of the Law. Nevertheless, in "The Opening of the Eyes," while expressing this firm conviction, the Daishonin also speaks of serious doubts. He writes: "And yet the people doubt me, and I too have doubts about myself. Why do the gods not assist me? . . . Does their failure to do so mean that I am in fact not a votary of the Lotus Sutra?" (WND-1, 243).

He is asking why the heavenly deities do not protect him, the votary of the Lotus Sutra. Surely they had vowed in the presence of Shakyamuni to rigorously protect anyone who practiced the Lotus Sutra in the Latter Day, no matter who that person might be. Does the absence of their protection therefore mean that he is not the votary of the Lotus Sutra?

This doubt is closely related to Nichiren's purpose in composing this treatise.

The government's harsh crackdown on the Daishonin, which culminated in the Tatsunokuchi Persecution (Nichiren's near-execution on September 12, 1271) and his ensuing Sado Exile, was also directed at his community of believers as a whole. Many of his followers were harassed and persecuted. The authorities punished them with fines, banishment or confiscation of their lands. As a result, a large majority of his followers in Kamakura abandoned their faith. He writes, "Among my disciples and followers, however, those who are cowards have for the most part either given in or retreated at heart" ("The Great Battle," WND-2, 465), and "999 out of 1,000 people . . . gave up their faith when I was arrested" ("Reply to Niiama," WND-1, 469).

Many in society scathingly asked why, if Nichiren were truly the votary of the Lotus Sutra as he claimed, he and his followers did not enjoy protection from the heavens. Many of his erstwhile followers may have also entertained the same doubt. His remaining followers, meanwhile, though they continued to put their trust in him and carried on valiantly in their Buddhist practice, did not know how to rebut the criticisms of ex-followers and others in society. Perhaps many of them were bitterly frustrated by this and wished they knew how to respond based on correct Buddhist doctrine.

In order to dispel people's negativity and instill them with confidence, it was imperative that Nichiren provide clear answers to the doubts raised by both his followers and the general populace. The greater part of this treatise is devoted to clarifying such doubts.

Here, in addition to addressing the doubts held by others, Nichiren also speaks of his own doubts. Of course, this does not mean that he had doubts in the sense of being confused or lacking faith. While the public and many of his followers had their doubts, the Daishonin naturally blazed with the powerful conviction that he and no other was the votary of the Lotus Sutra in the Latter Day of the Law.

If he were indeed the votary as he said, however, an important question had to be answered—that is, why the heavenly deities did not rise into action to protect him. It seems clear that Nichiren's own doubts center around the issue of the heavenly deities' promise to lend their protection to those who uphold the Lotus Sutra.

The doubts of others as to whether the Daishonin was in fact the votary of the Lotus Sutra and his own doubts as to why the heavenly deities did not act to protect him—these two points are inextricably bound.

"This Doubt Is the Most Important Concern of My Entire Life"

The Daishonin writes with regard to this two-sided question of why, if he is the votary of the Lotus Sutra, he does not receive protection: "This doubt lies at the heart of this piece I am writing. And . . . it is the most important concern of my entire life" (WND-1, 243).

Beyond the thick clouds of doubt that shroud people's hearts lies a brilliant blue sky of great conviction illuminated by the sun that shines serenely high above those clouds. Dispelling this doubt would also prepare the way for clarifying the "object of devotion in terms of the Person." Therefore, the Daishonin writes, "I will . . . emphasize it [this doubt] more than ever, before I attempt to answer it" (WND-1, 243). He aims to thoroughly resolve this doubt by first bringing it into sharp focus. His ensuing discussion on this subject in "The Opening of the Eyes" can be divided into two sections.

In the first section (WND-1, 243–61), he explains the profound debt owed to the Lotus Sutra by persons of the two vehicles (the voice-hearers and cause-awakened ones), bodhisattvas, heavenly and human beings, and others [who together function as heavenly deities, or protective forces], who were only able to attain enlightenment for the first time through its teaching. He then deliberately emphasizes the public's doubt that the failure of these beings to appear and protect him may indicate that he is not the sutra's votary.

While he seems to be reinforcing this doubt here, the Daishonin is in fact discussing the true nature of the protection of the heavenly deities. Namely, it is their debt of gratitude to the Lotus Sutra, the teaching by which they gained enlightenment, that prompts them to protect the sutra's votary. He also clarifies that the true essence of a votary of the Lotus Sutra is a person who practices the teaching for attaining Buddhahood.

In the second section (WND-1, 261–80), the Daishonin discusses such points as the three pronouncements in the "Treasure Tower," the 11th chapter of the Lotus Sutra, in which Shakyamuni urges the assembled bodhisattvas three times to propagate the sutra after his passing; the two admonitions in the "Devadatta," the 12th chapter, in which Shakyamuni teaches the enlightenment of all people; and the twenty-line verse section in the "Encouraging Devotion," the 13th chapter, which describes the three powerful enemies who will assail the votary of the Lotus Sutra in an evil age after the Buddha's passing.

In the course of this discussion, the Daishonin shows that he himself is practicing in complete accord with the sutra—in other words, that he is reading the Lotus Sutra with his life. At the same time, he also reveals the "ugly face" of the slander of the Law that is rampant throughout the land and that functions to obstruct the propagation of the Lotus Sutra, the teaching for attaining Buddhahood (see WND-1, 261). Here, Nichiren confirms his belief, based on the sutra's passages, that he is the votary of the Lotus Sutra, but given his apparent failure to receive protection from the heavenly deities, he once again reiterates his own doubt.

Nichiren then goes on to provide answers to these doubts from various perspectives. For the time being, suffice it to say that the main point he makes in it is that the heavenly deities fail to lend him their protection because they have abandoned the country on account of its being steeped in slander.

However, this is still just a partial answer. The true answer is found in the passage revealing Nichiren's great vow that begins: "This I will state. Let the gods forsake me. Let all persecutions assail me. Still I will give my life for the sake of the Law" (WND-1, 280). In other words, the issue is not whether one enjoys the protection of the heavenly deities. The true votary of the Lotus Sutra is someone who maintains the great desire for kosen-rufu, even in the face of enormous obstacles,

and ceaselessly struggles to lead people to enlightenment in a land filled with slander of the Law.

Ultimately, in the second section, it becomes clear that the votary of the Lotus Sutra encounters momentous persecutions by virtue of being a person who boldly fights against the evil of slandering the Law, the teaching for attaining Buddhahood. Further, such a genuine votary enjoys the true protection of the heavenly deities. I would like to take up this point again after discussing the first section in some detail.

The Profound Debt Owed to the Lotus Sutra by Persons of the Two Vehicles

In the first section of his discussion, Nichiren starts by clarifying that persons of the two vehicles, along with bodhisattvas and heavenly and human beings, owe a profound debt to the Lotus Sutra. This is because only when Shakyamuni finally expounds the Lotus Sutra are they able to attain enlightenment for the first time. To repay that immense debt of gratitude, they vow in the presence of Shakyamuni to protect those who practice the Lotus Sutra. That is why the Daishonin asserts that they would naturally come to the aid of the votary of the Lotus Sutra in the Latter Day of the Law.

Nichiren then discusses the importance of repaying debts of gratitude. Repaying debts of gratitude is the highest human virtue. Conversely, those who forget their debts are sure to deviate from the path that one should follow as a human being. The light of genuine humanity shines in recognizing and repaying one's debts of gratitude. Nichiren asserts that especially the persons of the two vehicles, bodhisattvas, heavenly beings and others who heard Shakyamuni preach the Lotus Sutra could not possibly have forgotten their profound debt of gratitude to that teaching.

The first group he takes up in this discussion is persons of the two vehicles. Here, he compares the pre-Lotus Sutra teachings with the Lotus Sutra. The former thoroughly denounces persons of the two vehicles as incapable of attaining Buddhahood, while the latter makes it possible for them to do so.

In the pre-Lotus Sutra teachings, Shakyamuni relentlessly castigates the voice-hearers. To offer a simple illustration of how harsh the Buddha's condemnation was, Nichiren says that when the voice-hearer Venerable Mahakashyapa was told he would never be able to gain enlightenment, the sound of his weeping and wailing echoed throughout the major world system (see WND-1, 245). Shakyamuni's rebukes actually arose out of his great compassion as the Buddha. The persons of the two vehicles had forgotten about benefiting others and were only interested in benefiting themselves. Shakyamuni thus wished to help them break free of their inner darkness and delusion.

In the Lotus Sutra, the voice-hearers acquire "the medicine of immortality" (WND-1, 243). Their inability to attain Buddhahood in earlier sutras had been tantamount to "death" as Buddhist practitioners. However, in the Lotus Sutra, they move beyond the provisional teaching of "reducing the body to ashes and annihilating the consciousness" in order to attain nirvana, and finally gain the wisdom of the Mystic Law. Herein lies their revival as Buddhist practitioners. Therefore, the Lotus Sutra is the "medicine of immortality."

In the Lotus Sutra, the four great voice-hearers,[1] who each receive a prophecy of attaining enlightenment, make a vow, saying, "Now we have become / voice-hearers in truth" (LSOC, 132). Transcending their earlier selves—that is, of voice-hearers who only listened superficially to the Buddha's voice and had a shallow understanding of what he was saying—they have now deeply comprehended the Buddha's true wisdom. They further declare that they will henceforth struggle as genuine voice-hearers to enable all people to hear the voice of the Buddha. This indicates their rebirth as bodhisattvas.

Theirs is a vow to fight together in a spirit of the oneness with their mentor. They break free from a narrow realm of self-absorption, where they concentrate only on liberating themselves from suffering, and soar into a realm as vast and boundless as the heavens, where they dedicate themselves to the cause of enabling all living beings to attain enlightenment. In the same sutra passage, they also emphasize again and again that the debt they owe to the Buddha is so enormous that they can never fully hope to repay it (see LSOC, 132).

Nichiren asserts that the persons of the two vehicles, having acquired the Buddha eye and the Dharma eye, with which they can penetrate any of the worlds in the ten directions, could not possibly fail to see a votary of the Lotus Sutra in this strife-filled saha world. Should a votary exist in the Latter Day, he says, then these sages would definitely come to his side and battle to protect him, even if they may have to pass through a great fire to do so. Otherwise, the prediction in the Lotus Sutra about widespread propagation in the fifth five-hundred-year period[2] after the Buddha's passing would be "mere nonsense" (WND-1, 247).

Nichiren further asks why, in spite of this, the persons of the two vehicles of the Lotus Sutra fail to protect the sutra's votary who is undergoing great persecution. He wonders if they are the allies of slanderers of the Law. While keenly censuring them for their inaction, the Daishonin repeatedly raises the question of why he has not received their protection, and concludes his discussion on this subject with the words, "My doubts grow deeper than ever" (WND-1, 248).

The Profound Debt Owed to the Lotus Sutra by Bodhisattvas and Heavenly and Human Beings

Next, Nichiren discusses the profound debt owed to the Lotus Sutra by bodhisattvas and heavenly and human beings.

While here again pointing out the differences between the pre-Lotus Sutra teachings and the Lotus Sutra, Nichiren further clarifies the doctrines expounded in the Lotus Sutra, the teaching for attaining Buddhahood. He specifically discusses the doctrine of the mutual possession of the Ten Worlds[3] found in the "Expedient Means," the 2nd chapter, and the doctrine of Shakyamuni's actual attainment of enlightenment in the remote past elucidated in the "Life Span," the 16th

chapter. He then explains the profound debt of gratitude owed to the Lotus Sutra by the bodhisattvas and heavenly and human beings who were able to attain Buddhahood through this teaching.

Nichiren notes that none of the bodhisattvas who appear in the pre-Lotus Sutra teachings were disciples of Shakyamuni. For example, the bodhisattvas who appear in the Flower Garland Sutra have traveled from Buddha lands in the ten directions to gather before Shakyamuni just after he first attained enlightenment under the bodhi tree in India; they are not his disciples. The Daishonin further states that, in the pre-Lotus Sutra teachings, Shakyamuni does not expound any teaching surpassing the doctrines that these bodhisattvas preached.

In the Lotus Sutra, these bodhisattvas press their palms together in reverence to Shakyamuni and request to hear the "teaching of perfect endowment" (LSOC, 61). Nichiren explains that "teaching of perfect endowment" means the doctrine of the mutual possession of the Ten Worlds, and is none other than Nam-myoho-renge-kyo. He writes, "In the phrase 'perfect endowment,' endowment refers to the mutual possession of the Ten Worlds, while perfect means that, since there is mutual possession of the Ten Worlds, then any one world contains all the other worlds, indicating that this is 'perfect'" (WND-1, 250).

Through the mutual possession of the Ten Worlds, it becomes clear that each of the Ten Worlds manifests its own Buddhahood and that all people therefore equally have the potential to attain enlightenment. With regard to the passage in the "Expedient Means" chapter, "the Buddhas . . . wish to open the door of Buddha wisdom to all living beings" (LSOC, 64), Nichiren writes: "The term 'all living beings' here refers to Shariputra, and it also refers to icchantikas, persons of incorrigible disbelief. It also refers to the nine worlds" (WND-1, 250). Here, the Daishonin clearly points out that it was not only the voice-hearer Shariputra who was able to attain enlightenment through the teaching of perfect endowment, but also all people in the nine worlds, including persons of incorrigible disbelief.

He further explains that by opening up the way for all people to attain enlightenment, Shakyamuni fulfilled his "vow to save innumerable living beings,"[4] and that all the bodhisattvas and heavenly beings understood that they had heard for the first time the Lotus Sutra's unsurpassed doctrine of three thousand realms in a single moment of life (see WND-1, 251).

Even at this point of Shakyamuni's preaching in the Lotus Sutra, there is sufficient reason for the bodhisattvas to regard the sutra as the supreme teaching. However, the profound debt they owe the sutra only becomes truly apparent when Shakyamuni reveals in the "Life Span" chapter that he has actually attained enlightenment in the remote past. This revelation indicates that all the other Buddhas who appear in the different sutras are in fact emanations of Shakyamuni. Consequently, the bodhisattvas who are the disciples of these Buddhas are ultimately all Shakyamuni's disciples (see WND-1, 256).

Thus, in the "Life Span" chapter, all Buddhas of the pre-Lotus Sutra teachings are unified in the Buddha who actually attained enlightenment in the remote past. It also becomes apparent that the Shakyamuni who attained enlightenment in the remote past is the Buddha who can be regarded as the teacher of all bodhisattvas who aspire for enlightenment.

The Buddha who attained enlightenment in the remote past is the eternal Buddha who is one with the eternal Mystic Law. The fact that this Buddha is said to be the true identity of Shakyamuni, the Buddha who lived in ancient India, indicates that all people can bring forth in their own lives the power of the eternal Mystic Law, the fundamental law of the universe. A Buddha is a person who has activated the power of the eternal Mystic Law in his or her life; a Buddha is Myoho-renge-kyo. Myoho-renge-kyo is the true essence of the Buddha; it is the original Buddha.

Among all of the sutras said to have been expounded by Shakyamuni, the eternal Mystic Law is revealed as the seed of enlightenment for the first time in the form of the teaching of the "Life Span" chapter of the Lotus Sutra—that is, Shakyamuni's actual attainment of Buddhahood in the remote past. The Buddha of the "Life Span" chapter means Myoho-renge-kyo, which is the true essence of the Buddha. And Myoho-renge-kyo is the law of life inherent within all people, and it is the seed for all people to attain enlightenment. This seed is hidden in the depths of the "Life Span" chapter. That's why the "Life Span" chapter is the highest teaching among all the sutras.

Nichiren thus praises the "Life Span" chapter as follows, "If, among all the numerous sutras, this 'Life Span' chapter should be lacking, it would be as though there were no sun or moon in the sky, no supreme ruler in the nation, no gems in the mountains and rivers, and no spirit in human beings" (WND-1, 256).

This is the reason why all bodhisattvas who aspire to attain enlightenment should feel a deep debt of gratitude toward the Lotus Sutra.

Those Ignorant of Their Indebtedness Are Nothing More Than "Talented Animals"

The various Buddhas, bodhisattvas, and heavenly and human beings described in the sutras that preceded the Lotus may seem to have gained enlightenment through the particular sutras in which they appear. But in fact they attained enlightenment only through the Lotus Sutra. The general vow taken by Shakyamuni and the other Buddhas to save countless living beings finds fulfillment through the Lotus Sutra. That is the meaning of the passage of the sutra that states that the vow "has now been fulfilled."

In view of these facts, I believe that the devotees and followers of the Flower Garland, Meditation, Mahavairochana, and other sutras will undoubtedly be protected by the Buddhas, bodhisattvas, and heavenly beings of the respective sutras that they uphold. But if the votaries of the Mahavairochana, Meditation, and other sutras should set themselves up as the enemies of the votary of the Lotus Sutra, then the Buddhas, bodhisattvas, and heavenly beings will abandon them and will protect the votary of the Lotus Sutra (WND-1, 260–61) . . .

I, Nichiren, think as follows. The gods of the sun and moon and the other deities were present in the two places and three assemblies[5] when the Lotus Sutra was preached. If a votary of the Lotus Sutra should appear, then, like iron drawn to a magnet or the reflection of the moon appearing in the water, they will instantly come forth to take on his sufferings for him and thereby fulfill the vow that they made in the presence of the Buddha. But they have yet to come and inquire of my well-being. Does this mean that I am not a votary of the Lotus Sutra? If that is so, then I must examine the text of the sutra once more in light of my conduct and see where I am at fault. (WND-1, 261)

The various Buddhist schools of Nichiren's day were unaware that among all Shakyamuni's teachings, the Buddha of the "Life Span" chapter is the Buddha who should be taken as the object of devotion in one's Buddhist practice for attaining enlightenment. Not only were they ignorant of this, but they made their own arbitrary interpretations that further obscured and distorted the Buddha's true teaching.

The Latter Day of the Law is a time when evil monks appear and obscure the correct teaching. As a result, the truth of the Lotus Sutra is lost. And eventually the various schools of Buddhism become confused about the correct object of devotion.

The Daishonin strictly refutes the views held by the schools of his day about the object of devotion and about attaining enlightenment. He pronounces that they have gone astray, failing to recognize the fundamental Buddha expounded in the "Life Span" chapter who possesses the seed of enlightenment. He compares these misguided schools of Buddhism to the heir of the supreme ruler of a state who, confused about the identity of his own father, disparages him and believes someone else to be the real king (see WND-1, 258). And just like the child who does not know his own father, the adherents of schools who are ignorant of the Buddha of the "Life Span" chapter likewise "do not understand to whom they are obligated" (WND-1, 258). While they might appear to be knowledgeable about Buddhism, Nichiren sharply denounces them as no more than "talented animal[s]" (WND-1, 258).

Returning to our main subject about the heavenly deities protecting the Lotus Sutra, Nichiren voices his belief that the bodhisattvas who attained enlightenment through hearing the Lotus Sutra would surely come forth instantly to protect the votary of the Lotus Sutra, in keeping with the vow they made in the presence of the Buddha (see WND-1, 261). That being the case, however, why was it that they failed to appear to protect him? In summing up the first section, Nichiren once more emphasizes this doubt, asking, "Does this mean that I am not a votary of the Lotus Sutra?" (WND-1, 261).

He also goes so far as to say, "If that is so, then I must examine the text of the sutra once more in light of my conduct and see where I am at fault" (WND-1, 261). In this way, he sets the stage for the next section of his discussion, which I will take up in detail another time.

"The Object of Devotion Is the Entity of the Life of the Votary of the Lotus Sutra"

Nichiren's discussion in the first section focuses on the promise of protection for those who uphold the Lotus Sutra by the persons of the two vehicles, bodhisattvas and others who first learned of the teaching for attaining Buddhahood in the Lotus Sutra and achieved enlightenment as a result. His purpose, we can surmise, is to highlight the fact that the protective workings of the heavenly deities are activated through the power of the Mystic Law, the teaching for attaining Buddhahood.

Put another way, the fundamental nature of enlightenment[6] manifests as the heavenly deities, or the protective workings of the universe. That's why the heavenly deities are said to abandon a land that is filled with slander of the Law. However, even in an evil age rife with such slander, if there is a votary of the Lotus Sutra who protects and spreads the Mystic Law, the heavenly deities will protect that person.

No matter how evil the times, the heavenly deities will search out a person who struggles for the sake of Buddhism and will rigorously protect him or her. This is because such a person is embraced by the Mystic Law throughout the three existences of past, present and future, and becomes an entity that is one with the Mystic Law.

In discussing the protection extended by the persons of the two vehicles, bodhisattvas and others, Nichiren proclaims his view that the votary of the Lotus Sutra is a person who practices the Mystic Law, the teaching for attaining Buddhahood, and who fights against slander of the Law.

In the Latter Day, the Mystic Law manifests only in the life of a votary of the Lotus Sutra. Both the doctrine of the mutual possession of the Ten Worlds (revealed in the "Expedient Means" chapter) and the Mystic Law that is the seed of enlightenment (elucidated through the explanation of the Buddha's

actual attainment in the remote past in the "Life Span" chapter) exist nowhere but in the life of a votary of the Lotus Sutra.

Therefore, in *The Record of the Orally Transmitted Teachings*, Nichiren says, "The object of devotion is thus the entity of the entire life of the votary of the Lotus Sutra" (p. 142). We can find the object of devotion—which serves as a mirror and guide in our Buddhist practice for attaining enlightenment—in the life of the votary of the Lotus Sutra. That is why Nichiren says of these questions concerning the protection of the heavenly deities and the identity of the votary of the Lotus Sutra: "This doubt lies at the heart of this piece I am writing. And . . . it is the most important concern of my entire life" (WND-1, 243). It is also why "The Opening of the Eyes" is said to reveal the "object of devotion in terms of the Person."

8

The Six Difficult and Nine Easy Acts—To Discard the Shallow and Seek the Profound Is the Way of a Person of Courage

By tasting a single drop, one can tell the flavor of the great ocean, and by observing a single flower in bloom, one can predict the advent of spring. One does not have to cross the water to far-off Sung China, spend three years traveling to Eagle Peak in India, enter the palace of the dragon king the way Nagarjuna did, visit Bodhisattva Maitreya [in the Tushita heaven] the way Bodhisattva Asanga did, or be present at the two places and three assemblies when Shakyamuni preached the Lotus Sutra, in order to judge the relative merits of the Buddha's lifetime teachings. It is said that snakes can tell seven days in advance when a flood is going to occur. This is because they are akin to dragons [who make the rain fall]. Crows can tell what lucky or unlucky events are going to take place throughout the course of a year. This is because

in a past existence they were diviners. Birds are better at flying than human beings. And I, Nichiren, am better at judging the relative merits of sutras than Ch'eng-kuan of the Flower Garland school, Chia-hsiang of the Three Treatises school, Tz'u-en of the Dharma Characteristics school, and Kobo of the True Word school. That is because I follow in the footsteps of the teachers T'ien-t'ai and Dengyo. If Ch'eng-kuan and the others had not accepted the teachings of T'ien-t'ai and Dengyo, how could they have expected to escape the sin of slandering the Law?[1]

I, Nichiren, am the richest man in all of present-day Japan. I have dedicated my life to the Lotus Sutra, and my name will be handed down in ages to come. If one is lord of the great ocean, then all the gods of the various rivers will obey one. If one is king of Mount Sumeru, then the gods of the various other mountains cannot help but serve one. If a person fulfills the teaching of "the six difficult and nine easy acts" of the Lotus Sutra, then, even though he may not have read the entire body of sutras, all should follow him. (WND-1, 268)

Struggling for the Law in Accordance With the Buddha's Will and Decree

In "The Opening of the Eyes," Nichiren Daishonin establishes that he is the votary of the Lotus Sutra in the Latter Day of the Law, the current era, by examining various passages of that sutra. In particular, he considers the three pronouncements of "Treasure Tower," the 11th chapter; the two admonitions of "Devadatta," the 12th chapter; and the description of the three powerful enemies in the twenty-line verse section of "Encouraging Devotion," the 13th chapter.

The three pronouncements of the "Treasure Tower" chapter represent three viewpoints Shakyamuni expresses on the importance of spreading the Lotus Sutra after his passing, each accompanied with a call to the gathered bodhisattvas to shoulder this mission. We'll examine these pronouncements in detail shortly.

The two admonitions of the "Devadatta" chapter refer to Shakyamuni's disclosure that even evil people and women can attain Buddhahood. He thus indicates that after his passing the assembled bodhisattvas should spread the Lotus Sutra—the teaching of enlightenment—and work to enable all people living in the evil age of the Latter Day of the Law to obtain this supreme state of life.

Nichiren refers to the three pronouncements and the two admonitions collectively as the "five proclamations" (WND-1, 269). The specific term he uses for *proclamation* originally meant "the words or decree of an emperor." He uses it here to indicate "words expressing the Buddha's will" or "the Buddha's injunction." Propagation of the Lotus Sutra in the Latter Day is the Buddha's will and decree.

After hearing this will and decree, the eight hundred thousand million *nayutas* of bodhisattvas gathered at the assembly respond in the "Encouraging Devotion" chapter by vowing to propagate the Lotus Sutra after Shakyamuni's passing. Their vow contains the description of the three powerful enemies. That is, they pledge to widely spread the sutra even if they should encounter intense persecution at the hands of such formidable adversaries.

Citing these sutra passages, the Daishonin demonstrates that he is the votary of the Lotus Sutra in the Latter Day. It also becomes evident from these passages that the hallmark of a votary is fighting against slander of the Law in this defiled age. In other words, a true votary is one who responds to the Buddha's will and decree by actively taking on the challenge to propagate the sutra, fully aware that great trials and obstacles lie ahead.

The Daishonin indicates this concisely in "On Practicing the Buddha's Teachings":

"This is indeed an accursed time to live in this land! However, the Buddha has commanded me to be born in this age, and it is impossible for me to go against the decree of the Dharma King. And so, as the sutra dictates, I have launched the battle between the provisional and the true teachings"[2] (WND-1, 392).

By writing, "This is indeed an accursed time to live in this land!" however, Nichiren isn't actually lamenting his misfortune at having been born in a troubled time. Rather, he is indicating his readiness and determination to battle the evil that abounds in it.

But when the Daishonin was being harshly persecuted and seemingly not receiving protection from the heavenly deities, many in society—even some of his disciples—doubted whether he could really be the Lotus Sutra's votary. In response, he asserts that the votary described in the Lotus Sutra is one who is personally prepared to launch the "battle between the provisional and the true teachings," knowing that great persecution is inevitable.

The onslaught of persecutions that befell the Daishonin were certainly not a result of passivity; it was a consequence of the struggle he set into motion by seeking to fulfill the Buddha's intent. This proactive approach to life is a key point that the Daishonin teaches his followers in "The Opening of the Eyes."

The SGI has initiated just such a committed struggle in order to realize kosen-rufu, the Buddha's will and decree. Those who join in this struggle live in accord with the Buddha's will; they carry out the work of the Thus Come One.[3] Therefore, the infinite benefit of the Mystic Law, the essence of the Buddha's enlightenment, manifests in the lives of SGI members.

The Three Pronouncements of the "Treasure Tower" Chapter

In "The Opening of the Eyes," as I mentioned earlier, Nichiren cites the sutra passages containing the "three pronouncements" of the "Treasure Tower" chapter (WND-1, 261–62; LSOC, 215–20).

In the first pronouncement, Shakyamuni declares his wish to entrust the Lotus Sutra to those who will spread it in the strife-filled saha world after his passing, and he exhorts the bodhisattvas present to come forward and vow to carry out this mission. In fact, the entire Ceremony in the Air, which begins in the "Treasure Tower" chapter [and ends in the "Entrustment," the 22nd chapter], is a ceremony to entrust the Bodhisattvas of the Earth with the mission of propagating the Lotus Sutra.

In the second pronouncement, Shakyamuni indicates that the reason all Buddhas of the ten directions—that is to say, throughout the universe—have gathered at the assembly of the Lotus Sutra in the saha world is to "make certain the Law will long endure" (LSOC, 216), and he urges those present to openly state their vow to propagate the sutra after his passing. In other words, the perpetuation of the Law in this troubled world is the will of all Buddhas throughout the universe—that in itself underscores just how important it is that the Law endures. The struggles of the Buddha, who awoke to this Law of universal enlightenment and seeks to share it with others, would all come to naught if living beings in this troubled world could not attain Buddhahood.

In the third pronouncement, Shakyamuni sets forth the "six difficult and nine easy acts." Explaining how difficult it will be to propagate the sutra in the age after his passing, he commands the bodhisattvas to arouse a great aspiration and proclaim their vow to undertake this arduous challenge.

Shakyamuni's Evaluation of the Relative Merit of the Sutras

Of these three pronouncements, Nichiren devotes the greatest discussion to the teaching of the six difficult and nine easy acts, focusing on this teaching as a means for judging the relative merits of the different sutras. He goes on to consider the various sutras in the light of whether they fall into the category of the "six difficult acts" (a teaching that should be propagated after the Buddha's passing) or the category of the "nine easy acts" (an inferior teaching) (WND-1, 263–64).

In short, the reason Shakyamuni expounds the six difficult and nine easy acts and urges the bodhisattvas to propagate the Lotus Sutra after his demise is that this sutra constitutes the foremost teaching in that it assures enlightenment for all people of the evil age to come.

As Nichiren writes in the first part of "The Opening of the Eyes," the doctrine of the true "mutual possession of the Ten Worlds" and the true "three thousand realms in a single moment of life"—the essential teaching for ordinary people to attain Buddhahood—is hidden in the depths of the "Life Span" chapter of the Lotus Sutra. That is why the Lotus Sutra surpasses all other teachings.

In *The Outstanding Principles of the Lotus Sutra,*[4] the Great Teacher Dengyo, founder of the Japanese Tendai school of Buddhism, writes with regard to the significance of the six difficult and nine easy acts: "Shakyamuni taught that the shallow is easy to embrace, but the profound is difficult. To discard the shallow and seek the profound is the way of a person of courage" ("The Selection of the Time," WND-1, 558). In other words, Shakyamuni set forth the six difficult and nine easy acts to teach that spreading a shallow teaching is easy, while propagating a profound teaching is difficult. Here we have Shakyamuni's own evaluation of the relative merits of the various sutras—a comparative classification—based on which the Lotus Sutra is deemed profound and all other sutras shallow. Hence Dengyo writes, "Shakyamuni taught that the shallow is easy to embrace, but the profound is difficult."

The various other sutras are easy to believe and easy to understand because the Buddha expounded them according to the capacity of beings of the nine worlds; a method known as "preaching in accordance with the minds of others." The Lotus Sutra is difficult to believe and difficult to understand because the Buddha directly revealed his own enlightenment. In other words, he employed "preaching in accordance with his own mind." Thus Dengyo continues, "To discard the shallow and seek the profound is the way of a person of courage."

These are important words. By setting forth the six difficult and nine easy acts and urging those gathered to take up the mission of propagation after his passing, Shakyamuni indicates his wish that his followers discard shallow teachings and spread the profound teaching of the Lotus Sutra.

Here, "a person of courage" means a "trainer of people"[5]—the Buddha—while "the way of a person of courage" means "the Buddha's will." With regard to the propagation of his teachings after his death, the Buddha's will is that people should reject the shallow teachings, which are easy to believe and understand, and instead adhere to the profound teaching of the Lotus Sutra, which is difficult to believe and understand.

Shakyamuni himself established that the Lotus Sutra is his paramount teaching. Therefore, bodhisattvas who make the Buddha's intent their own will abide by this evaluation after his passing, discarding all other sutras and upholding and spreading this one supreme teaching.

Ignorance of the Correct Object of Comparison

After quoting the sutra passages containing the three pronouncements, Nichiren writes, "The meaning of these passages from the sutra is right before our eyes" (WND-1, 262). As he suggests, the Buddha's intent in making these pronouncements is quite obvious—as clear and unmistakable as the sun shining in the sky. But people with strong attachments or biases cannot see even something as obvious as the sun; it is as if they are blindfolded.

The Daishonin then highlights the distorted views of the Lotus Sutra held by the founders of the Flower Garland, Dharma Characteristics, Three Treatises and True Word schools. These men formulated some of the main comparative classifications of the sutras that existed in Nichiren's day.

Why did the founders of these schools classify the sutras erroneously? Nichiren says it was because they did not know the right object or focus of comparison.[6] The sutras of these various schools each claimed they were foremost among all teachings, but this could not be so, because their claims of supremacy were only based upon a limited framework.[7]

In contrast, as indicated in "The Teacher of the Law," the 10th chapter, with Shakyamuni's declaration about "the sutras I have preached, now preach, and will preach" (LSOC, 203),[8] the Lotus Sutra is the highest among the teachings he has expounded. The "Teacher of the Law" chapter clearly explains that among all his lifetime teachings the Lotus Sutra is the most difficult to believe and understand. Precisely because it is the profoundest and the most difficult teaching to accept and comprehend, Shakyamuni sets forth the six difficult and nine easy acts.

The founders of the various other Buddhist schools lost sight of this and instead relied on passages in other sutras that claimed preeminence. As a result, they devised systems of classification counter to the Buddha's intent. And the later priests of these schools remained confused about the relative merits of the various sutras and misinterpreted the principles found in them. The Daishonin severely refutes their mistakes, saying, "Unless one can perceive the relative profundity of the various writings, one cannot judge the worth of the principles they reveal" (WND-1, 267).

In other words, blind to the six difficult and nine easy acts that Shakyamuni personally clarified and to his statement about "the sutras I have preached, now preach, and will preach," these people failed to grasp the true relative merits of the various sutras. Naturally, this resulted in confusion about the depth of the teachings contained in those sutras.

"The Richest Person in All of Present-Day Japan"

Put another way, by understanding the six difficult and nine easy acts, one can judge the merits of the various sutras, as well as establish which teachings are most profound. That is Nichiren Daishonin's position. Accordingly, he says that his own judgment of the sutras far surpasses that of Ch'eng-kuan of the Flower Garland school, Chia-hsiang of the Three Treatises school, Tz'u-en of the Dharma Characteristics school and Kobo of the True Word school.[9]

To follow the teaching of the six difficult and nine easy acts and apprehend which teachings are shallow and which profound is to dedicate one's life to upholding and propagating the Lotus Sutra as described in the six difficult acts. When doctrinal comparisons of the teachings are not accompanied by actual practice, they become mere intellectual games. The Daishonin declares that because, without begrudging his life, he has struggled in exact accord with the spirit of the Lotus Sutra, his name will surely be handed down in ages to come. Based on this immense state of life, he writes, "I, Nichiren, am the richest man in all of present-day Japan" (WND-1, 268).

There is no greater spiritual wealth than to read with one's life—to put into action— the Lotus Sutra, which is the highest teaching. Through our practice of Nichiren Buddhism, we of the SGI also come to savor this vast state of life.

How remarkable it is that Nichiren, although exiled on Sado Island, can declare himself the richest person in all Japan. In other letters written while on Sado, he also exclaims: "Though we may be exiles, we have cause to be joyful in both body and mind!" ("Reply to Sairen-bo," WND-1, 312), and "I feel immeasurable delight even though I am now an exile" ("The True Aspect of All Phenomena," WND-1, 386).

Certainly, no authority or persecution could suppress or contain his immense state of life. Viewed from the life state of Buddhahood, not even the most hellish circumstances could pose a restraint. This was his spirit.

Selfless practice carried out without begrudging one's life is the key to achieving such a lofty, unhindered state of being, as Nichiren indicates when he writes, "I have dedicated my life to the Lotus Sutra, and my name will be handed down in ages to come" (WND-1, 268). By devoting ourselves to the Lotus Sutra, we can tap Myoho-renge-kyo from within and bring it to bloom in our lives.

The Daishonin compares one who lives based on the six difficult and nine easy acts to being the "lord of the great ocean" and the "king of Mount Sumeru" (WND-1, 268).[10] He says that just as the "lord of the great ocean" is obeyed by the gods of the various rivers, and as the "king of Mount Sumeru" is served by the gods of the various other mountains, one who internalizes the teaching of the six difficult and nine easy acts, according to Buddhism, reigns supreme. That sort of person can correctly discern Buddhism's highest teaching or ultimate truth because he or she embodies the Mystic Law—the teaching implicit in the depths of the "Life

Span" chapter and the foundation of all sutras expounded by Shakyamuni—and strives to spread it widely, expressed in the concrete form of Nam-myoho-renge-kyo.

A Person of Courage Seeks the Profound

Let us return once more to Dengyo's passage, "To discard the shallow and seek the profound is the way of a person of courage."

"To seek the profound" refers to our challenge in bravely standing as protagonists of kosen-rufu. We of the SGI have steadfastly taken on this most difficult challenge in the present age. From the pioneering days of our movement, despite being showered with slander, criticism and abuse, our members have summoned up their courage and told others about the greatness of Nichiren's teachings and about our noble cause—all out of the desire to help others become happy. In these compassionless and self-centered times, where people are only concerned about themselves and give little thought to others, we of the SGI have chanted for the happiness of our friends, prayed for the prosperity of our local communities and society, and wholeheartedly exerted ourselves for kosen-rufu.

In this way, day after day, with courage and conviction, we have nobly sought to "propagate the Lotus Sutra widely in an evil age," "teach it even to one person" and "inquire about its meaning"—all of which are described among the six difficult acts. This intrepid spirit to fight for kosen-rufu is itself "the way of a person of courage," and becomes the heart of the Buddha. We have succeeded in opening an unprecedented age of worldwide kosen-rufu, thanks to our members' valiant struggles that resonate with the Buddha's spirit.

Viewed in terms of human life, "shallow" means inertia, idleness and cowardice. Bravely defeating such inner weakness and seeking deep conviction and profound human greatness is "the way of a person of courage." To seek the shallow or the profound—this inner battle takes place in our hearts many times each day.

Life, too, is a struggle. We need to defeat our weaknesses and courageously stand up, based on faith, with the resolve to continue growing in our lives, to keep moving forward and to be victorious in the challenges we encounter. When we live with such depth and meaning, we can become true winners in life. That is the purpose of our daily practice of faith and our SGI activities.

9

The Two Admonitions of the "Devadatta" Chapter—A Call To Lead All People to Enlightenment Based on the Teachings of Changing Poison Into Medicine and Attaining Buddhahood in One's Present Form

The widespread propagation of the Mystic Law in the Latter Day—this is the great vow expressed in the Lotus Sutra, representing not only the individual wish of Shakyamuni but the shared aspiration of Many Treasures Thus Come One and all Buddhas and bodhisattvas throughout the ten directions and three existences.

In the three pronouncements[1] of the "Treasure Tower" chapter of the Lotus Sutra, Shakyamuni calls out in a loud voice to those gathered in the great assembly, urging them to propagate the Lotus Sutra after his passing. He says in effect: "Many Treasures Buddha roars the lion's roar because of his great vow. All of you should likewise make a great vow to uphold and spread this sutra" (see LSOC, 217).

This vow the Buddhas and bodhisattvas made in response to Shakyamuni's call for the sutra's widespread propagation in the Latter Day of the Law began to be fulfilled in a true sense with the appearance of Nichiren Daishonin.

In "The Opening of the Eyes," Nichiren discusses the transmission section[2] of the theoretical teaching (first half) of the Lotus Sutra—that is, "Treasure Tower," the 11th chapter, "Devadatta," the 12th, and "Encouraging Devotion," the 13th. In these chapters, Shakyamuni urges the assembly to spread the sutra after his passing. Nichiren clarifies that he is the votary of the Lotus Sutra of the Latter Day of the Law because he has internalized and read these three chapters with his life and is practicing exactly as Shakyamuni teaches.

In my last lecture, I focused on how the Daishonin propagated the Lotus Sutra, a teaching that is "difficult to believe and the most difficult to understand" (LSOC, 203), in perfect accord with the intent of the Buddha reflected in the three pronouncements and the six difficult and nine easy acts, which appear in "Treasure Tower."

This time, we will look at how the Daishonin opened the great path for ordinary people to attain Buddhahood and for changing poison into medicine in this troubled age of the Latter Day of the Law, based on the teachings contained in the two admonitions of the "Devadatta" chapter.

Two Key Teachings: The Enlightenment of Evil People and the Enlightenment of Women

In addition to the three pronouncements of the Buddha in the "Treasure Tower" chapter of the Lotus Sutra, the "Devadatta" chapter contains two enlightening admonitions. [The first reveals that Devadatta will attain Buddhahood.] Devadatta was a man of incorrigible disbelief, of the type called icchantika,[3] and yet it is predicted that he will in the future become a Buddha called the Thus Come One Heavenly King. The forty volumes of the Nirvana Sutra state that [all beings, including the icchantikas, possess the Buddha nature, but] the actual proof of that is found in this chapter of the Lotus Sutra. There are countless other persons such as the monk Sunakshatra[4] or King Ajatashatru who have committed the five cardinal sins[5] and slandered the Law, but Devadatta is cited as one example to represent all the countless others; he is the chief

offender, and it is assumed that all lesser offenders will fare as he does. Thus it is revealed that all those who commit the five or the seven cardinal sins[6] or who slander the Law or who are icchantikas inherently opposed to taking faith will become Buddhas like the Thus Come One Heavenly King. Poison turns into sweet dew,[7] the finest of all flavors.

[The second admonition concerns the fact that the dragon king's daughter attained Buddhahood.] When she attained Buddhahood, this does not mean simply that one person did so. It reveals the fact that all women will attain Buddhahood. In the various Hinayana sutras that were preached before the Lotus Sutra, it is denied that women can ever attain Buddhahood. In the Mahayana sutras other than the Lotus Sutra, it would appear that women can attain Buddhahood or be reborn in the pure land. But they may do so only after they have changed into some other form. It is not the kind of immediate attainment of Buddhahood that is based on the doctrine of three thousand realms in a single moment of life. Thus it is an attainment of Buddhahood or rebirth in the pure land in name only and not in reality. The dragon king's daughter represents "one example that stands for all the rest."[8] When the dragon king's daughter attained

Buddhahood, it opened up the way to attaining Buddhahood for all women of later ages. (WND-1, 268–69)

The two admonitions of the "Devadatta" chapter refer to two teachings: the enlightenment of evil people, who are represented by Devadatta; and the enlightenment of women, who are represented by the dragon king's daughter.[9] They are called "admonitions" because Shakyamuni admonishes the assembled bodhisattvas to widely propagate the Lotus Sutra in the Latter Day so that all people may attain Buddhahood.

The enlightenment of evil people and women was not taught in the provisional pre-Lotus Sutra teachings. Consequently, the fact that it is expounded in the Lotus Sutra underscores again that the sutra is the one supreme teaching by which all people in this defiled age of the Latter Day of the Law can attain Buddhahood.

This is where we find the Lotus Sutra's true greatness. If the Lotus Sutra could not open the way to enlightenment for the unfortunate beings denied Buddhahood in the provisional teachings, then it could not possibly enable all people of the Latter Day to attain that state of life either. The hallmark of a votary of the Lotus Sutra in this age is bringing the true greatness of the Lotus Sutra to shine forth, responding to Shakyamuni's call by actually striving to realize the Buddha's wish and intent.

It is important that we actively engage in the challenge of guiding those around us to happiness. Without that struggle, any ambition of achieving happiness for all humanity is meaningless. A religion is as good as dead if it cannot provide an answer to the vital question of how we can arouse the joy of living in the hearts of those experiencing the deepest suffering and despair, those who have lost all hope.

The teachings of the Lotus Sutra and the Buddhism of Nichiren Daishonin, with their life-affirming quality, represent a philosophy of revitalization that views all things as having infinite value and potential. They also constitute a philosophy of hope that can inspire fresh optimism and zest for life in the hearts of those suffering intensely.

This philosophy of hope is the core of a genuinely humanistic religion, for it teaches how we can develop deep appreciation for being alive at each moment. It also allows us to repay our gratitude to our parents who raised us and to all in our environment to whom we are indebted. And it makes it possible for all humankind to lead happy, fulfilling lives.

The enlightenment of evil people and women expounded in the "Devadatta" chapter is therefore very closely tied to the true purpose of religion.

Opening the Path To Attaining Buddhahood in an Evil Age

We can identify three main points in Nichiren's explanation of the two admonitions in this treatise.

First, Devadatta—an evil person and *icchantika*—is predicted to attain Buddhahood.

Icchantikas were people of incorrigible disbelief who in the provisional pre-Lotus Sutra teachings were said to have the least possibility of attaining Buddhahood. Then, the dragon girl—a female who suffered discrimination in society and in the religious tenets and customs of Shakyamuni's time—swiftly gives an actual demonstration of her ability to attain Buddhahood. This highlights the fact that the Lotus Sutra is the scripture that opens the path to enlightenment for all people living in an evil age.

It is the votary of the Lotus Sutra who leads this trailblazing struggle to unlock the Buddhahood of all human beings.

Second, as a doctrinal basis for the teaching of universal enlightenment, the Daishonin emphasizes the "immediate attainment of Buddhahood that is based on the doctrine of three thousand realms in a single moment of life"[10] (WND-1, 269). This concept of instantly attaining Buddhahood is found only in the Lotus Sutra. Here Nichiren clarifies the transformative power that makes this feat possible. In the case of evil people attaining enlightenment, he explains this power lies in the potential to "change poison into medicine," that is, to transform even the greatest evil into the greatest good. In the case of women attaining enlightenment, this power, he explains, lies in the actual proof of attaining Buddhahood in one's present form, that is, without having to undergo a physical transformation or rebirth.

Consequently, the votary of the Lotus Sutra is one who embodies the principle of "the immediate attainment of Buddhahood that is based on the doctrine of three thousand realms in a single moment of life."

Third, by expounding that evil people and women can attain Buddhahood—thereby establishing the potential for all human beings in an evil age to become enlightened—Nichiren also opens the way to the "attainment of Buddhahood by all fathers and all mothers" (see WND-1, 269). He therefore calls the Lotus Sutra "*The Classic of Filial Piety* of Buddhism" (WND-1, 269), a teaching that makes it possible for us to truly repay our debt of gratitude to our parents.

The spirit and practice of gratitude, underpinned by a philosophy of hope, are the very heart of human society; they give rise to true bonds between people. The votary of the Lotus Sutra is one who strives to realize the principle of establishing the correct teaching for the peace of the land, who perseveres in the fundamental struggle to build a peaceful and prosperous society.

Even Icchantikas Can Attain Buddhahood Through the Mystic Principle of Changing Poison Into Medicine

In discussing the significance of the attainment of Buddhahood by evil people, which is taught in the "Devadatta" chapter, Nichiren writes: "Devadatta was a man of incorrigible disbelief, of the type called icchantika, and yet it is predicted that he will in the future become a Buddha called the Thus Come One Heavenly King. The forty volumes of the Nirvana Sutra state that [all beings, including the icchantikas, possess the Buddha nature, but] the actual proof of that is found in [the 'Devadatta'] chapter of the Lotus Sutra" (WND-1, 268).

Devadatta, of course, was an extremely evil individual who turned against his teacher Shakyamuni, slandered the correct teaching, and committed several of the five cardinal sins, including that of causing disunity among the community of Buddhist believers.

The actual principle for the attainment of Buddhahood by all people is found in the concept of the "true aspect of the ten factors of life"[11] in "Expedient Means," the 2nd chapter of the Lotus Sutra. In light of that principle, even the enlightenment of Devadatta is already assured in this chapter.

But whether an icchantika—one who lacks faith and disparages the Law—could actually attain Buddhahood was a crucial question for many people. This theme particularly occupies the Nirvana Sutra, in which Shakyamuni states that all people possess the Buddha nature, including even the icchantika. Nevertheless, he also explains that their disbelief in and slander of the correct teaching prevent them from actually attaining enlightenment, so that this state exists for them merely as a potential.[12]

How then could Devadatta, the arch icchantika, attain Buddhahood? It is curious, to say the least. Why was it that he—a person who was said to have fallen into the hell of incessant suffering and been destined to remain there for infinite *kalpas*—received a prediction of future enlightenment from Shakyamuni Buddha at the assembly of the Lotus Sutra?

Nichiren writes, "How astounding, then, that in the 'Devadatta' chapter of the Lotus Sutra Shakyamuni Buddha should reveal that Devadatta was his teacher in a past existence and should predict that he would attain enlightenment in the future as a Thus Come One called Heavenly King!" ("The Daimoku of the Lotus Sutra," WND-1, 147).

It is amazing indeed. Ultimately, we see here the power of the Mystic Law. Nichiren says that the prophecy of Devadatta's enlightenment guarantees that all evil people can likewise attain the Buddha way, telling us, "Therefore, the Lotus Sutra is called *myo* [mystic or wondrous]" (WND-1, 147).

Myo has three meanings: "to open," "to be fully endowed" and "to revive."[13] Explaining how those who had been despised in the pre-Lotus Sutra teachings—persons of the two vehicles, icchantikas and women—can attain Buddhahood through the Lotus Sutra, Nichiren writes, "*Myo* means to revive, that is, to return to life" (WND-1, 149). He also says, "The Lotus Sutra . . . can cure the dead as well as the living, and therefore it has the character *myo* [mystic or wondrous] in its title [Myoho-renge-kyo]" (WND-1, 149).

Here, "the dead" refers to the condition of persons of the two vehicles and the icchantika, who had allowed their Buddha nature to wither and die on account of attachment to mistaken beliefs, ideas and teachings. The Lotus Sutra has the power to revive even the lives of such people. This is because the Lotus Sutra serves as the ultimate elixir for revitalizing and reactivating the Buddha nature. That is why "The Life Span of the Thus Come One," the 16th chapter, describes the sutra as "a highly effective medicine" (LSOC, 269).

In the Lotus Sutra, Shakyamuni and Many Treasures, as well as all Buddhas and bodhisattvas gathered at the assembly from throughout the universe, praise the Mystic Law that led them to enlightenment and rejoice at revealing their Buddha nature through the power of that Law. They also vow to guide all people to enlightenment and devote themselves to this great undertaking with the spirit of not begrudging their lives.

Indeed, it could be said that the whole purpose of the Lotus Sutra is to inspire people to bring forth their Buddha nature. The sutra is like a paean to the Buddha nature. Thus, when people hear it, when their lives encounter the sublime symphony of the Mystic Law and the noble life states of bodhisattva and Buddhahood, no matter how steeped they may be in evil or misery, they can awaken their innate Buddha nature. The Lotus Sutra teaches that even a person of immense evil such as Devadatta is not excluded.

In "The Opening of the Eyes," Nichiren writes that the Lotus Sutra's prediction of Devadatta's future enlightenment is proof that an icchantika can in fact attain Buddhahood. Moreover, he says that Devadatta's example indicates the potential for all evil people in the Latter Day to gain this supreme state of life, as well. He sums up by saying, "Poison turns into sweet dew, the finest of all flavors" (WND-1, 268).

Devadatta's attainment of Buddhahood serves as actual proof of the principle of changing poison into medicine found in the Lotus Sutra.

Opening the Way to Buddhahood for Women of the Latter Day

Next, we'll look at the attainment of Buddhahood by the dragon king's daughter.

As in the case with Devadatta, Nichiren asserts that the dragon girl's enlightenment does not merely signal one person's attainment of Buddhahood but, rather, indicates that all women have the potential to do so. He writes, "When the dragon king's daughter attained Buddhahood, it opened up the way to attaining Buddhahood for all women of later ages" (WND-1, 269). Nichiren emphasizes here that the individual's ability attain enlightenment assures the same potential for all people.

Everything starts with one person. As an ancient Chinese saying goes, "One is the mother of ten thousand." Kosen-rufu cannot be achieved without an ardent desire to help others become happy, irrespective of who they may be.

Furthermore, from a doctrinal standpoint, the Daishonin refutes the provisional Mahayana sutras that at a glance might seem to teach that women can attain Buddhahood. While acknowledging that these teachings may recognize women's potential for enlightenment, he denounces them for limiting women to "attaining Buddhahood through transformation"—in other words, insisting that a woman can only attain enlightenment after first being reborn as a man.

In contrast, the dragon king's daughter instantly attains Buddhahood in accord with the doctrine of three thousand realms in a single moment of life—she manifests the life state of Buddhahood in her present form, as a living being in the nine worlds. In short, she becomes a Buddha while retaining her form as the eight-year-old daughter of the dragon king.

The "Devadatta" chapter of the Lotus Sutra records the doubts expressed by

Shariputra, the wisest of Shakyamuni's ten major disciples. When Shariputra is confronted with the dragon girl's attainment of enlightenment, he is incredulous, saying that it is "difficult to believe" (LSOC, 227). He rather rudely interrogates her, demanding to know, "How . . . could a woman like you be able to attain Buddhahood so quickly?" (LSOC, 227).

Even Shariputra, who earlier in the Lotus Sutra had been predicted to attain Buddhahood, could not completely abandon the notion that one could only attain enlightenment after undertaking austere practices for countless eons. As a result, he could not readily accept the idea of attaining Buddhahood in one's present form.

What the enlightenment of Devadatta and the dragon girl shows is the beneficial power of the Mystic Law to enable one to change poison into medicine and attain Buddhahood in one's present form. Only through this beneficial power can all people in the defiled age of the Latter Day achieve genuine happiness. This is because the Mystic Law is the highly effective medicine that can make this a reality on the most fundamental level.

Believing in the Transformative Power of the Mystic Law

Nichiren also describes this immediate attainment of Buddhahood, writing: "The heart of the Lotus Sutra is the revelation that one may attain supreme enlightenment in one's present form without altering one's status as an ordinary person. This means that without casting aside one's karmic impediments one can still attain the Buddha way" ("Reply to Hakiri Saburo," WND-1, 410).

"Attaining supreme enlightenment in one's present form" means that one's life, just as it is, is an entity of the Mystic Law, while "not altering one's status as an ordinary person" means that becoming a Buddha does not require changing into something or someone else.

We can summon forth our Buddhahood without altering our form as ordinary people and give expression to our Buddha nature through our conduct. The way to genuine happiness for people of this age, the Latter Day of the Law, lies solely in this path of human revolution and the attainment of Buddhahood in one's present form.

Also, this is a time when people's lives and society are wracked unceasingly by negative causes and effects. The above-cited passage includes the phrase *without casting aside one's karmic impediments*. If one could not attain Buddhahood without discarding such hindrances, then it would remain an unreachable goal for people of the Latter Day of the Law. The principle of changing poison into medicine thus gives people the power to bring forth innate hope and overcome feelings of despair and helplessness in this evil age, with its endless cycle of negative causation.

The famous Indian Mahayana scholar Nagarjuna,[14] whom Nichiren frequently cites, declared: "[The Lotus Sutra is] like a great physician who can change poison into medicine" ("Hell Is the Land of Tranquil Light," WND-1, 458). This clearly expresses the Lotus Sutra's superiority and describes "the blessing of the single character *myo*" (WND-1, 458).

In "What It Means to Hear the Buddha Vehicle for the First Time" (WND-2, 741–45),[15] addressed to his lay follower Toki Jonin, Nichiren explains in depth the meaning of "changing poison into medicine." He writes that *poison* refers to the three paths—earthly desires, karma and suffering—while *medicine* indicates the three virtues—the Dharma body, wisdom and emancipation. Changing poison into medicine, he explains, is the principle whereby people living amid the negative causality of the three paths can manifest the positive benefit of the three virtues in their own lives through the power of the Mystic Law.

Earthly desires, karma and suffering—the three paths—describe the web of negative causation in people's lives that gives rise to evil and suffering. *Earthly desires* include such things as the three poisons—greed, anger and foolishness; they are illusions that bring about suffering. *Karma* arises from earthly desires; it indicates three categories of action—mental, verbal and physical—that lead to suffering. These actions include the five cardinal sins, ten evil acts,[16] and four grave prohibitions.[17] *Suffering* is the result of earthly desires and karma; it takes the form of physical and spiritual retribution, and includes the four sufferings and the eight sufferings.[18] Because of all these, people's lives are shackled by illusion and suffering (see GZ, 983–84).

In contrast to the three paths, the three virtues—the Dharma body, wisdom and emancipation—are great benefits that manifest in the life of a Buddha; they indicate ultimate truth, pure wisdom and a life state of infinite freedom.

The earthly desires, karma and suffering of ordinary people give rise to lives filled with illusion and torment, whereas the Dharma body, wisdom and emancipation of Buddhas make for lives replete with freedom and joy that accords with ultimate truth and wisdom. The two couldn't be more different. Through the marvelous power of the Mystic Law, however, we can dramatically transform the three paths into the three virtues. This is the principle of changing poison into medicine.

The life of an ordinary person engaged in a cycle of cause and effect based on the three paths is the seed for attaining the exact opposite state of life, one pervaded by the three virtues. In other words, it is the seed for Buddhahood. The key to changing poison into medicine is to believe in the Lotus Sutra, which elucidates the mystic nature of life whereby the three paths are instantly transformed into the three virtues (see GZ, 983). Faith, or confidence, in the Mystic Law unlocks this wondrous and unfathomable power inherent in our lives.

Tsunesaburo Makiguchi, the first Soka Gakkai president, discussing the principle of changing poison into medicine, stressed that no matter what may happen, we should always look to the future: "Our daily practice of the Mystic Law is one of changing poison into medicine. As long as we are human beings, we are bound at times to meet with accidents or misfortune, or encounter business setbacks . . . But we can change any situation from poison into medicine as long as we do not doubt the Gohonzon and continue to devote ourselves to this practice, with the Mystic Law and the Gohonzon as our basis.

"For example, you may fall ill. But merely worrying that it is retribution for a negative cause you made in the past solves nothing. You should say to yourself with confidence and determination, 'I will take this illness and change poison into medicine! I will unlock the door to great good fortune and benefit in the form of good health!' and continue to exert yourself steadfastly in faith. This is important.

"The power of the Mystic Law, with its ability to change poison into medicine, cannot only cure your illness but enable you to experience even greater good health than before, when you finally recover."[19]

The principle of changing poison into medicine serves as a wellspring of hope, making it possible for people to live with optimism in a troubled age.

"The Lotus Sutra Is The Classic of Filial Piety of Buddhism"

Confucianism preaches filial piety and care for one's parents, but it is limited to this present life. It provides no way for one to assist one's parents in their future lives, and the Confucian sages and worthies are therefore sages and worthies in name only and not in reality. Brahmanism, though it recognizes the existence of past and future lives, similarly offers no means to assist one's parents to a better life in the future. Buddhism alone can do so, and thus it is the true way of sages and worthies. But in the Hinayana and Mahayana sutras preached before the Lotus Sutra, and in the schools based on these sutras, to gain the way even for oneself is impossible. One can hardly hope to do anything for one's parents either. Though the texts of these sutras may say [that they can bring about enlightenment], in reality that is not the case. Only with the preaching of the Lotus Sutra, in which the dragon king's daughter attained Buddhahood, did it become evident that the attainment of Buddhahood was a possibility for all mothers. And when it was revealed that even an evil man such as Devadatta could attain Buddhahood, it became evident that Buddhahood was a possibility for all mothers. And when it was revealed that even an evil man such as Devadatta could attain Buddhahood, it became evident that Buddhahood was a possibility for all fathers. The Lotus Sutra is *The Classic of Filial Piety* of Buddhism. This ends my discussion of the two admonitions contained in the "Devadatta" chapter. (WND-1, 269)

Nichiren concludes his discussion of the attainment of Buddhahood by evil people and women in "The Opening of the Eyes" by saying that the Lotus Sutra opens the path to enlightenment for all fathers and for all mothers, and as such can be regarded as "*The Classic of Filial Piety* of Buddhism."

As he explains: "Only with the preaching of the Lotus Sutra, in which the dragon king's daughter attained Buddhahood, did it become evident that the attainment of Buddhahood was a possibility for all mothers. And when it was revealed that even an evil man such as Devadatta could attain Buddhahood, it became evident that Buddhahood was a possibility for all fathers" (WND-1, 269).

Earlier, I cited the writing "What It Means to Hear the Buddha Vehicle for the First Time." In this letter, written to Toki Jonin for the third memorial of his mother's death, Nichiren discusses the principle of changing poison into medicine to explain that both mother and child attain Buddhahood together.[20] He closes by writing: "Not only will ordinary people who hear this teaching attain Buddhahood themselves, but also their fathers and mothers will do so in their present form. This, he encourages Toki, is the ultimate expression of filial devotion" (WND-2, 745).

"Doctrines" in this passage refers to the principles of changing poison into medicine and attaining Buddhahood in one's present form.

The Daishonin was prompted in part to become a priest by the filial desire to enable his parents to attain Buddhahood. Wishing for the happiness of all people in the Latter Day of the Law and actually ensuring the happiness of one's own parents are very closely connected. The Daishonin writes: "Since he [Maudgalyayana, one of Shakyamuni's ten major disciples] himself had not yet attained Buddhahood, it was very difficult for him to relieve the sufferings of his parents. And how much more difficult would it have been for him to do so for anyone else!" ("On Offerings for Deceased Ancestors," WND-1, 819).

Nichiren repeatedly emphasizes the importance of us ourselves manifesting Buddhahood, if we are truly intent on repaying our debt of gratitude to our parents. He also explains that if it weren't possible to secure our own parents' enlightenment, there would be no way we could help others gain it. Nichiren taught his followers that only through the Lotus Sutra could they demonstrate true filial devotion and care for their parents.

The Mystic Law of Nam-myoho-renge-kyo is the driving force for changing poison into medicine and attaining Buddhahood in one's present form. As such, it is the supreme teaching for bringing genuine happiness to all humankind and the noble path of true filial piety for leading all parents to enlightenment.

10

The Three Powerful Enemies, Part 1—The Anatomy of Persecution Arising From Fundamental Darkness

Kosen-rufu is a struggle to spread the Lotus Sutra so that all people in the evil age of the Latter Day of the Law can attain enlightenment. Obstacles and devilish forces of every imaginable kind are sure to assail the votaries of the Lotus Sutra who take up this challenge. In particular, the three powerful enemies will appear without fail as a concrete manifestation of the devilish nature inherent in life. Precisely by battling and triumphing over these formidable enemies, however, we can attain Buddhahood in this lifetime and make kosen-rufu a reality.

The greatest persecution that befell Nichiren Daishonin in his efforts to spread the Law—an onslaught that saw the three powerful enemies attack him on an unprecedented scale—was the Tatsunokuchi Persecution and Sado Exile.[1] But ultimately none of the devilish forces arrayed against him could bring about his demise. The Daishonin says, "I survived even the Tatsunokuchi Persecution" (GZ, 843). Not only had he surmounted countless other hardships in the course of his endeavors, but he had triumphed, he declares,

in this most harrowing persecution in which the authorities had tried to execute him.

Even though the devil king of the sixth heaven, the personification of fundamental darkness, had mobilized forces "possessed by evil demons" (see LSOC, 233)—arrogant lay people, arrogant priests and arrogant false sages (the three powerful enemies)—and tried to eliminate Nichiren and destroy kosen-rufu, the devil king could not succeed. The triumphant life condition of the Daishonin, who had won over every attack by these malevolent forces, is nothing short of a manifestation of his true identity as the Buddha of limitless joy enlightened since time without beginning.

In "The Opening of the Eyes" so far, the Daishonin has discussed various passages from "Treasure Tower," the 11th chapter of the Lotus Sutra, and "Devadatta," the 12th chapter, to demonstrate that he is the sutra's votary in the Latter Day of the Law. Next, he turns his attention to the twenty-line verse section[2] regarding the three powerful enemies in "Encouraging Devotion," the 13th chapter

95

(LS, 232–34). Having personally battled these daunting adversaries, he concludes that he himself is the votary of the Lotus Sutra of the Latter Day (see WND-1, 268–78).

In "Encouraging Devotion," the eight hundred thousand million *nayutas* of bodhisattvas respond to Shakyamuni's five proclamations—the three pronouncements of the "Treasure Tower" chapter and the two admonitions of the "Devadatta" chapter—by pledging to spread the Lotus Sutra after his passing. And in the course of making that vow, they describe the three powerful enemies.

It could be said that "Treasure Tower" and "Devadatta" represent the "decree of the mentor," while "Encouraging Devotion" expresses the "vow of the disciples."

In any case, to win over obstacles and devilish functions is the true path of mentor and disciple dedicated to accomplishing kosen-rufu in the Latter Day of the Law.

"The Opening of the Eyes" Is a Paean of Victory

Awed by the five proclamations of the Buddha [made in the "Treasure Tower" and "Devadatta" chapters], the countless bodhisattvas promised the Buddha that they would propagate the Lotus Sutra, as described in the "Encouraging Devotion" chapter. I will hold up this passage [twenty-line verse section] of the sutra like a bright mirror so that all may see how the present-day priests of the Zen, Precepts, and Nembutsu schools and their lay supporters are guilty of slandering the Law.

On the twelfth day of the ninth month of last year [1271, on the occasion of the Tatsunokuchi Persecution], between the hours of the rat and the ox (11:00 P.M. to 3:00 A.M.), this person named Nichiren was beheaded. It is his soul that has come to this island of Sado and, in the second month of the following year, snowbound, is writing this to send to his close disciples. [The description of the evil age in the "Encouraging Devotion" chapter seems] terrible, but [one who cares nothing about oneself for the sake of the Law has] nothing to be frightened about. Others reading it will be terrified. This scriptural passage is the bright mirror that Shakyamuni, Many Treasures, and the Buddhas of the ten directions left for the future of Japan, and in which the present state of the country is reflected. (WND-1, 269)

At the beginning of his discussion on the twenty-line verse section, the Daishonin explains the significance of his undergoing the Tatsunokuchi Persecution. In other words, he starts by revealing his state of life in having vanquished the three powerful enemies. It is a declaration of spiritual triumph. This important passage signifies that "The Opening of the Eyes" as a whole can be viewed as a pacan of victory.

In writing "this person named Nichiren was beheaded," he is declaring that his status up to that time—in which he conducted himself as an ordinary person—came to an end at Tatsunokuchi.

The Daishonin is indicating here that at Tatsunokuchi he cast off his transient status and revealed his true identity. He uses the word *soul* to refer to that true identity—the Buddha of limitless joy enlightened since time without beginning. His soul, he says, has come to Sado. This represents a declaration of his state of life, his towering resolve from his place of exile to henceforth, as the original Buddha of the Latter Day, take the lead for the widespread propagation of the Mystic Law.

He continues, "[Nichiren] in the second month of the following year, snowbound, is writing this to send to his close disciples" (WND-1, 269). The Daishonin began composing "The Opening of the Eyes" immediately upon arriving at Tsukahara on Sado Island in early November 1271, and completed it in February 1272. The "close disciples" to whom he sent this treatise specifically refers to Shijo Kingo, who, with the spirit of not begrudging his life, had accompanied Nichiren during the Tatsunokuchi Persecution, but in a broader sense, it refers to all who had followed and fought alongside him up to that point.

Next, the Daishonin says: "[The description of the evil age in the 'Encouraging Devotion' chapter seems] terrible, but [one who cares nothing about oneself for the sake of the Law has] nothing to be frightened about. Others reading it will be terrified" (WND-1, 269). The first sentence is a statement of encouragement that although what is described may appear frightening, there is in fact nothing to fear.

Certainly, the persecutions by the three powerful enemies predicted in "Encouraging Devotion" are frightening. But once we understand the essence of the devilish forces behind these persecutions, it becomes obvious that what is truly terrifying is the devilish nature inherent in human beings.

In this treatise, however, the Daishonin, having risked his life to fight for kosen-rufu and subsequently triumphing over all obstacles and devilish functions, displays an indomitable spiritual state. Thus he says there is nothing to fear, not even amid the most terrible persecution or hardship caused by devilish functions.

The spirit to battle powerful enemies is the heart of the lion king. As long as we possess the readiness and courage to confront these negative forces, we can manifest our inherent Buddhahood and bring forth the necessary fighting spirit, wisdom and life force to achieve victory. For that reason alone, we have nothing to fear.

Accordingly, "there is nothing to be frightened about" (WND-1, 269) expresses the heart of the Daishonin (the lion king) and his disciples (the lion king's cubs) who fight alongside him with the same selfless spirit.

"Others . . . will be terrified" (WND-1, 269), meanwhile, refers to the hearts of those who do not practice with an ungrudging spirit and who are in danger of abandoning their faith out of cowardice. In other words, Nichiren was concerned that people who lacked firm resolve and commitment in faith would read the passage about the three powerful enemies in "Encouraging Devotion" and be overcome by fear and apprehension.

Cowardice is a state in which people have succumbed to inner devilish functions.

This can progress to such a profound level that they eventually lose their vitality and wisdom and even find their whole lives tumbling inexorably toward defeat. The Daishonin sternly warns that we should not let this happen to us.

Ultimately, unless we undertake the same resolve as our mentor in faith, we will be defeated by devilish functions. This is why the Daishonin's call to his disciples to rise into action with a vow equal to his resonates throughout this treatise.

A Bright Mirror Reflecting the Present State of the Country

The "Encouraging Devotion"
chapter states:
> "We beg you not to worry.
> After the Buddha has passed into
> extinction,
> in an age of fear and evil
> we will preach far and wide.
> There will be many ignorant people
> who will curse and speak ill of us
> and will attack us with swords and
> staves,
> but we will endure all these things.
> In that evil age there will be monks
> with perverse wisdom and hearts
> that are fawning and crooked
> who will suppose they have attained
> what they have not attained,
> being proud and boastful in heart.
> Or there will be forest-dwelling
> monks

> wearing clothing of patched rags and
> living in retirement,
> who will claim they are practicing
> the true way,
> despising and looking down on all
> humankind.
> Greedy for profit and support,
> they will preach the Law to white-
> robed laymen
> and will be respected and revered by
> the world
> as though they were arhats who
> possess the six transcendental
> powers.[3]
> These men with evil in their hearts,
> constantly thinking of worldly
> affairs,
> will borrow the name of forest-
> dwelling monks
> and take delight in proclaiming our
> faults . . .
> Because in the midst of the great
> assembly
> they constantly try to defame us,
> they will address the rulers, high
> ministers,
> Brahmans, and householders,
> as well as the other monks,
> slandering and speaking evil of us,
> saying, 'These are men of perverted
> views
> who preach non-Buddhist
> doctrines!' . . .
> In a muddied kalpa, in an evil age
> there will be many things to fear.
> Evil demons will take possession of
> others

and through them curse, revile, and
heap shame on us . . .
The evil monks of that muddied age,
failing to understand the Buddha's
expedient means,
how he preaches the Law in accordance with what is appropriate,
will confront us with foul language
and angry frowns;
again and again we will be banished." (WND-1, 269-70;
see LSOC, 232–34)

The Daishonin next cites principal extracts from the twenty-line "Encouraging Devotion" verse section that describes the three powerful enemies. The section begins with the bodhisattvas making a powerful pledge. Addressing Shakyamuni, they say: "We beg you not to worry. / After the Buddha has passed into extinction, / in an age of fear and evil / we will preach far and wide" (LSOC, 232).

They then explain in detail the characteristics of those who will persecute them, as well as what form those attacks will take. Based on this verse section, the Great Teacher Miao-lo of China later classified the persecutors into three groups and named them the "three powerful enemies."

The first enemy is arrogant lay people. Ignorant of Buddhism, they curse and speak ill of the practitioners and attack them with swords and staves, thus persecuting them through both verbal and physical violence.

The second enemy is arrogant priests. These are priests of an evil age who possess perverse wisdom and are fawning and crooked,

who suppose they have attained enlightenment when they have not and who are attached to their own preconceived ideas and beliefs.

The third enemy is arrogant false sages. These are people who try to pass themselves off as sages. The sutra describes them as having the following traits:

- They live apart from others, don robes and make a show of religious authority.
- While claiming to practice the correct way of Buddhism themselves, they disparage others. In the words of the sutra, they "despise and look down on all humankind" (see LSOC, 232).
- Greedy and avaricious, they expound the Law to lay people in order to seek personal profit and gain.
- They are revered by people in society as if they were arhats possessing the six transcendental powers.
- They harbor malice toward practitioners of the Lotus Sutra and cause them to be persecuted in various ways.
- They use their religious authority to discredit practitioners of the Lotus Sutra.
- They make false allegations about the Lotus Sutra practitioners to the authorities and to influential people in society.
- They denounce the Lotus Sutra practitioners as people of "perverted views who preach non-Buddhist doctrines" (LSOC, 233).

The Daishonin called forth each of the three powerful enemies and overcame them all. His declaration of victory over them is the pronouncement cited earlier where he says, "I survived even the Tatsunokuchi Persecution" (GZ, 843).

Who, specifically, constituted the three powerful enemies that appeared during the Daishonin's lifetime? The Daishonin discusses this in detail in "The Opening of the Eyes," but for now here are his conclusions.

First, with regard to arrogant lay people— the first category—he says this refers to important lay believers who support priests in the second and third categories (see WND-1, 273). This indicates the key government figures who, in the Daishonin's day, supported high-ranking priests of Kamakura's main Buddhist temples.

Next, he says arrogant priests are people like the Pure Land (or Nembutsu) priest Honen[4] who "disregard the precepts and hold perverse views" (WND-1, 274). This signifies the Nembutsu priests throughout Japan who draw their lineage from Honen.

As for arrogant false sages, from one standpoint he says this refers to people such as "Shoichi of Kyoto[5] and Ryokan of Kamakura[6]" (WND-1, 275), while from another he says it refers to "Ryokan, Nen'a,[7] and others" (WND-1, 277). Of those whom the Daishonin specifically lists in this category, the name of Ryokan stands out. He no doubt wishes to underscore that Ryokan is the one person who most aptly fits the description of an "arrogant false sage."

Indeed, both the Tatsunokuchi Persecution and Sado Exile can be traced to the maneuverings of this arrogant false sage. Ryokan along with Nembutsu priests such as Nen'a joined forces with the powerful government official Hei no Saemon[8] and other authorities to do away with the Daishonin and destroy his community of followers.

In "The Opening of the Eyes," the Daishonin ends his discussion in this section by indicating that the appearance of the three powerful enemies offers conclusive proof that he is the votary of the Lotus Sutra in the Latter Day of the Law (see WND-1, 278).

As we have seen, the bright mirror of the "Encouraging Devotion" chapter not only depicts those who will carry out the persecution but also describes the future votaries of the Lotus Sutra. That is why the Daishonin calls it a bright mirror that reflects the country's present state, while also indicating that it is a prophecy made by Shakyamuni, Many Treasures and other Buddhas (see WND-1, 269).

Persecutions Arise From Ignorance, Perverse Wisdom and Malice

Considered in that light, how significant this mirror, this prophecy is. The Lotus Sutra predicts that persecution will befall its votaries in the evil age to come, even describing in detail that it will be carried out by arrogant lay people, arrogant priests and arrogant false sages. And the Daishonin in fact underwent persecutions that perfectly matched the sutra's descriptions.

The next chapter will discuss the significance of the concordance between the sutra and the Daishonin's practice. Here, let's address the question why this close symmetry is possible. There are two main points we should consider. One is that the Lotus Sutra offers a detailed explanation of the workings of the devil king of the sixth heaven that are activated by the fundamental darkness inherent in life. And the other is that the

Daishonin, in exact accord with the Lotus Sutra and without begrudging his life, actually strove to spread the teaching of universal enlightenment in the Latter Day.

As he describes in "The Opening of the Eyes," the Latter Day of the Law is undoubtedly an age when "conditions in the world decline, and people become increasingly shallow in wisdom" (see WND-1, 226), and when "sages and worthies gradually disappear from the scene, and deluded people increase in number" (WND-1, 238). The true crisis of the Latter Day lies in the fact that people, subserviently adhering to authoritarian teachings or beliefs, reject the Lotus Sutra's profound religious philosophy, causing their minds to grow increasingly distorted.

It is even more difficult, therefore, for people of the Latter Day, an age of unceasing human conflict and mistrust, to accept the Lotus Sutra—a teaching of universal enlightenment conveying the message that all living beings are equal and worthy of respect. They shun it simply because they have difficulty understanding it. Further, they even come to bear animosity toward Lotus Sutra practitioners who courageously spread this profound teaching and earnestly endeavor for the genuine enlightenment of all people.

This is analogous to how someone whose eyes have become accustomed to the darkness cannot look directly at the sun's rays. People consumed by hatred and jealousy despise and resent both the Lotus Sutra, which expounds the infinite potential of all human beings, and those who propagate it. This is the frightening reality of people whose lives are steeped in slander of the Law.

The "Encouraging Devotion" chapter states that persecution of the Lotus Sutra's votaries is initiated by arrogant lay people out of "ignorance," by arrogant priests out of "perverse wisdom," and by arrogant false sages out of "evil in their hearts" or malice. This indicates that when fundamental darkness manifests itself in the world, it does so in three phases: ignorance, perverse wisdom and malice.

In other words, ignorant people are readily swayed and incited by those of perverse wisdom and malice (the second and third enemies). That is why it is most often lay people who directly attack the practitioners of the Lotus Sutra through verbal abuse and even physical violence.

Next are those hostile people in whom fundamental darkness manifests as perverse wisdom. While they leave secular life in order to pursue the Buddha way, they regard only the limited teachings they can understand as absolute and erroneously conclude that these alone are correct. In particular, when it comes to the Lotus Sutra with its promise of enlightenment for all, they cannot accept it, believing it undermines the absolute status of the particular provisional Buddhas in which they have misguidedly placed their faith. As a result, in various ways they try to demean the Lotus Sutra's significance. Such priests come to harbor strong enmity toward the practitioners correctly spreading the Lotus Sutra.

Finally, there are those in whom fundamental darkness manifests as malice, similar to the devilish nature inherent in power and authority. It could also be described as the great arrogance of those who employ religious authority to fulfill their personal desires and ambitions.

The Lotus Sutra states that arrogant false sages, proud of their authority, "despise and look down on all humankind" (see LSOC, 232). This is the exact opposite of the spirit of the Lotus Sutra, which teaches respect for all people. Not surprisingly, false sages bear bitter hatred toward the sutra's votaries, fabricating outrageous accusations to discredit them. As the ultimate expression of this malice, these false sages incite influential secular leaders to persecute the Lotus Sutra's practitioners.

Because their fundamental darkness is so deep, people of malice, with evil in their hearts, become the devilish nature personified. They stop at nothing to achieve their ends and therefore become the root cause of persecution of the Lotus Sutra practitioners.

Genuine practitioners correctly spread the teaching of universal enlightenment and fight without retreating against the devilish forces that seek to fundamentally distort the spirit of Buddhism. When we understand the true nature of this struggle, we can naturally foresee that ignorance of the correct teaching—namely, fundamental darkness—will manifest in the form of arrogant lay people, arrogant priests and arrogant false sages who will persecute the votaries of the Lotus Sutra.

11

The Three Powerful Enemies, Part 2—Confronting the Most Formidable Enemy: Arrogant False Sages

In "The Opening of the Eyes," Nichiren Daishonin writes, "If there exists a votary of the Lotus Sutra, then the three types of enemies are bound to exist as well" (WND-1, 278). Persecution by the three powerful enemies—arrogant lay people, arrogant priests and arrogant false sages—arises in response to efforts by the sutra's practitioners to propagate the Mystic Law. The fundamental darkness in people's lives reacts with hostility to such efforts and manifests in the form of devilish functions of various kinds.

Furthermore, if the practitioners of the Lotus Sutra persist in spreading the Law undeterred by obstacles resulting from such devilish functions, then the fundamental darkness will appear in the form of arrogant false sages, who embody extreme evil. In other words, to call forth arrogant false sages and triumph over them is proof that one is a true votary of the Lotus Sutra.

In this chapter, we will continue to examine the three powerful enemies, focusing particularly on the third—arrogant false sages—while citing various relevant passages in "The Opening of the Eyes."

The Evil Actions of Arrogant Lay People and Arrogant Priests

In "The Opening of the Eyes," Nichiren Daishonin clarifies in detail who signifies each of these enemies in his lifetime. He also describes specifically why they may be considered evil, finally indicating that the third enemy—arrogant false sages—is the most formidable or pernicious of all. Three times in the course of his treatise, the Daishonin cites the Great Teacher Miao-lo of China as saying: "The third [group] is the most formidable of all. This is because [the second and the third ones are] increasingly harder to recognize for what they really are" (WND-1, 270, 275, 277).

Arrogant lay people, the first powerful enemy, are ordinary people in society who are influenced by the spurious accusations of arrogant false sages and as a result directly attack the Lotus Sutra's practitioners with slander, insults and physical violence. In "The Opening of the Eyes," the Daishonin merely describes them as being "important lay believers who support monks in the second and third categories" (WND-1, 273) and does not specify why they are evil. This is essentially because the reason is self-evident and also because, in terms of their capacity to deceive others and destroy the Law, the second and third enemies are far more destructive.

Next, the Daishonin turns to the second powerful enemy, arrogant priests, indicating that this refers to "men like Honen who disregard the precepts and hold perverse views" (WND-1, 274). He then outlines in some detail why they can be considered evil.

The Pure Land (Nembutsu) school of Buddhism, which was founded by Honen, belittles people's capacity for understanding the Lotus Sutra in the Latter Day of Law, asserting that the sutra's "principles are very profound but human understanding is slight" (WND-1, 273), and urges them to "ignore, abandon, close, and discard" the sutra (WND-1, 274). Cutting people off from the means of attaining genuine enlightenment through the Mystic Law of the Lotus Sutra in this manner constitutes slander of the Law. Therefore, the Daishonin denounces Honen and other Nembutsu priests as persons of "perverse views."

He also refers to them as people who "disregard the precepts." The Nembutsu adherents of the day desperately pinned their hopes on salvation after death based on Honen's teaching [which said that all could attain rebirth in the Pure Land by simply chanting Amida Buddha's name]. Since their lives were already steeped in negative karma and there was nothing they could do about it, they saw no point in exercising self-discipline or leading virtuous lives. As a result, they gave themselves over to decadent and dissolute behavior.

The second enemy—arrogant priests who commit slander of the Law and other evil actions—is relatively easy to recognize. But the third—arrogant false sages who carry on as if they were saints—is the most difficult to discern, and also the most pernicious.

The Buddha Eye Can Identify the Three Powerful Enemies

The six-volume Parinirvana Sutra says, "The extreme is impossible to see. That is, the extremely evil deeds done by the icchantika are all but impossible to perceive." Or, as Miao-lo has said, "The third [group] is the most formidable of all. This is because [the second and third ones are] increasingly harder to recognize for what they really are."

Those without eyes, those with only one eye, and those with distorted vision cannot see these three types of enemies of the Lotus Sutra who have appeared at the beginning of the Latter Day of the Law. But those who have attained a portion of the Buddha eye can see who they are. ["Encouraging Devotion," the 13th chapter of the Lotus Sutra (LSOC, 232), says:] "They will address the rulers, high ministers, Brahmans, and householders." And *Tung-ch'un*[1] states, "These men will appeal to the government authorities, slandering the Law and its practitioners."

In the past, when the Middle Day of the Law was coming to an end, Gomyo, Shuen,[2] and other priests presented petitions to the [imperial] throne in which they slandered the Great Teacher Dengyo. Now, at the beginning of the Latter Day of the Law, Ryokan, Nen'a, and others drew up false documents and presented them to the shogunate. Are they not to be counted among the third group of enemies of the Lotus Sutra? (WND-1, 277)

In "The Opening of the Eyes," the Daishonin cites many sutras and commentaries to clarify the true, insidious nature of "arrogant false sages," the third of the three powerful enemies. The following quotations sum up his key points:

- "Icchantikas who resemble arhats." (Parinirvana Sutra)
- "There will be monks who will give the appearance of abiding by the rules of monastic discipline. But they will scarcely ever read or recite the sutras and instead will crave all kinds of food and drink to nourish their bodies." (Nirvana Sutra)
- "Outwardly they will seem to be wise and good, but within they will harbor greed and jealousy." (Nirvana Sutra)

- "They are not true monks—they merely have the appearance of monks. Consumed by their erroneous views, they slander the correct teaching." (Nirvana Sutra)
- "Members of the clergy who act as leaders of all the other evil people." (Tung-ch'un)
- "Some Zen masters give all their attention to meditation alone. But their meditation is shallow and false, totally lacking in the nine ways." (Great Concentration and Insight)
- "'Priests who concentrate on the written word' refers to men who gain no inner insight or understanding through meditation, but concern themselves only with characteristics of the doctrine. 'Zen masters who concentrate on practice' refers to men who do not learn how to attain the truth and the corresponding wisdom, but fix their minds on the mere techniques of breath control." (Annotations on "Great Concentration and Insight")
- "All of them regretted what they had done when they were on their deathbed." (Great Concentration and Insight)
- "The extreme is impossible to see. That is, the extremely evil deeds done by the icchantika are all but impossible to perceive." (Parinirvana Sutra)
(see WND-1, 275–77)

Quotations one through four from the Nirvana Sutra and the Parinirvana Sutra all express the sharp disparity between the arrogant false sages' outward guise of saintliness and their actual inner reality.

"Icchantikas who resemble arhats" refers to false sages who give the appearance of being arhats—sages who have reached the highest stage in the Hinayana teachings—but in reality they are nothing more than icchantikas who are ruled by desires and disbelief. The next three quotes—two through four—all say approximately the same thing.

The term *icchantika* expresses the true nature of arrogant false sages. A Sanskrit word that originally meant "desire," it refers to people who are steeped in desire and incapable of believing that they and others possess the Buddha nature, and who, because they are ruled by that profound disbelief, slander the correct teaching.

The "Encouraging Devotion" chapter explains that arrogant false sages persecute the votary of the Lotus Sutra because of "evil in their hearts" (LSOC, 232). This ill will, or malice, characterizes the essence of icchantikas.

Point five—"Members of the clergy who act as leaders of all the other evil people"— signifies the ignorant and corrupt individuals, including arrogant lay people and arrogant priests, who join the arrogant false sages in persecuting the Lotus Sutra practitioners. In other words, arrogant false sages function as the chief instigators of persecution. We'll examine this point in greater detail a little later in relation to Ryokan, the main culprit behind the persecutions that plagued the Daishonin.

Points six through eight are passages from T'ien-t'ai's *Great Concentration and Insight* and Miao-lo's commentary on that treatise. In T'ien-t'ai's China, there were many Zen masters who practiced meditation and many ordinary priests who studied the sutras and treatises. But in nearly every case, they failed to attain the ultimate truth of Buddhism. Even so, there were those who inspired reverence

from lay people. But the Daishonin says that the people who followed these teachers could not gain any benefit, and died regretting the course they had chosen.

In other words, fraudulent religious figures like arrogant false sages bring irrevocable misery on the people. That is truly the greatest evil. This evil, however, is extremely difficult to discern. To highlight this, the Daishonin cites the passage listed in point (9): "The extremely evil deeds done by the icchantika are all but impossible to perceive."

Arrogant false sages perpetrate "extremely evil deeds" (WND-1, 277). While acting as if they are saints, their hearts are filled with greed and disbelief. They are perverse villains who have no compunction about exploiting Buddhism or sacrificing others' happiness in order to protect their own positions and fulfill their selfish desires. Arrogant false sages are indeed enemies of Buddhism pretending to be Buddhists, and enemies of humanity feigning an air of compassion.

The Daishonin says that the extreme evil that characterizes arrogant false sages can only be recognized by "those who have attained a portion of the Buddha eye" (WND-1, 277). The evil of these false sages is a manifestation of fundamental darkness, and so can only be discerned by those who have broken free of that darkness of ignorance and who have revealed the state of Buddhahood in their lives. For only such people have the strength to keep fighting against the onslaughts of this formidable enemy to the very end.

Ryokan—"Leader of All Other Evil People" in Nichiren's Day

In Nichiren Daishonin's time, how did the arrogant false sages contrive to inspire veneration from society? Let's look briefly at the circumstances of the various other religious schools of that era.

With regard to the twenty-line verse describing the three powerful enemies in the "Encouraging Devotion" chapter, the Daishonin writes in "The Opening of the Eyes," "We can discern without a trace of obscurity the ugly faces of the priests of the various schools of present-day Japan, especially the Zen, Precepts, and Nembutsu schools" (WND-1, 271).

"The various schools of present-day Japan" refers to the established schools of Buddhism at the time. These numbered eight: the six schools of Nara[3] plus the Tendai and True Word schools. All of these schools enjoyed the patronage and protection of the imperial court or the nobility.

Also, having been presented with vast land holdings, they wielded immense influence in society as lords of large estates. Those in control of the temples of the different schools had by and large forgotten the original purpose of helping people attain enlightenment and had become degenerate in their ways. Witnessing the appearance of the warrior monks at such leading temples as Enryaku-ji and Onjo-ji (the suffix -ji denotes a temple), people sensed the decline of Buddhism. Further, amid a succession of natural disasters and warfare, people began to feel more strongly that the Latter Day of the Law had indeed arrived.

With the onset of the Kamakura period (1192–1333), the Zen, Precepts and Nembutsu schools came to flourish as influential new forces of the day. Many people, dissatisfied with the established Buddhist schools, which had grown corrupt and decadent, found the newer schools a breath of fresh air because of their commitment to maintaining the precepts, which focused on regulating daily life and restoring rigor to practice. Though the word *precepts* conjures images of the Precepts school, one of the six established schools of Buddhism, in this particular period it refers not to one particular school but to the emergence of a general movement to restore the precepts throughout the Japanese religious world.

Among the key proponents of this movement were the Zen priest Shoichi of Kyoto as well as the True Word Precepts priest Eizon[4] of Saidai-ji in Nara and his disciple Ryokan. Influenced by these developments, the Nembutsu adherents in Kamakura also began to place greater importance on the precepts. The leading Nembutsu priests Doa (also known as Doamidabutsu) and Nen'a,[5] who enjoyed the patronage of the ruling Hojo clan, were at the forefront of this movement.

In the midst of this, Ryokan welcomed his teacher Eizon to Kamakura, making it possible for key people in the government and priests of the Nembutsu and other schools to receive the precepts. As a result, Ryokan succeeded in bringing important government figures and followers of the Nembutsu and other schools under his fold, and established his authority in Kamakura. This clearly reflected the words of Chih-tu's *Tung-ch'un* where, commenting on the three powerful enemies described in "Encouraging Devotion," he speaks of "members of the clergy who act as leaders of all the other evil people" (WND-1, 275).

While outwardly Ryokan conducted himself as the leader of the movement to revive the precepts, inwardly he, more than anyone, harbored attachments to secular things. Though he made a show of promoting charitable enterprises and public works projects, he used the profits reaped in connection with those activities to "hoard silks, wealth, and jewels" ("Conversation between a Sage and an Unenlightened Man," WND-1, 102).

The people of the day, unaware of Ryokan's true nature, revered him as "the living Buddha [of Gokuraku-ji]" ("Condolences on a Deceased Husband," WND-2, 777) and made offerings to him out of their desire for salvation through his teachings.

Ryokan perfectly matched the passage of the Nirvana Sutra cited earlier, "They are not true monks—they merely have the appearance of monks" (WND-1, 275). No matter how such people don robes and surplices and outwardly conduct themselves as priests, behind the façade they are devoid of priestly virtue.

Nevertheless, people are readily impressed and deceived by priestly robes. Unscrupulous priests cunningly take advantage of this, doing everything they can to enhance their august and venerable appearance. That's why the Great Teacher Miao-lo describes arrogant false sages as being the most difficult to recognize for what they really are (see WND-1, 227). Only the Daishonin could discern the true nature of the arrogant false sages of his age. He, therefore, waged a solitary and unremitting battle to expose their fraud.

In "Letter to Ryokan of Gokuraku-ji," one of the eleven letters of remonstration he sent to various influential government leaders and religious figures in 1268,[6] the Daishonin cites "Encouraging Devotion" and denounces Ryokan, saying: "You are nothing more than a sham, a traitorous 'sage' who pretends to the three types of learning, the precepts, meditation, and wisdom. A counterfeit sage, a person of overbearing arrogance in your present existence you will surely be marked out as a traitor to the nation, and in your next existence will fall into the region of hell" (WND-2, 324).

Also, in seeking to acquaint the ruling authorities with the true nature of this nefarious priest, the Daishonin challenged Ryokan to a public debate. Ryokan, however, ducked this proposal, showing himself unwilling to engage in open dialogue. Three years later, in 1271, when he was soundly defeated by the Daishonin in a contest to pray for rain, Ryokan increasingly revealed his devilish nature as an arrogant false sage. He "appeal[ed] to the government authorities, slandering the Law and its practitioners" (see WND-1, 277). "Government authorities" here indicates those who hold high public office, as well as other influential people in society. Ryokan sought to bring about the Daishonin's downfall by leveling false accusations against him.

Specifically, the priest Gyobin, a disciple of Nen'a, filed a lawsuit claiming that Nichiren was destroying the order of the Buddhist circle and the Shogunate government. At the start of his letter of rebuttal, Nichiren cites Ryokan, Nen'a and Doa, identifying them as the ones ultimately behind the spurious petition submitted in Gyobin's name.[7] When the lawsuit proved unsuccessful, Ryokan intensified his efforts to discredit the Daishonin in the eyes of key government officials and their wives. This resulted in the Tatsunokuchi Persecution and Sado Exile.

Driven by jealousy and anger, Ryokan plotted against Nichiren, making false accusations to the authorities in an attempt to bring great persecution down upon the votary of the Lotus Sutra. Nichiren's blistering refutations forced Ryokan to reveal his true colors and to act in perfect accord with the description of arrogant false sages, the third of the three powerful enemies, in the Lotus Sutra.

The Daishonin Read the Twenty-line Verse of the "Encouraging Devotion" Chapter With His Life

Because the predictions of the Buddha are not false, the three types of enemies of the Lotus Sutra already fill the country. And yet, as though to belie the golden words of the Buddha, there seems to be no votary of the Lotus Sutra. How can this be? How can this be?

But let us consider. Who is it who is cursed and spoken ill of by the populace? Who is the priest who is attacked with swords and staves? Who is the priest who, because of the Lotus Sutra, is accused in petitions submitted to the courtiers and warriors? Who is the priest who is "again and again banished," as the Lotus Sutra predicted? Who else in Japan besides Nichiren has fulfilled these predictions?

But I, Nichiren, am not a votary of the Lotus Sutra, because, contrary to the prediction, the gods have cast me aside. Who, then, in this present age will be the votary of the Lotus Sutra and fulfill the prophecy of the Buddha?

The Buddha and Devadatta are like a form and its shadow—in lifetime after lifetime, they are never separated. Prince Shotoku and his archenemy Moriya appeared at the same time, like the blossom and calyx of the lotus. If there exists a votary of the Lotus Sutra, then the three types of enemies are bound to exist as well. The three types of enemies have already appeared. Who, then, is the votary of the Lotus Sutra? Let us seek him out and make him our teacher. [As the Lotus Sutra says, to find such a person is as rare as for] a one-eyed turtle to chance upon a piece of driftwood [with a hole just the right size to hold him]. (WND-1, 278)

The Daishonin writes: "Because the predictions of the Buddha are not false, the three types of enemies of the Lotus Sutra already fill the country. And yet, as though to belie the golden words of the Buddha, there seems to be no votary of the Lotus Sutra. How can this be? How can this be?" (WND-1, 278).

He confirmed that the three powerful enemies had appeared in Japan in his day, exactly as predicted in the sutra. If so, he asks, then who was the votary of the Lotus Sutra who battles these enemies? Naturally, aside from the Daishonin there were no votaries who had fought relentlessly against the three powerful enemies.

To demonstrate this, he cites four kinds of persecution predicted in "Encouraging Devotion" and indicates that he has encountered all of them in the course of his own practice. They are: 1) cursed and spoken ill by the populace; 2) attacked with swords and staves; 3) accused in petitions submitted to the courtiers and warriors because of the Lotus Sutra; and 4) banished again and again (see WND-1, 278).

Each of these four types of persecution has profound meaning. Also, not one of the persecutions Nichiren underwent was of an ordinary scale. For example, while the sutra speaks of the votary being cursed and spoken ill of by ignorant people, Nichiren was continually vilified by people throughout Japan for more than twenty years. He writes: "Those who saw me scowled, while those who merely heard my name were filled with spite" ("The Izu Exile," WND-1, 35); "I am known throughout the country as a monk who transgresses the code of conduct, and . . . my bad reputation has spread throughout the realm" ("The Four Debts of Gratitude," WND-1, 42); and "Never have I heard of one hated to such a degree as is Nichiren because he is a votary of the Lotus Sutra!" ("Regarding an Unlined Robe," WND-2, 599).

The descriptions of the attacks by arrogant lay people indicate how difficult it is to change people's awareness. Nevertheless, the Daishonin stood up for the people's happiness, fully prepared to face storms of criticism and calumny. What an immensely lofty spirit!

This point alone tells us who the true votary of the Lotus Sutra is.

With regard to the second of the four persecutions cited by Nichiren—being attacked with sword and staves—he discusses this in detail in "Persecution by Sword and Staff," writing, "Only I, Nichiren, have read with my entire being the twenty-line verse [of the 'Encouraging Devotion' chapter of the Lotus Sutra]" (WND-1, 964). He thus indicates how, aside from himself, there was no one who had "met with persecution by both sword and staff" (WND-1, 964) for the sake of the Lotus Sutra.

Nichiren cites being attacked with swords during the Komatsubara Persecution in 1264 and the Tatsunokuchi Persecution in 1271. And as an instance of being attacked with staves, the Daishonin cites being struck in the face with a sutra scroll that was wielded like a staff at the beginning of the Tatsunokuchi Persecution. When Hei no Saemon and his forces descended on Nichiren's dwelling at Matsubagayatsu in Kamakura in 1271, a retainer named Sho-bo [an ex-follower of Nichiren], seized the scroll of the fifth volume of the Lotus Sutra that Nichiren was carrying and struck him with it.

The fifth scroll of the Lotus Sutra contains "Encouraging Devotion," which proclaims that the votary of the Lotus Sutra will be attacked with swords and staves. Because he was struck with this particular scroll, the Daishonin writes of the sutra's statement, "What a mysterious passage of prediction!" (WND-1, 964). All of these facts further corroborate Nichiren's claim that he has read the Lotus Sutra with his life.

The third persecution of the four cited by Nichiren is attacks by arrogant false sages, specifically in the form of unfounded accusations made to the authorities. As I mentioned earlier, the Tatsunokuchi Persecution and subsequent Sado Exile occurred as the direct result of such fabrications.

In other words, when evil people seek to bring down a person of justice, their only avenue is defamation and character assassination. Likewise, because arrogant false sages have no sound religious justification for attacking a genuine votary of the Lotus Sutra, their only recourse is to resort to dishonest, underhanded means.

Although Ryokan was supposed to be strictly upholding the precepts, including the injunction not to lie, he nevertheless tried to defame people through falsehoods. This starkly highlights his hypocrisy and duplicity, making him unqualified to be a priest.

The last of the four persecutions cited by Nichiren is that of exile, representing persecution by the authorities. The sutra clearly indicates that the votary will be driven out. Since the passage in "Encouraging Devotion" states, "Again and again we will be banished" (LSOC, 234), the Daishonin places great importance on the phrase *again and again*— signifying repeated exile.

The Daishonin discussed this important point at length earlier in "The Opening of the Eyes," writing: "If Nichiren had not been banished time and again for the sake of the Lotus Sutra, what would these words 'again and again' have meant? Even T'ien-t'ai and Dengyo were not able to fulfill this prediction represented by the words 'again and again,' much less was anyone else" (WND-1, 242).

Had it not been for him, what would these words *again and again* have meant, the Daishonin asks. He was exiled not once but twice (to Izu in 1261 and to Sado in 1271).

After he moved to Mount Minobu, there were rumors he would even be exiled a third time. Normally, it would have been unthinkable for a person who had been pardoned to be condemned to such a fate again. And it was all the more so in this case, given that exile in those days was tantamount to a death sentence.

It also shows how obstinate and persistent the devilish nature is. A votary of the Lotus Sutra is one who resolutely battles and triumphs over this devilish nature. The important thing is to maintain the spirit to keep on fighting with the unshakable resolve to overpower even the obstinate devilish nature.

Nichiren writes, "The Buddha and Devadatta are like a form and its shadow—in lifetime after lifetime, they are never separated" (WND-1, 278). The activities of the votary of the Lotus Sutra call forth the three powerful enemies—functions activated by the fundamental darkness that seeks to obstruct the votary's efforts. Just as a moving form is followed by its shadow, so the Lotus Sutra's votary is dogged by the three powerful enemies.

When evil flourishes and good is defeated, the function of the Dharma nature, or inherent enlightenment, is extinguished. But when good flourishes and evil is defeated, the function of fundamental darkness, or ignorance, is extinguished. A struggle between good and evil takes place in our lives at every moment. Nichiren writes, "Prince Shotoku and his archenemy Moriya appeared at the same time, like the blossom and the calyx of the lotus" (WND-1, 278). Accordingly, the only way to strengthen good is to wage a continuous struggle against evil.

Although we speak of the Buddhist Law,

the Law itself is invisible. The beneficent Law manifests in the conduct of the votary of the Lotus Sutra.

It is extremely rare, however, to encounter a votary who struggles against and triumphs over the three powerful enemies. It is difficult to encounter a genuine leader of Buddhism. Therefore, Nichiren writes: "Let us seek him out and make him our teacher. [As the Lotus Sutra says, to find such a person is as rare as for] a one-eyed turtle to chance upon a piece of driftwood" (WND-1, 278). He urges us to seek out the votary of the Lotus Sutra and make him our teacher, our mentor. The mentor-disciple relationship only comes into existence through the disciple's steadfast efforts to seek the mentor. Such efforts allow us to deeply sense the greatness of the mentor's struggles.

In that regard, we can view "The Opening of the Eyes" as a call for us to awaken to the true votary of the Lotus Sutra who battles fundamental darkness and arrogant false sages, as well as to our true selves as people who seek their mentor and join him in fighting unceasingly against life's inherent devilish nature.

12

Why the Votary of the Lotus Sutra Encounters Great Persecutions—The Votary's Battle Against the Fundamental Evil of Slander of the Law

Someone may raise this question: It would surely appear that the three types of enemies are present today, but there is no votary of the Lotus Sutra. If one were to say that you [Nichiren] are the votary of the Lotus Sutra, then the following serious discrepancies would become apparent. The Lotus Sutra states, "The young sons of heavenly beings will wait on him and serve him. Swords and staves will not touch him and poison will have no power to harm him."[1] It also reads, "If people speak ill of and revile him, their mouths will be closed and stopped up."[2] And it states, "They [who have heard the Law] will enjoy peace and security in their present existence and good circumstances in future existences."[3] It also states, "[If there are those who . . . trouble and disrupt the preachers of the Law], their heads will split into seven pieces like the branches of the arjaka[4] tree."[5]

Furthermore, it reads, "In this present existence they [the practitioners of the Lotus Sutra] will gain the reward of good fortune."[6] And it adds: "If anyone sees a person who accepts and upholds this sutra and tries to expose the faults or evils of that person, whether what he speaks is true or not, he will in his present existence be afflicted with white leprosy."[7] [How do you explain these discrepancies?]

Answer: These doubts of yours are most opportune. I will take the occasion to clear up the points that puzzle you. (WND-1, 278)

"The Opening of the Eyes" is a writing that announces the establishment of Nichiren Buddhism. The three virtues—sovereign, teacher and parent—form the main theme of this work. In the first part, the

Daishonin clarifies the teaching that can lead all people of the Latter Day of the Law, the current age, to enlightenment. In the second, he reveals the identity of the "teacher of the Latter Day" who spreads that teaching.

In the second part in particular, citing various passages from "Treasure Tower," the 11th chapter of the Lotus Sutra; "Devadatta," the 12th; and "Encouraging Devotion," the 13th; the Daishonin highlights how his propagation efforts and the persecutions that have befallen him match the sutra's predictions, thereby indicating that he is the votary of the Lotus Sutra of the Latter Day of the Law. This section, which I have already discussed in detail, might be termed his explanation based on "documentary proof"—one of the three proofs.[8]

What remains to be answered are the following questions: Why does the votary of the Lotus Sutra encounter persecution? And why is it that when persecution occurs, the heavenly deities don't protect him? The Daishonin says that these questions are "the heart of this piece I am writing . . . [and] the most important concern of my entire life" (WND-1, 243). He bases his ensuing explanation on reason and logic. In other words, he now seeks to show by means of "theoretical proof" that he is the votary of the Lotus Sutra in the Latter Day of the Law. This will be the focus of discussion in this chapter.

It is also important to note that at the end of the second half of "The Opening of the Eyes," after having completed his argument, Nichiren makes a declaration that opens with the lines: "This I will state. Let the gods forsake me. Let all persecutions assail me. Still I will give my life for the sake of the Law" (WND-1, 280). This represents his great vow

to continue waging an unremitting struggle as "the pillar of Japan," and conveys his towering state of life as the teacher of the Latter Day of the Law.

Nichiren then outlines the faith, benefit and practice of the Buddhism he has established for the enlightenment of all people of the Latter Day. Having revealed his own state of mind, he urges his followers to embrace faith in and practice the correct teaching in a spirit of the oneness with him as their mentor. In the closing section, therefore, he seeks to show that he is the teacher of the Latter Day based on "actual proof"—in terms of the reality of his own life.

True Peace and Security Lie in Struggling To Overcome Great Hardships

Now, let us turn to the section where Nichiren demonstrates through theoretical proof that he is the Lotus Sutra votary of the Latter Day. He starts by raising the question of why, if he is in fact the sutra's votary, events that apparently contradict the sutra are occurring.

He writes: "Someone may raise this question: It would surely appear that the three types of enemies are present today, but there is no votary of the Lotus Sutra. If one were to say that you [Nichiren] are the votary of the Lotus Sutra, then the following serious discrepancies would become apparent" (WND-1, 278).

Six Lotus Sutra passages that would seem to seriously contradict the Daishonin's earlier statements are then introduced. Their content can be divided into two basic assertions: 1) those who spread the sutra in the Latter Day will definitely be protected by the heavenly deities and enjoy "peace and security in their present existence and good circumstances in future existences" (LSOC, 136); and 2) those who attack its practitioners will suffer immediate retribution without fail.

In the preceding section, Nichiren quotes passages from "Encouraging Devotion" as documentary proof to assert that he is the true votary. He argues that the persecutions he is undergoing mirror those described in that chapter; and he says that, accordingly, all people should seek him out and make him their teacher. The ensuing question about apparent discrepancies is thus presented to dispute the Daishonin's claims.

In response, wishing to reaffirm his basic premise that a genuine Lotus Sutra votary invariably encounters great persecution, he first lists examples of such votaries from the past. He points out, for instance, that Shakyamuni underwent nine great ordeals[9]; Bodhisattva Never Disparaging[10] was attacked with sticks of wood or tiles and stones; and such foremost practitioners as Maudgalyayana,[11] Bodhisattva Aryadeva[12] and the Venerable Aryasimha[13] were murdered. Simply because people experience life-threatening attacks and do not receive the protection of the heavenly deities, he says, does not mean they are not votaries.

In *The Record of the Orally Transmitted Teachings*, the Daishonin says, "When one practices the Lotus Sutra [in the Latter Day of the Law], difficulties will arise, and these are to be looked on as 'peaceful' practices" (OTT, 115). For a votary, in other words, peace and security mean the genuine peace and security

that come from establishing the indomitable state of life with which to continue fighting dauntlessly against great persecution.

After citing examples of votaries persecuted in the past, Nichiren writes, "If we consider the second part of your question [that is, the heart of the matter], we must note the following points" (WND-1, 279). He then offers a three-point explanation as to why Lotus Sutra votaries come under fierce attack and do not receive the heavenly deities' protection and why the perpetrators of the attacks do not suffer immediate punishment. The three points can be summarized as follows.

First, votaries fail to receive protection from the heavenly deities when persecuted because they have incurred negative karma from slandering the Law in their previous existences. Nichiren says that if the votaries do not possess such negative karma, then those who persecute them will indeed suffer immediate punishment (see WND-1, 279).

Second, *icchantikas*, people of incorrigible disbelief, will suffer no immediate punishment even though they commit grave offenses in this life, because they are already destined to fall into hell in their next existence (see WND-1, 279).

Third, protection from the heavenly deities is not forthcoming because they have deserted the country on account of its widespread slander of the Law (see WND-1, 280).

Let us consider these points one at a time based on the following statements by the Daishonin:

If we consider the second part of your question, we must note the following points. Those who did not commit

the error of slandering the Lotus Sutra in their previous existences will become votaries of the Lotus Sutra in their present lives. If such persons should be subjected to persecution under a false charge of having committed worldly offenses, then those who persecute them ought to suffer some kind of immediate retribution. It should be like the case of the asuras who shoot arrows at Shakra or the garuda birds that try to eat the dragon of Anavatapta Lake,[14] but who both invariably suffer injury themselves instead.[15] And yet T'ien-t'ai says, "The ills and pains I suffer at present are all due to causes in the past, and the meritorious deeds that I do in my present life will be rewarded in the future."[16] Likewise, the Contemplation on the Mind-Ground Sutra states: "If you want to understand the causes that existed in the past, look at the results as they are manifested in the present. And if you want to understand what results will be manifested in the future, look at the causes that exist in the present." The "Never Disparaging" chapter of the Lotus Sutra says, "when his offenses had been wiped out [he attained the Buddha way]."[17] This indicates that Bodhisattva Never Disparaging was attacked with tiles and stones because he had in the past committed the offense of slandering the Lotus Sutra.

Next, we should note that persons who are inevitably destined to fall into hell in their next existence, even though they commit grave offenses in this life, will suffer no immediate punishment. The icchantikas are examples of this . . .

Through these various similes we can know that icchantikas of the most evil type will invariably fall into the hell of incessant suffering in their next life. Therefore, they do not suffer any immediate punishment in this life. They are like the evil rulers of ancient China, King Chieh of the Hsia dynasty and King Chou of the Yin dynasty. During their reigns, heaven did not display any unusual manifestations as a warning. That was because their offenses were so grave that their dynasties were already destined to perish.

Third, it would appear that the guardian deities have deserted this country, and this is probably one reason why offenders do not suffer any immediate punishment. In an age that slanders the Law, guardian deities will take their leave, and the various heavenly gods will cease to lend their protection. That is why the votaries of the correct teaching do not receive any sign of divine favor but, on the contrary, encounter severe difficulties. The Golden Light Sutra says, "Those who perform good deeds day by day languish and dwindle in number." We are living in an evil country and an evil age. I have discussed all this in detail in my work entitled *On Establishing the Correct Teaching for the Peace of the Land.* (WND-1, 279–80)

(1) The Votary of the Lotus Sutra's Own Karma

The Daishonin explains that even though the Lotus Sutra says that those who harass the sutra's votaries will incur immediate punishment, it only refers to cases where the votaries have not slandered the Lotus Sutra in past existences. If the votaries have slandered the sutra in previous lifetimes, however, they will meet with persecution as retribution for that offense.

Bodhisattva Never Disparaging, too, underwent great tribulations on account of his own past offenses. The sutra indicates that the four kinds of believers—monks, nuns, laymen and laywomen—who violently attacked him did not receive obvious punishment[18] until after "his offenses had been wiped out"[19] (LSOC, 312).

The law of cause and effect is central to Buddhism. Nichiren thus cites the famous words of the Contemplation on the Mind-Ground Sutra: "If you want to understand the causes that existed in the past, look at the results as they are manifested in the present. And if you want to understand what results will be manifested in the future,

look at the causes that exist in the present" (WND-1, 279).

Present effects are due to karmic causes from the past. But the causes we make in the present give rise to the effects we will experience in the future. It is always the present that counts. While the causes we have made in past lifetimes have contributed to shaping our present, what we do in the present moment decides our future. In fact, the Daishonin emphasizes that no matter what karmic causes we have made in the past, through the causes we make in the present, we can achieve a brilliant future. Here we find the true worth of Nichiren Buddhism. In explaining karma, Nichiren's purpose is always to show that we can definitely transform it.

We will delve into Nichiren's theory of karma in detail on another occasion. This discussion is simply to confirm his point that the causes for encountering great persecution need to be sought within the individual votary's own life. This perspective is integral to the concept of transforming karma.

Slandering the Lotus Sutra is actually an act of fundamental evil that arises from people's fundamental darkness or ignorance. There is no greater offense a human being can commit than denying the fundamental Buddha nature inherent in all people's lives, than slandering the Lotus Sutra—the teaching that enables us to manifest this Buddha nature—and those who spread it.

Fundamental darkness, the source of slander of the Law, is the root of all negative karma. By winning over our fundamental darkness in this lifetime through faith in the Mystic Law, we can break free of the cycle of transmigration in the evil paths and move into a cycle of transmigration in the paths of good based on the Mystic Law. This is the principle of transforming one's karma.

On the matter of punishment, Nichiren explains that persecutors of those votaries who are free of negative karma will in fact incur immediate retribution. Notably, this punishment is not meted out by some external agent like a deity; rather, it is the natural outcome of a person's own actions and occurs in accord with the law of cause and effect. The Buddhist concept of punishment is thus retribution based on the Law.

On the other hand, even though persecutors of those votaries guilty of past slander of the Law will not receive immediate punishment, this doesn't mean that they get off scot-free. It simply means that their punishment doesn't manifest right away; they still incur definite inconspicuous punishment.[20] This becomes clear in connection with the next point, regarding icchantikas.

(2) Icchantikas Who Are Destined To Fall Into Hell

The Daishonin explains that icchantikas, who are destined to fall into hell in their next lifetime, do not experience immediate punishment. He writes: "We should note that persons who are inevitably destined to fall into hell in their next existence, even though they commit grave offenses in this life, will suffer no immediate punishment. The icchantikas are examples of this" (WND-1, 279).

As this indicates, when persecutors are already destined to fall into the hell of incessant suffering, they do not receive immediately visible retribution for their deeds.

In "Letter to Horen," the Daishonin writes of such people: "They are like men who have already been sentenced to execution and are awaiting their turn in prison. While they are in prison, regardless of what evil acts they may commit, they will receive no further punishment other than the death sentence already passed upon them. However, with regard to people who are eventually to be released, if they commit evil acts in prison, then they will receive warnings" (WND-1, 522).

In "The Opening of the Eyes," Nichiren, citing the Nirvana Sutra, points out that while even a person of considerable evil may, through various influences, have a change of heart and come to regret his earlier actions, in the case of icchantikas, nothing of this kind takes place (see WND-1, 280).

Icchantikas are people whose lives are so deeply steeped in disbelief and slander of the Law that they have no regret or remorse for their actions. Of course, even icchantikas possess the innate Buddha nature—the direct cause for attaining the state of Buddhahood. Lacking the faith necessary for manifesting it, however, they cannot break through the darkness that shrouds their highest inner potential. As a result, they behave as if they did not possess the Buddha nature at all, evil instead filling their minds and their actions. They are like people who wander around in the dark even though the sun is shining, because their own lives are veiled in heavy clouds that block out any light.

The benighted cannot believe that the Buddha nature exists in their own lives and those of others. Numb to the fact that they are committing slander of the Law, they advance inexorably toward the abyss of hell.

Also, while such offenders may not receive immediate punishment, they are invariably racked by a fundamental fear and anxiety arising from their inability to believe in their own Buddha nature. The anxiety and fear gnaw at them, steadily destroying their lives. So even where their retribution is not immediately visible, such people are clearly already suffering inconspicuous punishment. Therefore, Nichiren declares, "People who despise the votaries of the Lotus Sutra seem to be free from punishment at first, but eventually they are all doomed to fall" ("On Persecutions Befalling the Sage," WND-1, 997).

(3) The Heavenly Deities Abandon the Land

Third, we have the problem of the departure of the heavenly deities. The Daishonin writes: "It would appear that the guardian deities have deserted this country, and this is probably one reason why offenders do not suffer any immediate punishment. In an age that slanders the Law, guardian deities will take their leave, and the various heavenly gods will cease to lend their protection. That is why the votaries of the correct teaching do not receive any sign of divine favor but, on the contrary, encounter severe difficulties" (WND-1, 280).

This passage refers to the concept of benevolent deities ascending to the heavens.[21] In other words, deprived of their sustenance— the "flavor of the Law"[22]—due to widespread slander of the correct teaching, they abandon the country and return to their original homelands. The Daishonin also speaks of this principle in "On Establishing the Correct Teaching for the Peace of the Land," where he says: "The people of today all turn their backs upon what is right; to a person, they give their allegiance to evil. This is the reason that the benevolent deities have abandoned the nation and departed together, that sages leave and do not return. And in their stead devils and demons come, and disasters and calamities occur" (WND-1, 7).

The departure of the heavenly deities means that they will no longer safeguard the votaries of the Lotus Sutra and punish slanderers of the Law. As a result, the latter do not suffer immediate retribution for their offenses.

The Vow and Practice To Dedicate One's Life to Propagating the Lotus Sutra

As discussed, in "The Opening of the Eyes," Nichiren offers a three-point explanation as to why votaries of the Lotus Sutra encounter persecution and why, moreover, those who harass them do not receive immediate punishment. Again, the three points are: 1) the votary in question has committed the offense of slandering the Lotus Sutra in a past existence; 2) icchantikas slander the Lotus Sutra through their incorrigible disbelief, an offense that destines them to hell in their next existence; and 3) the heavenly deities abandon the land when it becomes rampant with slander of the correct teaching. Slander of the Lotus Sutra— which is synonymous with slander of the Law or correct teaching—is thus the common denominator of all three.

The various evils that befall a votary of the Lotus Sutra are all deeply related to the fundamental evil of slander of the Law. This is because votaries practice the correct teaching or Law. Their practice, coupled with their active denunciation of slander, sparks a violent reaction from the fundamental darkness in the lives of icchantikas, who then appear as the three powerful enemies and launch a fierce assault on the votaries.

The struggle of votaries is a struggle to reform the realm of Buddhism in order to eradicate the evil of slander of the Law. That is why votaries of the sutra are destined to suffer hardships resulting from the attacks that inevitably arise to hinder their efforts. Such difficulties, however, serve to forge and temper the votaries' lives, enabling them to expiate their slander of the Lotus Sutra in past lifetimes. Moreover, all their trials are for the cause of enabling people of an evil age to establish Buddhahood in their lives. Because the votaries wage such a struggle, they attain a vast state of life in which they can view "difficulties . . . as 'peaceful' practices" (OTT, 115).

For icchantikas, on the other hand, persecuting the votaries of the Lotus Sutra causes the fundamental darkness in their lives to function even stronger. Their lives become utterly steeped in disbelief and slander of the Lotus Sutra, as a result of which they incur inconspicuous punishment that will lead them to fall into hell.

Also, the influence of icchantikas causes disbelief in the correct teaching and slander of the Law to spread throughout the entire land, in turn causing the protective functions of the heavenly deities to vanish.

Votaries of the Lotus Sutra who nevertheless strive undeterred to overcome difficulties and persevere in propagating the correct teaching can bring forth the world of Buddhahood in their own lives. The votaries' struggle to propagate the Mystic Law is not only a struggle to transform their individual karma and attain Buddhahood in this lifetime but also to "establish the correct teaching for the peace of the land" in order to revive the heavenly deities' functions and bring peace and security to society.

Nichiren Buddhism Forges "Fighting Spirit"

Both of the doubts we have been discussing— if Nichiren is a votary of the Lotus Sutra, why don't the heavenly deities lend him assistance? And why don't his attackers suffer immediate punishment?—spring from a passive view of Buddhist faith, where people simply implore the heavenly deities for protection and wait fervently for it to arrive.

Nichiren answers these doubts with reason and logic—in other words, he offers theoretical proof. He proclaims the Mystic Law as the key to transforming karma and realizing a peaceful society and therefore as the force that can reactivate even the heavenly deities, who have disappeared from the land. He expresses this toward the end of "The Opening of the Eyes" in his great vow that begins with the lines: "This I will state. Let the gods forsake me. Let all persecutions assail me. Still I will give my life for the sake of the Law" (WND-1, 280).

When viewed in the light of the Daishonin's immense state of life as the one who embodies the three virtues—sovereign, teacher and parent—of the Latter Day of the Law, Nichiren Buddhism is not a teaching that laments the absence of protection from the heavenly deities. On the contrary, it seeks to revive the powerful functions of the heavenly deities throughout the country and realize an ideal society by actively working to establish the correct teaching for the peace of the land.

In my mind, I can hear the Daishonin calling out vigorously to his followers: "If you are not going to fight now, then when will you fight? My followers, stand up with courage! If you fight with the heart of the lion king, you can expiate all past offenses and transform your karma! Let us lead to enlightenment even the icchantikas who persecute us, and help free humankind from fundamental darkness! Let us establish the correct teaching for the peace of the land and construct a world where all can live together happily and peacefully."

Nichiren Buddhism forges people's fighting spirit. This could be described as the essence of "The Opening of the Eyes."

Accordingly, on the fundamental level, the doubts about persecution and the lack of protection can only be resolved when we each stand up with a great desire and vow for kosen-rufu and dedicate our lives to spreading the Lotus Sutra with the spirit of "not begrudging one's life" and of "unselfish devotion to the propagation of the Law."

The Daishonin's treatise reveals the true meaning of "opening the eyes," because it awakens all people to the genuine Buddhist spirit and human path of living true to the Law based on a personal vow.

13

"I Will Be the Pillar of Japan"—Standing Alone and Dedicating One's Life to the Vow for Kosen-rufu

Those who lead victorious lives, striving with a stand-alone spirit and steadfastly upholding the correct teaching, are free of the slightest doubt or regret. Their state of mind is like a clear, cloudless blue sky.

"This I will state. Let the gods forsake me. Let all persecutions assail me. Still I will give my life for the sake of the Law" (WND-1, 280). Whenever I read this inspiring passage that could be called the climax of "The Opening of the Eyes," my entire life resonates with Nichiren's sublime spirit, and I feel the stirring of immense courage and joy. These are words I engraved deeply in my life at the time of my inauguration as third Soka Gakkai president on May 3, 1960.

The main theme here is the stand-alone spirit. Kosen-rufu forever depends upon courageous individuals rising into action on their own.

It can be said that the history of Buddhism commenced the moment Shakyamuni, having awakened to the supremely noble state of life that exists within all human beings, stood up alone with the resolve to awaken others. And the widespread propagation of the correct teaching into the eternal future of the Latter Day of the Law was set into motion when Nichiren Daishonin, the Buddha of the Latter Day, singularly resolved to undergo any and all hardships in order to teach the people of this defiled age how to base their lives on the supreme state of Buddhahood.

Carrying on Nichiren's spirit in modern times, the first and second presidents of the Soka Gakkai, Tsunesaburo Makiguchi and Josei Toda, each single-handedly pursued religious reform and human revolution. I, too, as a disciple united in a spirit of the oneness with these two great mentors, stood up alone to open an unprecedented path of worldwide kosen-rufu.

When one struggles while maintaining a genuine stand-alone spirit, other courageous people will definitely follow. In the Soka Gakkai, many honorable, nameless, ordinary people have stood up one after another, leading to the development of our present global network dedicated to the cause of good and the correct teaching of Nichiren Buddhism.

Dispelling People's Deep-Seated Doubts

This I will state. Let the gods forsake me. Let all persecutions assail me. Still I will give my life for the sake of the Law. Shariputra practiced the way of the bodhisattva for sixty kalpas, but he abandoned the way because he could not endure the ordeal of the Brahman who begged for his eye.[1] Of those who received the seeds of Buddhahood in the remote past and those who did so from the sons of the Buddha Great Universal Wisdom Excellence,[2] many abandoned the seeds and suffered in hell for the long periods of numberless major world system dust particle kalpas and major world system dust particle kalpas, respectively, because they followed evil companions.

Whether tempted by good or threatened by evil, if one casts aside the Lotus Sutra, one destines oneself for hell. Here I will make a great vow. Though I might be offered the rulership of Japan if I would only abandon the Lotus Sutra, accept the teachings of the Meditation Sutra, and look forward to rebirth in the Pure Land, though I might be told that my father and mother will have their heads cut off if I do not recite the Nembutsu—whatever obstacles I might encounter, so long as persons of wisdom do not prove my teachings to be false, I will never yield! All other troubles are no more to me than dust before the wind.

I will be the pillar of Japan. I will be the eyes of Japan. I will be the great ship of Japan. This is my vow, and I will never forsake it! (WND-1, 280–81)

In a sense, this section of the "The Opening of the Eyes" could be regarded as a key source of inspiration for today's magnificent spread of worldwide kosen-rufu. It is here that we are presented with the conclusion that Nichiren is indeed the votary of the Lotus Sutra of the Latter Day of the Law.

Let's begin with a quick review of the Daishonin's discussion leading up to this section. First, in terms of the overall structure of "The Opening of the Eyes," this section comprises the conclusion to Nichiren's lengthy answer to people's doubts as to how he could truly be the votary of the Lotus Sutra when he is constantly persecuted and fails to receive the protection of the "heavenly deities" [a metaphor in Nichiren Buddhism for the protective functions of life and the universe].

In the course of his answer, spanning almost forty pages (from WND-1, 243, third paragraph, through first two lines of WND-1, 281), he closely scrutinizes various sutra passages and confirms in detail that his own conduct completely accords with the Lotus Sutra. Especially in view of the twenty-line passage referring to the three powerful enemies in "Encouraging Devotion," the 13th chapter, he concludes that because he has called forth these formidable foes, he must, as described here, be a votary of the Lotus Sutra. Further, he explains logically from three different perspectives as to why the sutra's votary is persecuted and fails to receive the protection of the heavenly deities. By offering a finely drawn argument based on documentary and theoretical proof, he thoroughly answers the questions people have about him.

He does not stop there, however. This is because the fundamental delusion that produces doubts about him in the minds of the general public and also his followers has not yet been completely dispelled. This fundamental delusion boils down to ignorance about slander of the Law, and it is the root of people's doubts about the votary of the Lotus Sutra.

The votary of the Lotus Sutra in the Latter Day is committed to battling slander of the Law, the fundamental evil. There are those, however, who are ignorant of the meaning of this struggle. Even though the Lotus Sutra predicts that its practitioners will encounter great persecutions in the Latter Day, and even though Nichiren clearly and logically explains the reasons for the failure of the heavenly deities to lend their protection, people still cannot fathom why he goes out of his way to fight slander of the Law and experience unbelievable hardships. Because of this, the Daishonin conveys his personal vow, thereby revealing his state of life as a votary of the Lotus Sutra who battles slander of the Law.

Prior to this section, Nichiren addresses people's doubts through explanations based on documentary and theoretical proof. Here, however, he strives to break through the fundamental delusion in people's hearts by citing his own way of life, which is based on an unshakable vow. This section is like a compassionate lion's roar aimed at purifying and elevating the lives of all people.

Also in this section, Nichiren teaches that the fighting spirit with which he carries out his vow is the very essence of a votary. Here, he goes beyond documentary and theoretical proof. This entire passage pulses with the spirit of the votary of the Lotus Sutra that Nichiren embodies.

He opens with "This I will state," thus signaling that although he has offered various explanations of the persecutions faced by the Lotus Sutra's votary, he is now going to state the most important point. He then declares: "Let the gods forsake me. Let all persecutions assail me. Still I will give my life for the sake of the Law." In other words: "If the gods are going to abandon me, then let them. If I have to encounter many persecutions, then so be it! My sole desire is to stake my life on this struggle."

In this passage, the Daishonin reveals his immense state of life, rising high above the doubts and criticisms held by the general populace, as well as his followers. It shows his profound inner commitment as the votary of the Lotus Sutra, transcending the mundane desire for divine protection or freedom from difficulties. As far as Nichiren is concerned, there is something more important than whether we receive the protection of the heavenly deities—something we must risk our lives to accomplish, no matter how daunting the obstacles. And that is the attainment of Buddhahood by all people, the highest good, which is the great vow Shakyamuni proclaimed in the Lotus Sutra. In other words, it is kosen-rufu, the actualization of that vow.

This is what Nichiren fought to achieve, an aspiration beyond the realm of mundane cares and attachments that preoccupied all society, including his followers.

A votary of the Lotus Sutra is a person of fighting spirit who makes the Buddha's great vow his or her own, and who strives amid all manner of obstacles to accomplish that vow in the evil age after the Buddha's passing.

Especially in the defiled Latter Day, unless we spread Nam-myoho-renge-kyo (the Mystic Law)—the "heart of the Lotus Sutra" ("The Actions of the Votary of the Lotus Sutra," WND-1, 765) and the teaching for all people to attain Buddhahood—we cannot accomplish this great vow.

Nam-myoho-renge-kyo is a teaching of life's inner workings and essence. Slander of the Lotus Sutra, which causes disbelief in the Mystic Law to arise in people's hearts, functions as a negative influence that moves people away from attaining Buddhahood. By obstructing the realization of the Buddha's great vow, slander functions as an enemy; and therefore, by necessity the votary of the Lotus Sutra in the Latter Day must be a person who battles slander of the Law.

The vow for kosen-rufu is an expression of the fighting spirit of practitioners of the Lotus Sutra. That is why the Daishonin elucidates his vow as the sutra's votary in this section of "The Opening of the Eyes."

Nonregression Is the Essence of Faith

What, then, is the most indispensable requirement for leading a life dedicated to this vow?

It is a "spirit of nonregression." A vow can only be called true if we uphold it and strive to fulfill it throughout our lives. For precisely that reason, a spirit of nonregression is essential. This is what Nichiren teaches in the following passage: "Shariputra practiced the way of the bodhisattva for sixty kalpas, but he abandoned the way because he could not endure the ordeal of the Brahman who begged for his eye. Of those who received the seeds of Buddhahood in the remote past and those who did so from the sons of the Buddha Great Universal Wisdom Excellence, many abandoned the seeds and suffered in hell for the long periods of numberless major world system dust particle kalpas and major world system dust particle kalpas, respectively, because they followed evil companions. Whether tempted by good or threatened by evil, if one casts aside the Lotus Sutra, one destines oneself for hell" (WND-1, 280).

The most important thing in faith is a spirit of nonregression. One must not regress in deed, word or thought. Never losing the spirit to keep struggling for as long as we live—this is the spirit of Nichiren Buddhism and the heart of the Soka Gakkai.

In "The Opening of the Eyes," looking back on when he first established his teaching, Nichiren reaffirms his unwavering pledge to initiate a struggle to propagate the Law while fully aware of the consequences. "I vowed to summon up a powerful and unconquerable desire for the salvation of all beings and never to falter in my efforts" (WND-1, 240), he writes.

Today, we carry out our Buddhist practice in this impure realm of the saha world[3] "in a muddied kalpa, in an evil age" (LSOC, 233). We live in a world rife with "evil companions," or negative influences, that promote slander of the Law. We are forced to wage battle with the three obstacles and four devils and the three powerful enemies. To show actual proof of faith under such circumstances, it is vital that we develop the inner strength and fortitude with which to constantly fight and win over our own inherent negativity or fundamental darkness.

Unless we forge the spiritual strength and purity not to be swayed by anything, to stay true to our vow without faltering, the flame of our Buddhist practice will be quickly extinguished by the winds of dark, insidious forces. Cultivating and strengthening such a spirit is the key to nonregression. Without a profound commitment and resolve, we cannot defeat the obstacles caused by negative influences.

To highlight the fearfulness of negative influences, the Daishonin cites the examples of Shariputra discarding his Mahayana practice and of two other groups of people who abandoned the way: those who received the seeds of Buddhahood in the remote past, and those who received the seeds of Buddhahood from the sons of Buddha Great Universal Wisdom Excellence.

In Shariputra's case, the Brahman who begged for his eye was in fact a demon who deliberately intended to cause him to abandon faith. Here, Shariputra was defeated not by the Brahman's reprehensible behavior but rather by his own mind or inner weakness. The negativity or fundamental darkness that filled Shariputra's heart after the Brahman stomped on his eye was fueled by the thought: *Such people are too difficult to be guided toward enlightenment.* As a result, Shariputra abandoned the Mahayana bodhisattva way and regressed to being a

Hinayana practitioner focused solely on personal salvation.

Of course, this is an episode from when Shariputra was practicing the pre-Lotus Sutra Mahayana teaching of carrying out bodhisattva austerities over innumerable *kalpas*. There's no need for us to directly apply his example to our own practice. Nichiren teaches after all that Buddhist practice "should follow the time" (WND-1, 287). From one standpoint, however, it could be said that we of the Soka Gakkai regularly undergo spiritual trials just as trying, or even more so, in the course of our propagation activities in this evil latter age. The heart of the bodhisattva's supremely noble practice lies in continuing exertion for others' welfare. This is carried out with a truly selfless and even self-sacrificing dedication, despite hostility and rejection, and despite slander and abuse originating from the ignorance, malice and perversity of people in society.

No matter what happens, we of the SGI chant Nam-myoho-renge-kyo earnestly before the Gohonzon with a "mind that is gentle and forbearing" (LSOC, 205). We sincerely chant, thinking: *This person also has the Buddha nature. I will send Nam-myoho-renge-kyo to the pure reservoir of Buddhahood in his or her life,* and heroically continue engaging in dialogue and taking action for others' happiness. As a result, we can greatly expand our own state of life.

Ultimately, what Shariputra was lacking when he abandoned his faith was the spirit of the Lotus Sutra. If he had firmly believed that all people possess the Buddha nature, then he could certainly have remained impervious to the Brahman's insults. Shariputra should have been an indomitable champion of the human spirit, while the Brahman should have been pitied for his lack of faith in human goodness. At a crucial moment, however, Shariputra's fundamental problem was revealed—he could not maintain his belief in the teaching of universal enlightenment that liberates all people from their inner darkness and delusion.

We can also surmise that the two other groups of people who abandoned the way and fell into the hell of incessant[4] suffering for immeasurable kalpas were defeated by negative influences, which caused them to doubt the Lotus Sutra's teachings.

The genuine teachings of Shakyamuni and Nichiren Buddhism are based on the Lotus Sutra principle that all people can attain Buddhahood. At the opposite extreme of this truth is fundamental darkness, a bleak, benighted condition in which one cannot recognize that all people equally possess the supremely noble state of Buddhahood. Turning against the Lotus Sutra leads inexorably to the abyss of darkness. Therefore, Nichiren writes, "If one casts aside the Lotus Sutra, one destines oneself for hell" (WND-1, 280).

The Lotus Sutra recognizes the dignity of all people's lives. It is a teaching that enables us to bring forth our Dharma nature, or inherent enlightenment. It is also a teaching of value creation.

As the Lotus Sutra spreads, negative influences or evil companions appear without fail in order to stop its progress and topple its practitioners from the elevated state they have attained. Negative influences try to pull us into darkness and negativity and bring us under the influence of oppressive forces. Not only mustn't we be swayed by their workings, it is imperative that we wholeheartedly combat the evil of slander of the Law, which is an enemy of the true teaching.

A fighting spirit is a nonregressing spirit. If we do not fight energetically, we cannot prevail over the magnetic force of negative influences. Please remember this vital principle for victory in life.

Living True to One's Vow for Kosen-rufu Is the Noblest Path

Next, Nichiren writes, "Whether tempted by good or threatened by evil . . . " Evil companions or negative influences attack in both good and evil guises. Thoroughly grasping this principle, the Daishonin continues: "Here I will make a great vow. Though I might be offered the rulership of Japan if I would only abandon the Lotus Sutra, accept the teachings of the Meditation Sutra, and look forward to rebirth in the Pure Land, though I might be told that my father and mother will have their heads cut off if I do not recite the Nembutsu—whatever obstacles I might encounter, so long as persons of wisdom do not prove my teachings to be false, I will never yield! All other troubles are no more to me than dust before the wind. I will be the pillar of Japan. I will be the eyes of Japan. I will be the great ship of Japan. This is my vow, and I will never forsake it!" (WND-1, 280–81).

The Daishonin asserts that even if tempted with an offer to become the ruler of Japan, or threatened with the execution of his parents, he will never compromise his beliefs. Irrespective of whatever life-threatening hardships he may encounter, he says, he will sweep them away like dust before the wind. He also evinces a towering confidence that his teachings will not be proven false.

In fact, from the time he established his teaching, Nichiren waged a fearless and impassioned struggle of words while overcoming four major persecutions[5] and countless minor ones. By casting off his transient status and revealing his true identity as the Buddha of the Latter Day during the Tatsunokuchi Persecution, he proved that Nam-myoho-renge-kyo is the great Law for the enlightenment of all living beings of the ten thousand years and more of the Latter Day. Nothing could prove the Daishonin's teachings false.

In addition to his vow never to regress, Nichiren proclaims his long-held pledge: "I will be the pillar of Japan. I will be the eyes of Japan. I will be the great ship of Japan." In this lofty vow, we find the three virtues—sovereign, teacher and parent.[6]

It would appear that this is the great vow Nichiren Daishonin made in his heart on the day he established his teaching (April 28, 1253). This treatise, "The Opening of the Eyes," was written almost twenty years later. No matter what storms of obstacles and devilish forces assailed him, his spirit never wavered. He suffered countless instances of slander and abuse. He had been the target of malicious plots and intrigues. The authorities had attempted to execute him and had exiled him twice.

But not even the most furious onslaughts of the devil king of the sixth heaven[7] had succeeded in extinguishing the flame of kosen-rufu blazing in his heart. On the contrary, they only caused that inner flame to burn all the brighter. "This is my vow, and I will never forsake it!" he writes, declaring that he will never for all eternity break that vow.

Buddhahood manifests in the lives of people of strong faith who make the Buddha's vow their own and who dedicate their lives to its fulfillment. The Soka Gakkai has realized resounding victory in every endeavor because we have carried out this vow without begrudging our lives.

Our vow is central to our efforts to spread the Mystic Law in the evil Latter Day. Without a powerful commitment to uphold and spread the correct teaching throughout our lives, we cannot turn back the raging currents of this polluted age; we cannot defeat the destructive and devilish tendencies in human life.

Our vow to work for kosen-rufu serves as a fundamental source of strength, giving us the courage to remain undaunted by even the greatest hardships and trials. When we dedicate ourselves with this vow, then no matter what obstacles and devilish functions arise, our lives will shine with a lofty, invincible spirit. No matter what karma should assail us, our lives will glow with the spirit of invincible champions.

As long as our commitment to this vow remains steadfast, then absolutely no devilish functions or karma can defeat us. Those who abandoned their faith and turned against us in the past were invariably people who grew arrogant, became obsessed with fame and fortune, and lost sight of their commitment. All of them, however, have met with ignominious defeat. As Nichiren writes, "It is the heart that is important" ("The Strategy of the Lotus Sutra," WND-1, 1000). He teaches that having a nonregressing spirit and remaining true to one's vow are the essence of victory as a human being.

Pillar of the Spirit, Eyes of Wisdom, Ship of Salvation

The Daishonin declares that he will be the "pillar of Japan," the "eyes of Japan" and the "great ship of Japan." Needless to say, the reference to Japan here is not indicative of a Japan-centered worldview. Japan could be regarded as a typical land in the Latter Day of the Law where the entire country is guilty of slandering the Law, for it is a land symptomatic of a deeply evil age. If a teaching can free from suffering a people and a land enduring the most painful hardships in this trying saha world, then it can do the same for all humankind.

In Nichiren's day, Japan was on the verge of collapse, having lost its spiritual moorings. Evil priests spreading the poison of slander of the Law filled the land, and people were left adrift in a sea of suffering.

A house without pillars will collapse. Japan was a society with no spiritual foundation, teeming with negative influences, its people wandering along without purpose. In such a spiritual wasteland, Nichiren stood up alone. We can interpret his resolve as him declaring: "I will become the spiritual pillar of this devastated country. I will become its eyes so that it can distinguish true from false amid the prevailing confusion in Buddhist thought. I will become a great ship that can rescue those who are adrift." And he held fast to his great vow throughout his life.

Even when confronted with the violent aggression of Hei no Saemon, the powerful government official who persecuted him and even tried to have him killed, Nichiren declared with a lion's roar in "The Selection of the Time": "Nichiren is the pillar and beam of Japan. Doing away with me is toppling the pillar of Japan!" (WND-1, 579).

Also, in "The Actions of the Votary of the Lotus Sutra," he writes: "The essential message in this work [of my treatise "The Opening of the Eyes"] is that the destiny of Japan depends solely upon Nichiren. A house without pillars collapses, and a person without a soul is dead. Nichiren is the soul of the people of this country" (WND-1, 772).

But no insidious workings of power or authority could undermine Nichiren's commitment to the cause of leading all people to enlightenment. Moreover, he fought unceasingly for that end without begrudging his life. Such commitment and struggle qualified him to proclaim himself the "pillar of Japan." It is the Soka Gakkai—and, indeed, only the Soka Gakkai—that has carried on the Daishonin's spirit.

Some words by Josei Toda, spoken shortly before he became second Soka Gakkai president, are deeply engraved in my heart. He said: "For me, there is only kosen-rufu . . . I will stand up! No matter what anyone says, I will fear nothing! I'm not going to let anyone hold me back! . . . I will stand up alone!"

In any time and place, a kosen-rufu movement always begins with the stand-alone spirit. With that spirit, we can limitlessly activate the power of the Mystic Law. As President Toda's disciple, I stood up alone to blaze a path of worldwide kosen-rufu where none had existed before. A stand-alone spirit is the first requirement for propagating the Mystic Law, which never changes throughout past, present and future. An unwavering commitment to kosen-rufu is the heart of a votary of the Lotus Sutra and the foundation of Nichiren Buddhism.

After clarifying this foundation, Nichiren goes on in "The Opening of the Eyes" to explain the fundamental path of mentor and disciple courageously united in the vow for kosen-rufu. With great force and energy, he outlines the essence of several key Buddhist principles such as "lessening karmic retribution" and "gaining Buddhahood without seeking it" and also the compassionate spirit of propagation.

14

Lessening One's Karmic Retribution— The Principle of Changing Karma That Frees People From Suffering

In this chapter, we will look at the section of "The Opening of the Eyes" that outlines the benefits to be obtained by the votaries or practitioners of the Lotus Sutra. These benefits have the power to fundamentally free humankind from suffering in the defiled age of the Latter Day of the Law, and it was Nichiren Daishonin who opened the way for all people to attain them.

The benefits described in this writing are: 1) lessening karmic retribution, or changing one's karma; and, 2) gaining Buddhahood without seeking it[1]—in other words, attaining Buddhahood in this lifetime. These great benefits are inherent in the practice carried out by the votaries of the Lotus Sutra.

As the sutra's votary, Nichiren showed proof of these benefits in his own life by triumphing over countless daunting trials—the quintessence of which was his victory over the persecution at Tatsunokuchi, where he was nearly executed by the authorities. Similarly, anyone who practices Buddhism just as Nichiren teaches can definitely realize the same kind of benefits.

Earlier in "The Opening of the Eyes," as

we have already discussed in detail, Nichiren addresses his critics—in society and among his followers—who say his claim to being a votary of the Lotus Sutra was invalidated by the persecutions he encountered. Using documentary and theoretical proof to back his case, he explains at length that genuine votaries are attacked and harassed precisely because they battle slander of the Law—the fundamental evil—in order to lead all people to enlightenment. Also, they triumph over all obstacles.

When we take a stand against the fundamental evil, we will inevitably encounter persecution. This is why our vow for kosen-rufu is so important and must serve as the driving force behind our efforts to surmount our hardships.

In the section that begins: "This I will state. Let the gods forsake me. Let all persecutions assail me . . ." (WND-1, 280), the Daishonin articulates his own unyielding vow to persevere as a votary of the Lotus Sutra and lead all people of the Latter Day to enlightenment, irrespective of the difficulties this may entail. This vow lies at the heart of the votary's spirit.

What are the benefits gained by the votaries of the Lotus Sutra? They are inherent in the votaries' actions and lives because of their unceasing struggle to vanquish slander of the Law, the fundamental evil.

In *The Record of the Orally Transmitted Teachings,* Nichiren says, "The element *ku* in the word *kudoku* [benefits] . . . refers to the merit achieved by wiping out evil, while the element *toku* or *doku* refers to the virtue one acquires by bringing about good" (OTT, 148). Because we fight slander of the Law both within and outside the harmonious body of believers, striving to eradicate this fundamental evil, the limitless power of the fundamental good—the Mystic Law—manifests in our lives and produces immeasurable benefits. Through deep, strong faith, the infinite power of the Mystic Law is activated within us and the fundamental life state of Buddhahood that is Nam-myoho-renge-kyo wells forth.

Squarely Facing and Changing Karma

Question: How can you be certain that the exiles and sentences of death imposed on you are the result of karma created in the past?

Answer: A bronze mirror will reflect color and form. The First Emperor of the Ch'in dynasty had a lie-detecting mirror that would reveal offenses committed in this present life. The mirror of the Buddha's Law makes clear the causal actions committed in the past. The Parinirvana Sutra states: "Good man, because people committed countless offenses and accumulated much evil karma in the past, they must expect to suffer retribution for everything they have done. They may be despised, cursed with an ugly appearance, be poorly clad and poorly fed, seek wealth in vain, be born to an impoverished and lowly family or one with erroneous views, or be persecuted by their sovereign. They may be subjected to various other sufferings and retributions. It is due to the blessings obtained by protecting the Law that they can diminish in this lifetime their suffering and retribution."

This sutra passage and my own experience tally exactly. By now all the doubts that I have raised earlier should be dispelled, and thousands of difficulties are nothing to me. Let me show you phrase by phrase how the text applies to me. "They may be despised," or, as the Lotus Sutra says, people will "despise, hate, envy, or bear grudges against them"—and in exactly that manner I have been treated with contempt and arrogance for over twenty years. "They may be cursed with an ugly appearance," "They may be poorly clad"—these too apply to me. "They may be poorly fed"—that applies to me. "They may seek wealth in vain"—that applies to me. "They may be born to an impoverished and lowly family"—that applies to me. "They may be persecuted by their sovereign"—can there be any doubt that the passage applies to me? The Lotus Sutra says, "Again and again we will be banished," and the passage from the Parinirvana Sutra says, "They may be subjected to various other sufferings and retributions." [These passages also apply to me.]

The passage also says, "It is due to the blessings obtained by protecting the Law that they can diminish in this lifetime their suffering and retribution." The fifth volume of *Great Concentration and Insight* has this to say on the subject: "The feeble merits produced by a mind only half intent on the practice cannot alter [the realm of karma]. But if one carries out the practice of concentration and insight so as to observe 'health' and 'illness,' then one can alter the cycle of birth and death [in the realm of karma]." It also says, "[As practice progresses and understanding grows], the three obstacles and four devils emerge in confusing form, vying with one another to interfere." (WND-1, 281)

First, Nichiren discusses the benefit of lessening karmic retribution in order to clarify the significance of the hardships practitioners of the Lotus Sutra undergo.

He begins by explaining that, when viewed in the light of Buddhism, all the difficulties and persecutions he has encountered—including attempted execution and an exile tantamount to a death sentence—are the result of past karma. He then quotes a passage from the Parinirvana Sutra[3] enumerating eight major trials or hardships one may typically suffer as retribution for karma created in previous existences. These are: 1) to be despised, 2) to be cursed with an ugly appearance, 3) to be poorly clad, 4) to be poorly fed, 5) to seek wealth in vain, 6) to be born to an impoverished and lowly family, 7) to be born to a family with erroneous views and 8) to be persecuted by one's sovereign.[4]

Nichiren, who had been besieged by obstacles and persecutions for more than two decades, emphasizes that all eight perfectly describe his own situation. He writes: "This sutra passage and my own experience tally exactly. By now all the doubts that I have raised earlier should be dispelled, and thousands of difficulties are nothing to me. Let me show you phrase by phrase how the text applies to me" (WND-1, 281). He then goes over the eight kinds of retribution individually, confirming that each applies to him.

Possessing a spiritual state of Himalayan proportions, the Daishonin surveys all his trials of karma and suffering with serene composure; he had experienced all these hardships in full measure and had triumphed over each of them.

Naturally, when he points out how his situation matches the sutra passages, Nichiren's words are not filled with the slightest sorrow or self-pity over the harsh retribution he has incurred for offenses from his past existences. Instead, he communicates the indomitable state of life with which he boldly surmounts all negative karma.

Nichiren discerned the root cause of all evil karma accumulated from past existences, which creates suffering and misfortune in this present lifetime. He said it stems from the grave offense of slandering the Lotus Sutra— that is, violating and slandering the Mystic Law. Accordingly, he clearly apprehended that when we triumph over this fundamental evil in our present lifetime, we can overcome all manner of negative karma. This is why he emphasizes that he has slandered the Lotus Sutra innumerable times in past existences. He writes: "From the beginningless past I have been born countless times as an evil ruler who deprived the votaries of the Lotus Sutra of their robes and rations, their fields and crops, much as the people of Japan in the present day go about destroying the temples dedicated to the Lotus Sutra. In addition, countless times I cut off the heads of the votaries of the Lotus Sutra" (WND-1, 281).

The Daishonin says he is certain to have committed slander of the Law throughout his infinite past lives. He also explains that, through his present efforts to denounce such slander as the Lotus Sutra's votary, he is calling forth retribution for these past offenses. This is why he encounters persecution.

"General Causality" and "Greater Causality"

The root of all negative karma can be traced back to disbelief in and slander of the Mystic Law. Those offenses set in motion a perpetual cycle of rebirth in the evil paths. As long as the influence of this fundamental evil remains, we are destined to continue accumulating negative karma and ultimately incur the retribution of hellish suffering. That is how fearful the offense of slandering the Law is.

On a still more essential level, disbelief in and slander of the Lotus Sutra arise from the fundamental darkness existing in human life. All people possess the potential for Buddhahood; and by revealing this potential we can become Buddhas just as we are. This is the concept of attaining Buddhahood based on the "mutual possession of the Ten Worlds" principle. Those whose lives are dominated by fundamental darkness or delusion, however, not only reject this truth, but they envy, resent, hate and despise the Lotus Sutra's votaries striving tirelessly to bring forth everyone's Buddha nature.

By reflecting on slander of the Law, the cause of the gravest negative karma, we can more deeply grasp the true nature of fundamental darkness, the source of all evil in life. Nichiren Buddhism opens the way to changing karma by enabling us to gain profound insight into fundamental evil and to eliminate the root cause that gives rise to it.

This is a philosophy that accords with the true teaching of Buddhism. It resonates with the concept of dependent origination expounded by Shakyamuni, who taught that by awakening to the fact that the sufferings of aging and death stem from fundamental darkness or delusion and by breaking through that darkness, we can liberate ourselves from those sufferings.

The Buddhism originally transmitted to Japan, however, brought with it a concept of eliminating offenses based on a very passive view of causality. As with the eight kinds of retribution found in the Parinirvana Sutra, it taught that one receives retribution in this lifetime for past offenses, which are expiated one at a time. Nichiren terms this the "general law of cause and effect" ("Letter from Sado," WND-1, 305).

The Nichiren Buddhist concept of changing karma, however, is not based on such "general causality." As discussed earlier, the fundamental cause of negative karma is disbelief in and slander of the Mystic Law. To change our karma, therefore, the *cause* we must make is our effort or Buddhist practice directed toward eliminating such disbelief and slander, which brings about the *effect* of the sun of the Mystic Law rising in our hearts and the world of Buddhahood welling forth. In other words, we change our karma through the cause and effect of attaining Buddhahood.

In contrast to "general causality," the fundamental causality for attaining Buddhahood based on the Mystic Law could be termed *greater causality*, for it supersedes all negative causes and effects, as well as subsumes all good causes and effects as defined by the idea of general causality taught in the pre-Lotus Sutra teachings.[5]

Lessening Karmic Retribution, Expiating Past Offenses and Changing Karma

From the beginningless past I have been born countless times as an evil ruler who deprived the votaries of the Lotus Sutra of their robes and rations, their fields and crops, much as the people of Japan in the present day go about destroying the temples dedicated to the Lotus Sutra. In addition, countless times I cut off the heads of the votaries of the Lotus Sutra. Some of these grave offenses I have already paid for, but there must be some that are not paid for yet. Even if I seem to have paid for them all, there are still ill effects that remain. When the time comes for me to transcend the sufferings of birth and death, it will be only after I have completely freed myself from these grave offenses. My merits are insignificant, but these offenses are grave.

If I practiced the teachings of the provisional sutras, then these retributions for my past grave offenses would not appear. When iron is heated, if it is not strenuously forged, the impurities in it will not become apparent. Only when it is subjected to the tempering process again and again will the flaws appear. When pressing hemp seeds, if one does not press very hard, one will not get much oil from them. Likewise, when I vigorously berate those throughout the country who slander the Law, I meet with great difficulties. It must be that my actions in defending the Law in this present life are calling forth retributions for the grave offenses of my past. If iron does not come into contact with fire, it remains black,

but if it contacts fire, it turns red. If you place a log across a swift stream, waves will pile up like hills. If you disturb a sleeping lion, it will roar loudly. (WND-1, 281–82)

If we delve more closely into the Nichiren Buddhist principle of changing karma based on this "greater causality," it could actually be said to involve three aspects:

1) lessening karmic retribution,
2) expiating past offenses and
3) changing karma.

"Lessening one's karmic retribution" literally means "transforming the heavy and receiving it lightly." In other words, we can receive in a lighter form and expiate the heavy retribution we would normally receive over a long period of time for our grave offenses in past existences we can instead experience in a lighter form and expiate it. This is also explained as the principle of changing karma from the aspect of the severity of the retribution received.

"Expiating past offenses" means eradicating the influence of heavy negative karma created in previous existences.

"Changing karma" could be described as transforming the unceasing cycle of rebirth in the evil paths owing to slander of the Law in past existences into a cycle of rebirth in the paths of good. This could be thought of as altering the course of our lives on the vast dimension of past, present and future.

The following passage from Nichiren's writing "Lessening One's Karmic Retribution"[6]

includes the above three aspects of changing karma: "The Nirvana Sutra teaches the principle of lessening one's karmic retribution. If one's heavy karma from the past is not expiated within this lifetime, one must undergo the sufferings of hell in the future, but if one experiences extreme hardship in this life [because of the Lotus Sutra], the sufferings of hell will vanish instantly. And when one dies, one will obtain the blessings of the human and heavenly worlds, as well as those of the three vehicles [the worlds of voice-hearers, cause-awakened ones and bodhisattvas] and the one vehicle [the world of Buddhahood]" (WND-1, 199).

Here, Nichiren says, "the sufferings of hell will vanish instantly." In "The Opening of the Eyes," he also speaks of "completely freeing" himself from the grave offenses he has committed in the past (see WND-1, 281). What he means is the full eradication of the influence of his negative karma. This is the principle of changing karma from the aspect of expiating past offenses.

To give an analogy, when the sun rises in the morning, the brilliance of the stars that had sparkled in the night sky is subsumed in the light of the sun, and becomes invisible to our eyes on earth. In the same way, when our deep faith causes the sun of the Mystic Law to rise in our hearts and vanquish our past slander of the Law, the world of Buddhahood wells forth in our lives. When that happens, our previous hellish sufferings instantly vanish. All offenses completely disappear in the brilliant sunlight of the Mystic Law.

The sufferings of karma will definitely vanish! The sun of victory will rise, dispelling the darkness of misery! This is the Daishonin's great conviction. Indeed, Nichiren Buddhism, with its teaching of changing karma, is a religion of hope, one that allows us to achieve a "happiness revolution."

Also, Nichiren teaches that we can end the cycle of rebirth in the evil paths, realms of delusion and suffering, and can attain the benefit of the worlds of human beings (humanity), heavenly beings (heaven), voice-hearers (learning), cause-awakened ones (realization), bodhisattvas and Buddhas in lifetime after lifetime. In other words, based on our transformation in this life, we can enter a cycle of rebirth in the paths of good. This is the perspective of changing one's karma.

Lessening karmic retribution means transforming the karmic retribution and suffering that would normally continue over countless lifetimes and to put an end to it in this existence by waging a struggle against slander of the Law.

The Blessings Obtained by Protecting the Law

In connection with the power that makes it possible for us to change our karma and cause all sufferings to vanish instantly, Nichiren Daishonin focuses on the Parinirvana Sutra expression, "the blessings obtained by protecting the Law" (WND-1, 281).

"Protecting the Law" means upholding and practicing Buddhism, safeguarding the correct teaching. Because slander of the Law is the fundamental cause for falling into an endless cycle of rebirth in the evil paths, by defending the Law we can put a stop to that cycle.

The purpose of protecting the Law is human happiness. When we protect this Law for attaining Buddhahood inherent in the lives of all people, we receive great blessings and benefit as a result.

In other words, in the course of striving steadily as practitioners of the Lotus Sutra, the negative impulses in our lives to disregard the Law are driven out, and we can defeat our fundamental darkness. Specifically, this refers to active efforts to combat evil and error, that is, the practice of *shakubuku*, refuting the erroneous and revealing the true. Negative influences and so-called evil friends function to keep people in darkness and delusion, blind to the enlightened Dharma nature that exists within them. Our battle against such negative forces is a battle to defeat our own inner darkness and delusion.

In "The Opening of the Eyes," Nichiren declares of his own struggle: "When I vigorously berate those throughout the country who slander the Law, I meet with great difficulties. It must be that my actions in defending the Law in this present life are calling forth retributions for the grave offenses of my past" (WND-1, 282).

Herein lies the great path of changing karma in Nichiren Buddhism. Because Nichiren vigorously denounced slander throughout the country, he encountered harsh persecution. This was simply the manifestation of retribution for grave offenses in past existences. Therefore, only by completely expiating these offenses in his present lifetime could he transcend the suffering-filled cycle of birth and death (see WND-1, 281).

Actively denouncing and eliminating slander of the Law is itself the direct path to changing karma. Doing so requires courage.

By contrast, one cannot transform the sufferings of life and death by waging a weak and timid struggle.

To back up this point, Nichiren cites two passages from T'ien-t'ai's treatise *Great Concentration and Insight* (see WND-1, 281). The first passage, "The feeble merits produced by a mind only half intent on the practice cannot alter [the realm of karma]," indicates that if our actions in the cause of good are exceedingly weak, then we will be powerless to change the unending sufferings of the cycle of birth and death.

The second passage, on the other hand, points out that "the three obstacles and four devils [will] emerge in confusing form, vying with one another to interfere" when a person practices the correct teaching exactly as it is taught.

Hardships Forge and Strengthen Our Lives

Consequently, great persecutions that arise as a result of denouncing slander of the Law are not so much hardships as opportunities for forging and strengthening our lives. In "The Opening of the Eyes," Nichiren writes: "When iron is heated, if it is not strenuously forged, the impurities in it will not become apparent. Only when it is subjected to the tempering process again and again will the flaws appear. When pressing hemp seeds, if one does not press very hard, one will not get much oil from them" (WND-1, 281–82).

In "Letter from Sado," he observes: "It is impossible to fathom one's karma. Iron, when heated in the flames and pounded, becomes a fine sword. Worthies and sages are tested by abuse" (WND-1, 303). And in "Letter to the Brothers," he writes: "Both of you have continued believing in the Lotus Sutra; thus you are now ridding yourselves of your grave offenses from the past. For example, the flaws in iron come to the surface when it is forged" (WND-1, 497).

A life forged through efforts to protect the Law drives out the impurities of the negative karma created through slander and endures eternally over the three existences—past, present and future. From time without beginning, we have repeated the cycle of birth and death. In this lifetime, however, we have had the good fortune to encounter Nichiren Buddhism. Because we practice the correct teaching, denounce slander of the Law and forge inner strength, we can change our karma and establish the eternally indestructible state of Buddhahood in our lives. This is the attainment of Buddhahood in this lifetime.

Pure and committed practice of Nichiren Buddhism entirely changes the meaning of hardships in our lives. We no longer view challenges and trials as negatives to be avoided but as things which, when overcome, bring us closer to our attainment of Buddhahood. Of course, it may not be easy for those in the midst of painful challenges to appreciate this fact. No one wishes to experience hardships. It's human nature to prefer to avoid them.

But if we understand the ultimate, transformative teaching of the Mystic Law, we can recognize that our hardships have arisen from our efforts to combat evil and be confident that by overcoming those hardships, we can attain the supreme life state of Buddhahood. With this positive approach, we can live with fundamental strength and resilience in the face of any difficulty.

Members of the Soka Gakkai understand this ultimate Buddhist truth in the depths of their lives. As proof of this, when our members encounter hardships, they are strong and, above all, upbeat. That's because they have already experienced in their own lives the rhythm of fundamental good that accompanies the process of changing karma. Or even if they haven't yet experienced it themselves, they are constantly in contact with others who have.

Those who strive in faith for kosen-rufu while battling their karma embody the quintessential Buddhist principle of "voluntarily assuming the appropriate karma."[7] Our members, comrades from the distant past, summon forth the heart of the lion king—the spirit to bravely take on challenges, never fearing hardships or lamenting painful trials —as they struggle valiantly to transform their karma into their mission and enact the victorious drama of a great human revolution. They possess a truly lofty state of life.

Accordingly, defeat for a Buddhist lies not in encountering difficulties but rather in not challenging them. Difficulties only truly become our destiny if we run away from them. We must fight as long as we live. We must live and struggle tenaciously to the end. Nichiren's philosophy of changing karma, which teaches this important essence of life, is also a revolutionary teaching, in that it represents a radical departure from the way other religions tend to view difficulties.

To practice Nichiren Buddhism is to live with the unshakable conviction that the most painful and trying times are opportunities for changing karma, for carrying out our human revolution, and that no matter how difficult the situation, we can ultimately, and without fail, transform it into something positive.

And it is the Soka Gakkai, an organization directly connected to Nichiren Daishonin, that actually puts this teaching of changing karma into practice and takes this revolutionary philosophy to the world. With this pride and joy, let us continue in our efforts to share Nichiren Buddhism with others.

15

"I and My Disciples"—Attaining Buddhahood Through Steadfast Faith at the Crucial Moment

Although I and my disciples may encounter various difficulties, if we do not harbor doubts in our hearts, we will as a matter of course attain Buddhahood. Do not have doubts simply because heaven does not lend you protection. Do not be discouraged because you do not enjoy an easy and secure existence in this life. This is what I have taught my disciples morning and evening, and yet they begin to harbor doubts and abandon their faith.

Foolish men are likely to forget the promises they have made when the crucial moment comes. Some of them feel pity for their wives and children and grieve at the thought of parting from them in this life. In countless births throughout many long kalpas they have had wives and children but parted from them in every existence. They have done so unwillingly and not because of their desire to pursue the way of the Buddha. Since they must part with them in any case, they should remain faithful to their belief in the Lotus Sutra and make their way to Eagle Peak, so that they may lead their wives and children there as well. (WND-1, 283)

Difficulties make us stronger. Great hardships strengthen our faith. If we keep challenging obstacles and forging strong, invincible conviction, we can bring forth the state of Buddhahood in our lives.

Those who, with the heart of a lion king, continue struggling valiantly even when assailed by monumental challenges will definitely attain Buddhahood. The essence of Nichiren Buddhism is that faith leads directly to enlightenment.

The kind of faith indicated here is a deep confidence in the existence of the Buddha nature in our own lives and those of others. This is extremely important. At the same time, and equally crucial, it refers to steadfast faith that remains unwavering no matter what happens, and strong faith that will not be defeated by devilish functions. Whether we can attain Buddhahood hinges on the strength of our faith.

"The Opening of the Eyes" contains the following famous passage, which explains the profound principle that faith leads directly to enlightenment: "Although I and my disciples may encounter various difficulties, if we do not harbor doubts in our hearts, we will as a matter of course attain Buddhahood. Do not have doubts simply because heaven does not lend you protection. Do not be discouraged because you do not enjoy an easy and secure existence in this life. This is what I have taught my disciples morning and evening, and yet they begin to harbor doubts and abandon their faith. Foolish men are likely to forget the promises they have made when the crucial moment comes" (WND-1, 283).

No matter what painful trials we encounter, we must not harbor doubts in our hearts. Nor should we be discouraged or succumb to complaint if we don't enjoy the protection of the heavenly deities or an easy and secure existence in this life. Those who maintain faith with such a nonregressing spirit are true winners. This is one of Nichiren's most important points of guidance, illuminating the very heart of faith; it is an eternal guideline.

In this chapter, we will focus mainly on the above passage and discuss the true essence of faith in Nichiren Buddhism.

The Heart of the Mentor-Disciple Relationship

At the beginning of this passage, the Daishonin addresses himself and his followers, "I and my disciples . . ." (WND-1, 283).

As we have seen so far in "The Opening of the Eyes," the Daishonin indicates that he is: (1) the true votary of the Lotus Sutra, who battles the fundamental evil of slander of the Law; (2) the pillar of Japan, who forestalls the loss of the correct teaching and the ruin of the nation; and (3) the Buddha of the Latter Day, who illuminates the darkness of the age long into the distant future by revealing the supreme Law for the enlightenment of all people.

Ready to brave all consequences, he declares his resolve: "This I will state. Let the gods forsake me. Let all persecutions assail me. Still I will give my life for the sake of the Law" (WND-1, 280). Then, with an indomitable lion's roar, he makes the powerful pledge: "I will be the pillar of Japan. I will be the eyes of Japan. I will be the great ship of Japan. This is my vow, and I will never forsake it!" (WND-1, 280–81). Here, he reveals the core of his own spirit.

While these passages constitute declarations of his personal resolve and commitment, the intent of the passage "I and my disciples . . ." (WND-1, 283) is clearly to underscore the importance of having faith that responds to the spirit of the mentor, the Daishonin. It is as if he were saying: "Follow my example! Cast aside your doubts and laments as befits cubs of the lion king! Don't foolishly discard your faith at the crucial moment!"

The Daishonin indicates that his true disciples are those who, sharing his resolve, stand up to struggle alongside him and work energetically for kosen-rufu. All who become genuine "disciples of Nichiren" (see "The True Aspect of All Phenomena," WND-1, 385) by making his spirit and commitment their own—no matter who they are—have in fact already opened wide the path to attaining Buddhahood. And, as long as they follow this path to the end, they will attain Buddhahood "as a matter of course" (WND-1, 283).

The ultimate teaching expounded by all Buddhas reveals that all living beings possess the life state of Buddhahood. The Lotus Sutra also clearly states that Buddhas fulfill the purpose of their appearance in the world by opening for all living beings the door to the Buddha wisdom lying dormant in their lives, showing it to them, causing them to awaken to it and guiding them to enter its path (see LSOC, 65)[1]—in other words, enabling all to attain enlightenment. The essence of this ultimate teaching of the Buddhas is to help everyone actualize the same great enlightenment that they have achieved. That is why Buddhism is at all times concerned with raising disciples who will exert themselves in faith and practice with the same spirit as the mentor. Buddhism is none other than a philosophy of mentor and disciple.

And the spirit of this philosophy of mentor and disciple truly comes to life only when the disciples' hearts blaze with the same bright spiritual flame evinced by Nichiren, who proclaimed: "Let the gods forsake me. Let all persecutions assail me. Still I will give my life for the sake of the Law" (WND-1, 280).

In that sense, the Daishonin's focus on

"I and my disciples" in this passage can also be read as a call for the emergence of ranks of capable successors who will continue his struggle.

Selfless Dedication Is the Essence of the Mentor-Disciple Bond

Every time I read this passage, the expression "I and my disciples" stands out vividly with a golden brilliance.

Often, religious leaders address or direct their followers in a unilateral manner, uttering only, "My disciples . . ." But Nichiren says, "I and my disciples . . ." Including himself in his instructions to his disciples exemplifies an attitude imbued with the Buddhist spirit of unity of mentor and disciple.

And the backbone of this relationship is the spirit of "not begrudging one's life," or unselfish dedication. Because the mentor, Nichiren Daishonin, does not begrudge his own life in propagating the Law, he is qualified to be a leader of the people who opens the path of Buddhism to all. Similarly, in order for his disciples to spread the Law in their capacity as disciples, they must actively struggle for that cause with the same selfless dedication as their mentor.

Nichiren teaches this in the following passage: "Some of them feel pity for their wives and children and grieve at the thought of parting from them in this life. In countless births throughout many long kalpas they have had wives and children but parted from them in every existence. They have done so unwillingly and not because of their desire to pursue the way of the Buddha. Since they must part with them in any case, they should remain faithful to their belief in the Lotus Sutra and make their way to Eagle Peak, so that they may lead their wives and children there as well" (WND-1, 283).

The Daishonin made this statement while undergoing life-threatening persecution. Looking at more recent times, during World War II the Soka Kyoiku Gakkai (Value-Creating Education Society, forerunner of the Soka Gakkai)[2] suffered persecution at the hands of the Japanese militarist authorities. The Soka Gakkai's top leaders were arrested and imprisoned. All of them except Tsunesaburo Makiguchi and Josei Toda, the first and second presidents, caved in to government pressure and turned their backs on the Daishonin's admonition by abandoning their faith.

While in prison, Mr. Toda wrote in a letter to his family: "Do not doubt that the heavenly deities, the Buddhas and the Buddhist gods will protect you. They will! Don't lament that you do not enjoy ease and security in this life." His words embody the essence of "The Opening of the Eyes."

How should we live out our lives as human beings and Buddhists? Let us always remember that it is only through faith—through dedicating ourselves to the supreme Law and striving for Buddhism with a selfless, ungrudging spirit—that we can truly forge our lives and establish the indestructible state of Buddhahood.

Gaining Buddhahood Without Seeking It

In the passage cited at the beginning, the Daishonin says that even if we face many difficulties, as long as we persevere undefeated and remain steadfast in our faith, then the benefit of attaining Buddhahood will naturally come to us of itself. This is termed *gaining Buddhahood without seeking it.*[3]

Why can we attain Buddhahood even if we do not seek it? First, it is because the lives of all living beings are inherently entities of Myoho-renge-kyo (the Mystic Law). And second, it is because our strong faith causes the limitless functions of Myoho-renge-kyo that reside within our lives to manifest without impediment. When Myoho-renge-kyo comes to function freely in our lives, we attain the life state of Buddhahood. The Mystic Law's infinite power then operates unhindered and expresses itself as various human powers or capacities. These include, for example, the courage to stand up alone, the strength to persevere, the wisdom to surmount adversity, and concern and compassion for others. Qualities such as these, described in the sutra as attributes of the Buddha's life, manifest in appropriate form as needed. To reiterate, attaining Buddhahood means being able to freely call forth the power of the Mystic Law from our lives in the form of various human powers or capacities.

It is important to be aware that what prevents the power of the Mystic Law from manifesting in our lives is actually the fundamental illusion or darkness that resides within us—in other words, it means a profound ignorance of the Mystic Law. This ignorance causes people to be lost, deluded and ruled by negative impulses; it is the root cause of all unhappiness and suffering.

Accordingly, when we become awakened to the Mystic Law, this delusion or darkness instantly vanishes. The Mystic Law, then, is like the sun, while delusion is like dark clouds obstructing it. When the dark clouds clear, bright sunshine streams down. When we break through fundamental darkness, the power of the Mystic Law is immediately activated and manifests as various kinds of benefit and value-creative functions. Such diverse benefit and value derive from the workings of the "Law of the *renge*, or lotus" ("The Entity of the Mystic Law," WND-1, 425)—the principle of the "simultaneity of cause and effect."

Therefore, while it is true that all living beings are entities of the Mystic Law whose lives are inherently endowed with the state of Buddhahood, unless we strive in earnest to dispel the obstructing clouds of fundamental darkness, the world of Buddhahood will not actually manifest in our lives. It is not something we can hope to achieve if we are halfhearted, simply going through the motions of chanting Nam-myoho-renge-kyo. Much less will it be achieved by having priests chant for us instead! It is up to each person who chants Nam-myoho-renge-kyo to wage an individual struggle to dispel the darkness in his or her life. Because this darkness arises from our inner delusion, the struggle to defeat it must be waged within. In short, this struggle means persevering in faith.

Based on the Lotus Sutra, which reveals the Buddha's enlightenment, the Daishonin discovered the workings of the fundamental Law of Myoho-renge-kyo in his own life; he then went on to confirm and prove its power

through his own life struggles. For us to freely manifest the workings of the Law in our own lives, we need to chant with the same mind and attitude as the Daishonin. In other words, our chanting of Nam-myoho-renge-kyo—the *daimoku*—must be based on faith, the spirit to battle fundamental darkness. The daimoku that the Daishonin spread could be described as "fighting daimoku."

Fundamental darkness manifests in various forms—as doubt, anxiety, earthly desires and so on. The power to break through fundamental darkness is none other than faith or belief. The Daishonin says, "Belief means to be without doubt" (OTT, 54).[4] He also states, "The single word *belief* is the sharp sword with which one confronts and overcomes fundamental darkness or ignorance" (OTT, 119–20). Battling devilish functions and confronting the various difficulties of life must essentially be an intense struggle against our illusion. We use the sharp sword of belief against the devilish forces that obstruct kosen-rufu.

If we should lose our faith or belief in the Mystic Law—that is to say, if we lose the conviction that we can definitely become happy and attain Buddhahood, and if we lose the desire to accomplish kosen-rufu without fail—then we will also be defeated by hardships, obstacles and devilish functions on the path to kosen-rufu.

In "The Opening of the Eyes," the Daishonin says we must not succumb to doubt and pessimism, both of which are manifestations of fundamental darkness. A clear illustration of faith conquering illusion is provided by the Nirvana Sutra's parable of the poor woman who gives up her life to protect her child,[5] which Nichiren cites in this treatise.

The Parable of the Poor Woman in the Nirvana Sutra

The Nirvana Sutra states: "She [the poor woman] has no house to live in and no one to aid or protect her, and in addition she is beset by illness, hunger, and thirst; she wanders through various places, begging for a living. While staying at an inn, she gives birth to a baby, but the master of the inn drives her away. Though the baby has just been born, she takes it up in her arms and sets out, hoping to journey to another land. But along the way, she encounters fierce wind and rain, and she is troubled by cold and bitten by mosquitoes, gadflies, hornets, and poisonous insects. Coming at length to the Ganges River, she clasps her child in her arms and begins to cross it. Although the current is very swift, she will not let go of her child, and in the end both mother and child are drowned. But through the merit that the woman gained by her loving tenderness, she is reborn after her death in the Brahma heaven[6]" (WND-1, 282).

The parable teaches that the poor woman could transform her state of life through her strong compassion to try to protect her child even at the cost of her own life.

To us today, the mother's predicament and the fate of her and her child may seem sad and tragic, especially since Buddhism exists to enable all mothers and children to become happy. Moreover, from our perspective as practitioners of the Mystic Law, attaining Buddhahood and establishing a state of absolute happiness are assured to us in this lifetime. In that sense, this Nirvana Sutra parable reflects several basic assumptions that differ from the perspective of Nichiren

Buddhism. Why then does the Daishonin cite this tale in "The Opening of the Eyes"? Likely, it's because of the vital message contained in Shakyamuni's concluding remarks.

Shakyamuni guides his disciples, telling them in effect that they must defend the correct teaching as resolutely and selflessly as this mother protected her child (see WND-1, 282). The message is that the path to attaining Buddhahood lies in faith committed to steadfastly protecting the Law, no matter what—in other words, the selfless spirit of faith of "not begrudging one's life" and of "caring nothing for one's own life" taught in the Lotus Sutra (see LSOC, 229–33). In terms of our practice, however, "not begrudging or caring for one's life" does not mean throwing away our lives; it means thoroughly dedicating ourselves to the Law.

The "Jewel" of Three Thousand Realms in a Single Moment of Life

In this writing, the Daishonin succinctly describes the principle of attaining Buddhahood conveyed through this parable of the poor woman as the "jewel that is the doctrine of three thousand realms in a single moment of life" (WND-1, 283).

Let's briefly go over the main points of the Daishonin's explanation in "The Opening of the Eyes." He sums up the essential message of this parable as follows: "In the end it is nothing other than the loving kindness with which the woman cares for her child that makes the difference. Her concern concentrates on one thing just like the Buddhist practice of concentration. She thinks of nothing but her child, which is similar to Buddhist compassion. That must be why, although she created no other causes to bring it about, she was reborn in the Brahma heaven" (WND-1, 283).

Why is the poor woman reborn in the Brahma heaven without seeking it? Nichiren offers two explanations. First, it is because her "concentrating on one thing" is similar to the Buddhist practice of concentration. Second, it is because her "thinking of nothing but her child" is comparable to Buddhist compassion.

"Concentrating on one thing" means focusing one's mind on a single objective. The ultimate expression of this is the practice of "exhausting the pains and trials of millions of kalpas in a single moment of life" (see OTT, 214). When we practice with such concentrated effort, we can manifest the limitless life state of the Buddha eternally endowed with the three bodies.[7]

The Daishonin says that the doctrines for attaining Buddhahood expounded in various other sutras and schools—such as the Flower Garland doctrine of the phenomenal world as created by the mind alone, the eight negations of the Three Treatises school, the Consciousness-Only doctrine of the Dharma Characteristics school and the True Word school's meditation on five elements of the universe—are not "jewels" but merely "yellow stones,"[8] and that one cannot attain enlightenment by these means. He explains that the path to Buddhahood is only the Lotus Sutra's "jewel that is the doctrine of three thousand realms in a single moment of life" (see WND-1, 283).

Here, on one level, the "jewel that is the doctrine of three thousand realms in a single moment of life" may be taken to indicate the condition of simultaneity of cause and effect that we can realize through our concentrated prayer, or mind of faith. It is a condition in which the other nine of the Ten Worlds (cause) and the world of Buddhahood (effect) exist simultaneously in a single moment of life. The Daishonin likens such a state to a "jewel" because it embodies the mutual possession of the Ten Worlds and three thousand realms and shines with beautiful gemlike brilliance. The essence of such a state of life is simply strong faith in Myoho-renge-kyo (the Mystic Law). Our concentrated prayer manifests as a jewel that contains Buddhahood.

In some instances, the doctrines for attaining Buddhahood put forward by various other sutras and advanced by different schools are little more than simple ways of viewing the world and are limited to shallow self-affirmations. In other instances, they teach the importance of extinguishing delusions but are similar to the Hinayana teaching of eradicating earthly desires by "reducing the body to ashes and annihilating consciousness."[9] In either case, although they may appear similar, these doctrines are completely different from the "jewel that is the doctrine of three thousand realms in a single moment of life."

Nichiren concludes his discussion of the parable by citing once more the Nirvana Sutra passage, "Although they do not seek emancipation, emancipation will come of itself" (WND-1, 283). In other words, one naturally arrives at enlightenment even without seeking it.

Never Forget To Challenge Fundamental Darkness "at the Crucial Moment"

As the Daishonin indicates when he says, "If we do not harbor doubts in our hearts, we will as a matter of course attain Buddhahood" (WND-1, 283), we can only break through the darkness of doubt and pessimism and bring forth the power of Myoho-renge-kyo (the Mystic Law) in our lives through resolute faith.

Fundamental darkness, however, is also stubbornly powerful and deep-rooted. At the precise moment we need to battle illusion, it creeps into our hearts and invades our lives. The Daishonin admonishes against the folly of allowing this to happen, saying, "Foolish men are likely to forget the promises they have made when the crucial moment comes" (WND-1, 283).

To harbor doubt and disbelief and turn away from the correct teaching at the very time we should arouse strong faith is foolish indeed. The Daishonin's words seem to ring with the impassioned cry: "This is a chance to make great causes for attaining Buddhahood! Everlasting happiness lies on the other side of this momentous challenge!"

No matter what happens, we must not give in to doubt, we must not be discouraged. Those who possess such a robust spirit will not fear anything.

There have been many instances in the history of the Soka Gakkai when we have faced enormous obstacles—such as when President Makiguchi was imprisoned during the war, when President Toda's business enterprises fell into dire straits in the postwar period, and when we were attacked by the three powerful enemies embodied by the Nichiren Shoshu priesthood and others. Our true worth and mettle as disciples and practitioners of Nichiren Buddhism are revealed in what we do and how we act at such times.

We absolutely must never forget that Buddhahood shines in the faith of those who fight steadfastly at the crucial moment. This is one of the principal conclusions of "The Opening of the Eyes."

16

Shakubuku: A Lion's Roar of Great Compassion To Refute Error and Spread Good

Question: You insist that the followers of the Nembutsu [Pure Land] and Zen schools will fall into the hell of incessant suffering. This shows that you have a contentious heart. You yourself are in danger of falling into the realm of the asuras [the world of anger]. Moreover, it is said in the "Peaceful Practices" chapter of the Lotus Sutra, "He [a practitioner of the Latter Day] should not delight in speaking of the faults of other people or scriptures. He should not display contempt for other teachers of the Law." It is because you are going against this passage in the sutra that you have been abandoned by heaven, is it not? (WND-1, 283–84) . . .

Answer: . . . I suppose the learned priests of the time think it is only natural that one should have doubts about this. Therefore, no matter how I explain and try to persuade my own

disciples, they still cannot seem to overcome their doubts, but behave like icchantikas, or persons of incorrigible disbelief. Therefore, I have quoted these passages of explanation from T'ien-t'ai, Miao-lo, and others in order to silence their ungrounded criticisms.

These two methods of shoju and shakubuku are like water and fire. Fire hates water, water detests fire. The practitioner of shoju laughs with scorn at shakubuku. The practitioner of shakubuku laments at the thought of shoju. When the country is full of evil people without wisdom, then shoju is the primary method to be applied, as described in the "Peaceful Practices" chapter. But at a time when there are many people of perverse views who slander the Law, then shakubuku should come first, as described in the "Never Disparaging" chapter. It is like using cold water to cool yourself in the hot weather, or longing for a fire when the weather turns cold. Grass and trees are kindred to the sun—they suffer in the cold moonlight. Bodies of water are followers of the moon—they lose their true nature when the hot weather comes.

In the Latter Day of the Law, however, both shoju and shakubuku are to be used. This is because there are two kinds of countries, the country that is passively evil, and the kind that actively seeks to destroy the Law. We must consider carefully to which category Japan at the present time belongs. (WND-1, 285)

Compassion is the heart of Buddhism. It is not only an expression of the enlightened state of Buddhahood, it also lies at the foundation of bodhisattva practice.

As we have already seen earlier in "The Opening of the Eyes," Nichiren Daishonin asserts that a true votary of the Lotus Sutra is one who excels in compassion and forbearance. He writes, "As regards my ability to endure persecution and the wealth of my compassion for others, I believe they [the Great Teachers T'ien-t'ai and Dengyo] would hold me in awe" (WND-1, 242).

The Compassion of the Lotus Sutra Combines Both Love and Sternness

In the Latter Day of the Law, an age when evil is persistent and deep-rooted, those who take it upon themselves to lead people out of darkness must be prepared to battle unceasing obstacles. This will be even more so in the case of the votary of the Lotus Sutra, whose mission it is to lead all humanity to enlightenment. The votary's ability to endure hardship and persecution derives from what might be called a "stern fatherly compassion," or spirit of "tough love," to prevent people of the Latter Day from straying onto the path of slander of the Law.

In "The Opening of the Eyes," Nichiren emphasizes this "tough love" aspect of the Lotus Sutra. The Mystic Law is described as the "seed of Buddhahood of three thousand realms in a single moment of life"[1] (see "The Object of Devotion for Observing the Mind," WND-1, 365). It is the only means for freeing all people of the Latter Day from suffering. The Buddha's compassion in planting this seed in people's lives is not only characterized by a deep caring for their happiness and welfare but also by strict rebuke of slander of the Law. This is because people cannot actualize the principle of attaining Buddhahood in this lifetime as long as their hearts are clouded by the darkness of delusion and disbelief that causes them to denigrate the correct teaching.

Earlier in this treatise, the Daishonin discusses the "object of devotion of sowing"[2]—the Gohonzon of Nam-myoho-renge-kyo—by citing the Great Teacher Dengyo as saying: "The sutras that the other schools are based upon give expression in a certain measure to the mother-like nature of the Buddha. But they convey only a sense of love and are lacking in a sense of fatherly sternness. It is only the Tendai Lotus school that combines a sense of both love and sternness"[3] (WND-1, 258).

The "mother-like nature of the Buddha" refers to an infinite motherly kindness. We can find examples of this aspect of the Buddha's compassion in the pre-Lotus Sutra teachings, too. But Dengyo asserts that these other sutras "convey only a sense of love and are lacking in a sense of fatherly sternness," adding that the Lotus Sutra alone "combines a sense of both love and sternness."

In other words, the compassion of the Lotus Sutra naturally embodies an infinite kindness resembling a mother's love. At the same time, since this sutra does away with expedient means and clearly and precisely reveals the true means for all to attain Buddhahood, it also inevitably contains an uncompromising strictness with regard to the Law. This is an aspect of the Lotus Sutra's compassion not found in other sutras. The strictness or rigor we find here arises out of the desire to reveal the Mystic Law as the universal seed of Buddhahood. As such, it is strictness to enable all people to attain enlightenment; it is also an expression of compassion to make the Law available to all.

In order to clarify who possesses this compassion, which "combines both love and sternness," Nichiren discusses the three virtues—sovereign, teacher and parent—in "The Opening of the Eyes." The identity of that person is the votary of the Lotus Sutra, who battles slander of the correct teaching and

spreads the Mystic Law as the seed of Buddhahood for the enlightenment of all people of the Latter Day; it is none other than the Daishonin himself.

Let's save a detailed examination of the sovereign, teacher and parent of the Buddhism of sowing—the Buddha of the Latter Day of the Law—for later. In this chapter, we'll examine the passages relating to the subject of *shakubuku*—a method of expounding Buddhism by refuting another's attachment to erroneous teachings—which constitutes the last major focus of "The Opening of the Eyes" and forms the basis for the Daishonin's subsequent conclusion regarding sovereign, teacher and parent.

The Parable of the Poor Woman Revisited

In his writings (WND-1, 282–83), Nichiren outlined the spirit necessary for votaries of the Lotus Sutra to attain Buddhahood, citing the Nirvana Sutra's parable of the poor woman who gives up her life to protect her child. We saw him telling his disciples that as long as they maintain strong, doubt-free faith, no matter what difficulties may arise, then they will as a matter of course attain Buddhahood.

Now, let's turn once again to the cause that enabled the poor woman to gain great benefit without seeking it. We are told that this benefit was due to her "concentrating on one thing"—namely, "thinking of nothing but her child" (see WND-1, 283). The Daishonin says that this single-minded focus is similar to the Buddhist practice of concentration, while her selfless concern for her child resembles Buddhist compassion. In addition, he likens the poor woman's efforts to protect her child through all adversity to maintaining unswerving faith in the Lotus Sutra and never succumbing to doubts in the face of obstacles. He also compares the poor woman's rebirth in the Brahma heaven to attaining Buddhahood through persevering in faith.

To have unceasing faith in all people's potential to attain enlightenment is itself true compassion. And shakubuku can be seen as the primary practical means for implementing or giving expression to this compassion. Put another way, the practice of shakubuku is indispensable to attaining Buddhahood.

Clarifying the True Spirit of Shakubuku

Nichiren refuted the doctrines of the Nembutsu and Zen schools of his day as slander of the Law for their encouraging people to discard the Lotus Sutra. He condemned them as teachings that caused people to fall into the hell of incessant suffering. Here in "The Opening of the Eyes," he begins his discussion on the subject of shakubuku by asking whether his repudiation of these other schools reflects "a contentious heart" and a state of life verging on "the realm of the asuras"—the world of anger.[4]

Further, he brings up the questioner's assertion that the heavenly deities have presumably abandoned him because, in his insistence on pursuing shakubuku, he is ignoring the passage from "Peaceful Practices,"[5] the 14th chapter of the Lotus Sutra, which states: "[A practitioner in the Latter Day] should not delight in speaking of the faults of other people or scriptures. He should not display contempt for other teachers of the Law" (LSOC, 240).

This is probably representative of the kind of criticism actually directed at the Daishonin. Many people no doubt felt that it was not very "Buddhist" of him to censure and attack other schools. Such behavior also went against the prized Japanese virtue of maintaining *wa,* or harmony. In this treatise, Nichiren indicates that not only did the priests and followers of other schools rise up to condemn him, but that some of his own disciples also failed to understand his actions. He writes: "I suppose the learned priests of the time think it is only natural that one should have doubts about this. Therefore, no matter how I explain and try to persuade my own disciples, they still cannot seem to overcome their doubts" (WND-1, 285).

In "Letter from Sado," the Daishonin also denounces erstwhile followers who allowed themselves to be led astray by learned and influential people of the day, saying, "They not only have forsaken the Lotus Sutra, but also actually think themselves wise enough to instruct me" (WND-1, 306).

The real underlying problem here is obviously the deep and pervasive misconceptions about Buddhism that existed in society. People generally viewed Buddhism as a teaching that aspired to attaining a state of perfect inner tranquillity known as nirvana.[6] This gave rise to a tendency to seek escape from the real world, and it became common for Buddhist practitioners to seclude themselves in the mountains and yearn for a utopia or paradise far removed from this world of suffering. With that perspective, practitioners could not appreciate the real spiritual struggle that is the essence of the correct teachings of Buddhism.

Genuine Buddhism does not promote a utopia existing in some imaginary realm. On the contrary, it is a philosophy that seeks to enable us to transform reality and live an ideal life right here in this troubled saha world. It seeks to empower us, to help us develop the spiritual strength and inner fortitude with which to overcome all storms as we struggle amid the reality of our daily lives.

The essence of Buddhism, in a sense, is not to seek the placid existence of a still pond but to establish a towering state of happiness that not even the stormiest seas can destroy. Though we might wish for a humble happiness where nothing untoward ever occurs, it is impossible to avoid being buffeted by life's winds and waves when storms howl. Indeed, it is only by bringing forth our inherent strength to make our way dauntlessly through the maelstrom of fundamental darkness and karma that we can secure true happiness. In that respect, happiness is found only amid struggle.

Building genuine happiness for oneself and others necessarily entails battling erroneous thinking and mistaken beliefs that lead people to misery. This is what the practice of shakubuku is all about.

In response to the criticism that shakubuku involves "a contentious heart" and leads to one falling into "the realm of asuras," Nichiren explains that shakubuku is an expression of compassion and the will to fight evil. This in turn is the spirit of the Buddha. Therefore, shakubuku is a practice at one with the Buddha's heart and intent, and represents the way of bodhisattva practice for the Latter Day of the Law.

Shoju and Shakubuku

Rejecting the accusation that shakubuku involves "a contentious heart," the Daishonin first explains that Buddhist practice includes two methods of propagation: *shoju*,[7] or gentle encouragement, and shakubuku, or strict refutation. He thus indicates that shakubuku is a legitimate form of Buddhist practice.

He points out, however, that since the two propagation methods are exact opposites, those who practice one often tend to reject the other: "The practitioner of shoju laughs with scorn at shakubuku. The practitioner of shakubuku laments at the thought of shoju" (WND-1, 285). Here we see the fundamental illusion of egoism at work giving rise to misguided attachments that lead one to resent and negate the position of others.

Nichiren's concludes that both shoju and shakubuku are legitimate ways of spreading the Buddha's teachings, and says, citing the Great Teacher T'ien-t'ai, "The method chosen should be that which accords with the time" (WND-1, 284). He then offers the following guideline for deciding which is appropriate: "When the country is full of evil people without wisdom, then shoju is the primary method to be applied, as described in the 'Peaceful Practices' chapter. But at a time when there are many people of perverse views who slander the Law, then shakubuku should come first, as described in the 'Never Disparaging' chapter" (WND-1, 285).

The question put to the Daishonin earlier cited a passage from the "Peaceful Practices" chapter to imply that his active refutation of other Buddhist schools departed from the spirit of the Lotus Sutra. But this is simply based on a shallow, fragmentary understanding of the sutra that does not take into account its teachings as a whole.

The practice set forth in "Peaceful Practices"—in which one does not address the faults of other schools or their teachers and followers—is to be carried out when the country is filled with "evil people without wisdom,"[8] that is, people ignorant of Buddhism. In contrast, shakubuku is the preferred method when the country is filled with "people of perverse views who slander the Law."[9]

In the Lotus Sutra, this latter situation is illustrated through the example of Bodhisattva Never Disparaging, who—in a chapter named after him—is depicted as persevering in his practice of venerating others even when attacked with "sticks of wood or tiles and stones" (LSOC, 309).

Bodhisattva Never Disparaging's practice consisted of bowing to others in reverence and greeting them with words that make up what is known as "the twenty-four-character Lotus Sutra,"[10] a distillation of the Lotus Sutra's core teaching that all people possess the Buddha nature. He did not waver in his conviction even when he encountered negative reactions and persecution from people of overbearing arrogance among the four kinds of believers—monks, nuns, laymen and laywomen. His bold, unremitting efforts to proclaim the truth are comparable to refuting people's misguided and erroneous beliefs. Accordingly, the "Never Disparaging" chapter of the Lotus Sutra teaches the practice of shakubuku.

Determining the Method of Propagation According to the Age

As we have seen, it all depends on the age as to which propagation method should be used. What we are speaking of here is not the historical time period but rather the prevailing nature of the times or overall tendencies found in a particular society as shaped by its dominant ideas and belief systems, its citizens' attitudes and outlooks, and its existing social conditions and general environment.

Let us look at the conditions of the Daishonin's day as described in this treatise. Popular were schools such as True Word and Flower Garland, which had surreptitiously appropriated the Lotus Sutra doctrine of three thousand realms in a single moment of life, incorporating the concept but failing to put it into practice. Also enjoying wide support were schools such as Nembutsu and Zen, which urged people to cast aside the Lotus Sutra. Confusion reigned as to which were the true and which were the provisional teachings of Buddhism,[11] resulting in the Buddha's teaching of enlightenment for all people being obscured.

Nichiren also cites another major problem that existed at that time: Individuals whose duty it should have been to protect the correct teaching of the Lotus Sutra instead contributed to Buddhism's denigration. He writes in scathing reproof, "The learned priests of the Tendai and True Word schools fawn on the lay supporters of the Nembutsu and Zen schools the way a dog wags its tail before its master or fear them the way a mouse fears a cat" (WND-1, 286).

SHAKUBUKU—A LION'S ROAR OF GREAT COMPASSION

He further notes that the teachings these men preach to the ruler and other officials of the land will result in both the destruction of Buddhism and the ruin of the country. The widespread confusion about the correct teaching, he asserts, bodes ill for the country's future and is also the fundamental cause of the sufferings that afflict people throughout the land.

Which of the two methods of propagation—shoju or shakubuku—is appropriate is determined by the time. In a time like the Daishonin's, to just stand idly by and not speak out and address such wrongs would signify both spiritual defeat as a Buddhist and spiritual death as a person of religious conviction. The Tendai and True Word priests' failure to defend Buddhism when it was imperiled shows that they did not understand this point, and as such acted against the Buddha's spirit. They divorced themselves from the real world, instead retiring to mountain forests to carry out their solitary meditation practices. The Daishonin declares that they are destined to fall into the realm of hungry spirits, the world of hunger, in their present existence and, in their next, find themselves in the hell of incessant suffering. He rebukes them for their error, asking how they can possibly free themselves from the sufferings of life and death (see WND-1, 286).

Thus, the Japan of Nichiren's time was widely populated with priests who were hostile to the Lotus Sutra, followers of these priests and professed practitioners of the Lotus Sutra who did not challenge those who sought to destroy the correct teaching. Their combined negative influence was so pervasive that it poisoned the entire land, turning it into "a country filled with people of perverse views who slander the Law" (see WND-1, 285).

Such circumstances compel genuine votaries of the Lotus Sutra to stand up and fight to defend the correct teaching. Not only is such action vital for opening the path to enlightenment for all people, but it is the only way to carry out the Buddha's admonitions.

Wisdom That Guides People to Happiness Is Identical to Buddhist Wisdom

The Lotus Sutra embodies universal values. It is a teaching that expounds the dignity and equality of all people. The sutras other than the Lotus also to some degree present concepts and forms of practice that indicate the inherent nobility and preciousness of human beings. When these sutras are approached based on a firm grasp of the Lotus Sutra, we can also utilize their wisdom freely and appropriately. As seen in the doctrine of the "unification of the teachings,"[12] the Lotus Sutra is an all-encompassing scripture that brings all Buddhist teachings within its fold. For that reason, it continues to tower even today as an unparalleled teaching of humanism.

At the same time, the Lotus Sutra teaches that if anti-humanistic influences should arise in the realm of Buddhism, and if they were to distort the spirit of the Lotus Sutra, then its practitioners should actively and thoroughly repudiate such error. The sutra predicts that those who practice and propagate the correct teaching in the evil age of the Latter Day will inevitably face struggles against individuals and groups that will persecute and attack them. Various chapters warn that they will have to battle manifestations of fundamental darkness and arrogance. For instance, "Teacher of the Law," the 10th chapter, states, "Since hatred and jealousy toward this sutra abound even when the Thus Come One is in the world, how much more will this be so after his passing?" (LSOC, 203). And there are also lengthy descriptions set forth in the form of the "six difficult and nine easy acts" in "Treasure Tower," the 11th chapter, and the "three powerful enemies" in "Encouraging Devotion," the 13th chapter.

We see the same duality in the practice of shakubuku in Nichiren Buddhism. On the one hand, it demands a rigorous struggle against those who spread erroneous teachings that distort Buddhism and cause people suffering. On the other, it possesses the broadmindedness to try to find commonalities between Buddhism and philosophies and belief systems that likewise value human beings and put their welfare first. As an example of this, in one writing, Nichiren acclaims several statesmen in ancient China who worked for the happiness of their subjects or compatriots prior to Buddhism's transmission from India. He writes: "Though these men lived before the introduction of Buddhism, they helped the people as emissaries of Shakyamuni Buddha, the lord of teachings . . . [T]he wisdom of such men contained at heart the wisdom of Buddhism" ("The Kalpa of Decrease," WND-1, 1121–22). Thus the Daishonin indicates that wisdom that guides people to happiness is identical to the wisdom of Buddhism.

To conduct shakubuku is to carry out the Buddha's practice of compassion—to remove suffering and impart joy. Above all, shakubuku is founded on a profound and embracing respect for all people. Consequently, our efforts in this sphere will not be successful unless we have deep respect for those we seek to guide toward the correct teaching, as all of us who have earnestly undertaken this challenge keenly recognize.

In view of this, shakubuku is definitely not motivated by "a contentious heart" or other aggressive, negative emotions. Because of this, it is not in any way exclusivist or self-righteous. The heart of shakubuku is compassion; it is also the spirit to refute error because of the suffering it causes—a spirit that transforms our compassion into the courage to fight against that which is wrong.

When there is serious confusion regarding the Buddhist teachings in which people place their faith, with mistaken beliefs and tenets imperiling the spiritual welfare of society, nothing could be farther from Buddhist compassion than not taking action to rectify the situation. The schools that spread such confusion have forgotten Buddhism's original spirit of working for the people's welfare and helping them gain enlightenment. If their errors were allowed to go unchallenged, it would only plunge people into even greater suffering. Such permissiveness may seem like moderation and tolerance—free of any hint of "a contentious heart"—but remaining passive when faced with error is actually an extremely grave offense.

"If One Befriends Another Person But Lacks the Mercy To Correct Him, One Is in Fact His Enemy"

Question: When you berate the followers of the Nembutsu and Zen schools and arouse their enmity, what merit does that bring?

Answer: The Nirvana Sutra says: "If even a good monk sees someone destroying the teaching and disregards him, failing to reproach him, to oust him, or to punish him for his offense, then you should realize that that monk is betraying the Buddha's teaching. But if he ousts the destroyer of the Law, reproaches him, or punishes him, then he is my disciple and a true voice-hearer."

[The Great Teacher of China] Chang-an comments on this as follows: "One who destroys or brings confusion to the Buddha's teachings is betraying them. If one befriends another person but lacks the mercy to correct him, one is in fact his enemy. But one who reprimands and corrects an offender is a voice-hearer who defends the Buddha's teachings, a true disciple of the Buddha. One who rids the offender of evil is acting as his parent. Those who reproach offenders are disciples of the Buddha.

But those who do not oust offenders are betraying the Buddha's teachings." (WND-1, 286)

In "The Opening of the Eyes," Nichiren employs the above exchange to underline the enormous importance of the shakubuku spirit in addressing errors in the realm of Buddhism.

This section begins with the question: "When you berate the followers of the Nembutsu and Zen schools and arouse their enmity, what merit does that bring?" In response, the Daishonin addresses the issue by citing a Nirvana Sutra passage in which Shakyamuni declares that any of his disciples who do not engage in a rigorous struggle to reproach, oust or punish those who destroy the correct teaching are enemies of Buddhism, whereas those who undertake this struggle are his true disciples and true voice-hearers who defend the Law. The Daishonin then further cites a passage from *On the Nirvana Sutra* by Chang-an—a disciple of T'ien-t'ai—which states that whoever acts as a false friend and lacks the compassion to correct those who destroy the Buddha's teachings is in fact an enemy.

These passages make it clear that shakubuku is an act of compassion. True compassion means to awaken people from the darkness of ignorance or illusion that destroys their lives and to fundamentally free them from suffering.

Shakubuku is an irrepressible action that arises from faith and compassion. In "The Opening of the Eyes," Nichiren writes: "If someone is about to kill your father and mother, shouldn't you try to warn them? If a bad son who is insane with drink is threatening to kill his father and mother, shouldn't you try to stop him? If some evil person is about to set fire to the temples and pagodas, shouldn't you try to stop him? If your only child is gravely ill, shouldn't you try to cure him or her with moxibustion treatment?" (WND-1, 287).

Hypocrisy is the exact opposite of compassion—especially, the hypocrisy of knowing when wrong is being committed in the realm of Buddhism but doing nothing to address it. If such hypocrisy prevails, lies and pretense will become the norm and no one will speak the truth. This will ultimately lead to the spiritual and moral decay of society. Without a sound spiritual underpinning like that provided by a humanistic religion, the fabric of society will crumble. If erroneous teachings spread to where they enslave and exploit people, they will exert a harmful and poisonous effect on people's hearts and minds. That is why the Daishonin stresses the importance of steadfastly and resolutely battling the "enemies of the Lotus Sutra." He writes: "Even those with profound faith do not reproach the enemies of the Lotus Sutra. However great the good causes one may make, or even if one reads and copies the entirety of the Lotus Sutra a thousand or ten thousand times, or attains the way of perceiving three thousand realms in a single moment of life, if one fails to denounce the enemies of the Lotus Sutra, it will be impossible to attain the way" ("Encouragement to a Sick Person," WND-1, 78).

Shakubuku, an act of supreme compassion, is a lion's roar directed toward the goal of reviving the goodness in people's hearts and bringing dynamic vitality and creativity to society for the benefit of all. It is a spiritual struggle of the loftiest dimension, one that seeks to conquer devilish functions, break through darkness and delusion and actualize true, lasting happiness for humankind. And it is powered by a fighting spirit that resembles that of a fearless lion king.

This struggle enables us to forge an indestructible, diamond-like state of life. Citing the Nirvana Sutra, the Daishonin notes that obtaining a "diamond-like body"[13] (WND-1, 285) is the benefit of practicing shakubuku.

By embarking on this compassionate struggle, we can rid our own lives of the rust of inertia, carelessness and cowardice—the dull patina that prevents our true brilliance from shining forth. Those who tap the depths of their wisdom and persevere in their efforts to lead even one person to happiness can break through the binding chains of all kinds of preconceived ideas and prejudices and defeat the alienating ignorance of disbelief and disrespect. Those who battle negativity and delusions can cleanse and polish their lives with a purifying stream that washes away spiritual decay; they can develop an infinitely vast and expansive state of life that desires the happiness of all humanity. Moreover, those who remain committed to this cause can create the most wonderful and everlasting memories of their lives in this human world.

The glory of a life dedicated to kosen-rufu is found in the midst of tireless struggle. The indestructible, diamond-like state of being we attain through winning resolutely in every challenge for kosen-rufu not only adorns our lives in this present existence but will shine on for all eternity.

The Sovereign, Teacher and Parent of the Buddhism of Sowing of the Latter Day of the Law, Part 1

Spreading the Fragrant Breeze of Compassion in a Defiled Age

From this chapter, we will finally begin an in-depth discussion of the three virtues—sovereign, teacher and parent—in terms of the Buddhism of sowing of the Latter Day of the Law—the subject that occupies the conclusion of "The Opening of the Eyes."

With the passage, "I, Nichiren, am sovereign, teacher, and father and mother to all the people of Japan" (WND-1, 287), the Daishonin declares that it is he who possesses all three virtues—sovereign, teacher and parent of the Latter Day. This passage also forms the basis for "The Opening of the Eyes" being designated as the writing that clarifies the object of devotion in terms of the Person.

While this is a passage of manifold significance, let's focus on the fact that compassionate action constitutes the essence of these three virtues.

Compassion is the heart of Buddhism and the essence of the Lotus Sutra. Lack of compassion totally contradicts the spirit of Buddhism.

In an early Buddhist scripture, the *Sutta-nipata*, Shakyamuni, the founder of Buddhism, explains that "loving-kindness"[1]—namely, compassion—is proof of enlightenment. He says that one who is "skillful in respect of the [ultimate] good" and has "attained the peaceful state"[2]—the enlightened state of a Buddha—evinces the following benevolent sentiments: "Let all [living beings] indeed be happy (and) secure; let them be happy-minded . . . Whichever are seen or unseen, whichever live far or near, whether they already exist or are going to be, let all [living beings] be happy-minded . . . Just as a mother would protect with her life her own son, her only son, so one should cultivate an unbounded mind [of loving-kindness] towards all beings, and loving-kindness towards all the world."[3]

In other words, those who have attained true enlightenment feel infinite compassion toward all living beings and the entire world.

Without such a spirit, one cannot be called genuinely enlightened. True enlightenment is the wellspring of inexhaustible compassion, and compassion is the proof of true enlightenment.

Nichiren took on the challenge of spreading this spirit of compassion in the Latter Day of the Law, a defiled age when people are indifferent to others' suffering and succumb easily into the life state of anger, constantly quarreling and fighting among themselves and growing ever more arrogant. The votary of the Lotus Sutra assumes the noble role of a courageous spiritual pioneer who, undaunted by adversity, spreads the fragrant breeze of compassion in this dark and troubled age.

Infinite Encouragement and Strict Refutation

If we examine the "Treasure Tower" chapter of the Lotus Sutra, we find Shakyamuni Buddha, Many Treasures Buddha, and the Buddhas of the ten directions who are emanations of Shakyamuni Buddha gathering together. And why? As the sutra itself says, "Each . . . has come to this place on purpose to make certain the Law will long endure." Shakyamuni, Many Treasures, and the other Buddhas intend to insure the future propagation of the Lotus Sutra so that it can be made available to all the children of the Buddha in times to come. We may surmise from this that their concern and compassion are even greater than those of a father and mother who see their only child inflicted with great suffering. [The Nembutsu priest] Honen, however, shows not the least concern about their compassion, but would tightly shut the gates to the Lotus Sutra in the Latter Day of the Law so that no one would have access to it. Like a person who tricks a demented child into throwing away a treasure, he tries to induce people to discard the Lotus Sutra, a shameless thing to do indeed!

If someone is about to kill your father and mother, shouldn't you try to warn them? If a bad son who is insane with drink is threatening to kill his father and mother, shouldn't you try to stop him? If some evil person is about to set fire to the temples and pagodas, shouldn't you try to stop him? If your only child is gravely ill, shouldn't you try to cure him or her with moxibustion treatment? To fail to do so is to act like those people who see but do not try to put a stop to the Zen and Nembutsu followers in Japan. [As Chang-an says,] "If one befriends another person but lacks the mercy to correct him, one is in fact his enemy."

I, Nichiren, am sovereign, teacher, and father and mother to all the people of Japan. But the men of the Tendai school [who do not refute misleading teachings] are all great enemies of the people. [As Chang-an has noted,] "One who rids the offender of evil is acting as his parent." (WND-1, 286–87)

Compassion is the hallmark of all Buddhas. Awakened to the truth that the ultimate Law of the universe exists within their own lives, Buddhas are aware that this Law also resides in the lives of all others.

All people are inherently entities of this fundamental Law, and as such have the potential to manifest the life state of Buddhahood. When deluded by ignorance, however, people fail to realize this. They are swayed by various phenomena and suffer as a result.

Recognizing that all human beings are entities of the Mystic Law and individuals endowed with the potential for Buddhahood, Buddhas feel loving-kindness toward them similar to that of a mother toward her child. People's suffering derives from their ignorance of the dignity of their own lives. Buddhas grieve when they see such suffering and overflow with a profound empathy that causes them to feel others' pain and anguish as if it were their own.

Tears of grief, smiles, sadness, joy—Buddhas share all of these. They place absolute trust in people and believe in their potential. They love them and have boundless affection for them. Their compassion is entirely free of discrimination and extends to all. Accordingly, it is as broad and vast as the universe. As we see in the quote I cited earlier

from the *Sutta-nipata,* this benevolent goodwill of Buddhas is not only directed toward everyone they encounter in their immediate environment but also to all imaginable people unseen and unknown—encompassing the whole of humankind and all sentient and insentient beings. This is the reality of the three thousand realms in a single moment of life demonstrated by Buddhas.

In short, Buddhas are not simply enlightened to their own inherent power. They recognize the potential of all beings and continually devote their energies to helping them actualize that potential. "Unlock your true humanity! Awaken to your own potential!"—this is the fervent wish of Buddhas. Their compassionate encouragement is an unending paean to the human being and a reverent salute to life itself.

This is also why Buddhas seek to vanquish ignorance and fundamental darkness, and why they sternly denounce the arrogance of those who denigrate others and do not believe in life's potential. All Buddhas' benevolent and courageous actions for others are infused with compassion and empathy; they are dedicated to relieving suffering and imparting joy, as well as encouraging positive growth and rebuking error and wrongdoing.

The Three Virtues as Expounded in the Lotus Sutra

The Lotus Sutra, which is the essence of Shakyamuni's Buddhism, is a teaching that elucidates the supreme compassion of the

Buddha who strives to lead all people to enlightenment. Nichiren refers to the Lotus Sutra as the "ultimate principle of compassion" ("On Reciting the Daimoku of the Lotus Sutra," WND-2, 235).[4] In the Lotus Sutra, this ultimate compassion of the Buddha is expounded as the three virtues—sovereign, teacher and parent.

"Simile and Parable," the 3rd chapter, which appears in the theoretical teaching (first half) of the Lotus Sutra contains the well-known passage: "There is no safety in the threefold world; / it is like a burning house" (LSOC, 105). This actual world in which we dwell is like a burning house; it is filled with suffering, pains and trials. The sutra explains that the Buddha acts tirelessly to save the inhabitants of this perilous realm, and the section that follows the above quote contains passages that clearly correlate with the three virtues. "Now this threefold world/ is all my domain" (LSOC, 105) represents the virtue of sovereign; "The living beings in it / are all my children" (LSOC, 106) indicates the virtue of parent; and "I am the only person / who can rescue and protect others" (LSOC, 106) points to the virtue of teacher.

"Life Span," the 16th chapter, which appears in the essential teaching (latter half) of the Lotus Sutra, meanwhile, reveals that Shakyamuni actually attained enlightenment in the remote past[5] and has been continuously in the world taking compassionate action to help all people become Buddhas. In a compilation of Nichiren's teachings on the Lotus Sutra, *The Record of the Orally Transmitted Teachings,* passages are cited from the *jigage* verse section[6] of the "Life Span" chapter that indicate the three virtues embodied by the Shakyamuni of original attainment in the remote past (see

OTT, 137). Here, "This, my land, remains safe and tranquil" (LSOC, 272) corresponds to the virtue of sovereign; "Constantly I have preached the Law, teaching [and] converting" (LSOC, 270) corresponds to the virtue of teacher; and "I am the father of this world" (LSOC, 273) corresponds the virtue of parent.

As we can see, the meaning of the three virtues is roughly the same in both the theoretical and essential teachings of the Lotus Sutra. Now, let's examine the key points relating to these passages.

Virtue of Sovereign

"Now this threefold world / is all my domain." (LSOC, 105)

"This, my land, remains safe and tranquil." (LSOC, 272)

Virtue of Parent

"The living beings in it [this threefold world] / are all my children." (LSOC, 106)

"I am the father of this world." (LSOC, 273)

Virtue of Teacher

"I am the only person / who can rescue and protect others." (LSOC, 106)

"Constantly I have preached the Law, teaching [and] converting." (LSOC, 270)

In the passages relating to the virtue of sovereign, the Buddha says that the actual world of suffering is his domain and that it is inherently a safe and tranquil Buddha land. This can be read as expressing the Buddha's resolve to take personal responsibility for realizing and protecting the peace and security of the land and the people living in it.

In the passages referring to the virtue of parent, the Buddha states that living beings are his children. This expresses, as I mentioned earlier, the Buddha's loving compassion for all living beings and his profound empathy for their sufferings.

In the passages corresponding to the virtue of teacher, the Buddha speaks of his actual efforts to teach people about the Law, lead them to the Buddha way, free them from suffering and protect them from harm. Expounding the Law and guiding people to enlightenment is the key to genuine salvation in Buddhism.

The Practice of the Votary of the Lotus Sutra Embodies the Three Virtues

The passage "I, Nichiren, am sovereign, teacher, and father and mother to all the people of Japan" (WND-1, 287) clarifies that the Daishonin's practice as the votary of the Lotus Sutra embodies the three virtues as an expression of the compassion of the Buddha expounded in the Lotus Sutra.

In terms of Nichiren's practice, his efforts to establish the correct teaching in order to bring peace and security to the land correspond to the virtue of sovereign. He may also be said to possess this virtue, which is characterized by a commitment to protect and save all humankind, because of his far-reaching vision for the widespread propagation of the Mystic Law throughout the entire world and for the westward transmission of Buddhism.[7]

Next is the virtue of parent. The sufferings of the Latter Day arise from the fundamental evil of slander of the Law. Therefore, Nichiren's pursuit of the *shakubuku* method of propagation—strict refutation of slander of the Law—is a struggle to empathize with and to relieve people's sufferings, and so corresponds to the virtue of parent. As I discussed in the last chapter, shakubuku is not motivated by "a contentious heart" but by a fighting spirit to oppose evil. Accordingly, shakubuku is not a manifestation of the world of anger—or "the realm of the asuras," as Nichiren terms it—but of the world of bodhisattva, characterized by the compassionate desire to free people from suffering.

Lastly, the virtue of teacher derives from the fact that Nichiren revealed and left for all future humankind the great Law of Nam-myoho-renge-kyo, which opens the door to universal enlightenment. If shakubuku—refuting slander of the Law—is a struggle to relieve people's suffering, then propagating Nam-myoho-renge-kyo is a struggle to impart joy.

In this way, Nichiren's actions as the votary of the Lotus Sutra are themselves compassionate actions embodying the three virtues.

All People Can Practice Compassion

It is vital to note that Nichiren Daishonin did not simply manifest these three compassionate virtues and work to save all living beings in the evil age of the Latter Day, he also established shakubuku and chanting

Nam-myoho-renge-kyo as a concrete practice so that all people could lead lives with compassion for others. In other words, he not only lived a compassionate life himself but also showed the way for all people to do so. We may interpret this as being the true reason Nichiren is regarded as the Buddha of the Latter Day of the Law.

President Toda explained the significance of Nichiren's appearance in the world as follows: "As human beings, it's normal that we find it difficult to embark on a life of conscious compassion. That's where the importance of Nichiren's appearance comes in. The Latter Day of the Law is an age when evil people abound and when acts of compassion are desperately needed. The reality, however, is that the world is lacking in compassion to the extreme. Even if the inherent essence of our lives is compassion, we cannot become truly happy as human beings unless we cultivate the wisdom of the Buddha. Cultivating the wisdom of the Buddha and living with true compassion is the key to all happiness. This wisdom is gained only through faith. We need to bear this deeply in mind."[8]

It is far from easy for ordinary people of the Latter Day to live with compassion. But unless a way can be established for them to do so, the original purpose of Buddhism will never be accomplished. In this case, leading people to enlightenment in this polluted age could only be achieved by a Buddha of outstanding compassion appearing from time to time to save people weary from suffering. With this kind of sporadic salvation, however, subsequent generations after the Buddha's passing would gradually forget the benefit of the Buddha's teaching and succumb once more to the malaise from which they previously suffered. This means that another Buddha would have to appear and once more help guide people to enlightenment. An alternative scenario is that people might put their faith in an imagined Buddha dwelling in some pure land far removed from this world and aspire to be reborn there. If such cycles continue repeatedly, it will be impossible to transform the real world of the Latter Day of the Law.

The fundamental error here is thinking that only a special Buddha can serve as a compassionate liberator of human suffering. To accept this belief shows a failure to grasp the true significance of Shakyamuni Buddha entrusting the Bodhisattvas of the Earth with the mission of widespread propagation—kosen-rufu—in the Latter Day of the Law. If the idea of a fixed relationship between an absolute savior and practitioners who need saving takes hold, then it will be impossible to create a world of mutual compassion, which is the goal of Buddhism. Essential to truly freeing people from suffering in this cold, cruel Latter Day is the appearance of a votary of the Lotus Sutra who inherits the three virtues of the Buddha, along with countless similar votaries—agents and practitioners of compassion—who unite their efforts around the central votary.

In "The Opening of the Eyes," immediately before declaring that he possesses the virtues of sovereign, teacher and parent in the Latter Day of the Law, Nichiren indicates that shakubuku is the correct method of propagation in a country like Japan that is filled with people of perverse views who slander the Law,[9] and he enjoins his followers to pursue the same course of practice as he. His true intent here is to teach that, by dedicating ourselves to the practice of shakubuku, each of us can come to embody compassion and then spread that compassion throughout the world. Nichiren indicates that ordinary people, through the function of compassion, can form positive connections with others.

Certainly, it's difficult for us ordinary people to readily bring forth compassion, but we can summon courage instead. When we courageously practice and spread the Law of compassion, those very efforts are equivalent to our having taken compassionate action. And such efforts will naturally lead to the development of infinite, positive human relationships based on compassion, spreading from one person to another. Our challenge lies in infusing the realm of fundamental darkness with the warm, life-affirming current of compassion and working dauntlessly to create a world where people have compassion for one another based on the Buddhist teaching of dependent origination—the principle of the interconnection of all things. By doing so, we carry on the legacy of Buddhism that originates from Shakyamuni and can further build on it into the future.

Safeguarding the World of Compassion of the Lotus Sutra

The Latter Day of the Law is characterized by the appearance of evil people who function to undermine this compassionate world of the Lotus Sutra. These evil people include not only those who actively seek to destroy Buddhism but also individuals who, though they ought to protect and perpetuate the correct teaching of the Lotus Sutra, stand idly by and allow such destruction to take place. The presence of the second group is the root cause of the ills of the Latter Day of the Law. Such irresponsible, passive bystanders create a climate where destroyers of the Law can flourish. Since it should be their mission to safeguard the correct teaching, the offense of these people is actually greater than that of those who actively seek to destroy the Law.

Hence, in the closing section of "The Opening of the Eyes," immediately after his statement on the three virtues, the Daishonin denounces the Japanese Tendai school,[10] saying, "The men of the Tendai school [who do not refute misleading teachings] are all great enemies of the people" (WND-1, 287). Because their school was originally based on the Lotus Sutra, they ought to have spread that sutra's message and ideals for the welfare and happiness of the people and stood up to refute the erroneous teachings of the Nembutsu priest Honen and others. Instead, they chose to curry favor with those in positions of status and authority. Nichiren reprimands such followers of the Tendai school, calling them "great enemies" of all the people of Japan. This refutation lies at the heart of Nichiren's religious revolution.

In modern times, the Nichiren Shoshu priesthood should have risen into action to defend Nichiren Buddhism when it was threatened by the militarist authorities during World War II. Instead, they acquiesced to the forces of slander and even tried to oust and disassociate itself from our first Soka Gakkai president, Tsunesaburo Makiguchi, who had stood up to protect the correct teaching. Nichiren Shoshu priests are the spiritual descendants of the "great enemies" of Nichiren's time and deserve to be condemned as such. Those passive, self-serving bystanders gave birth to the corrupt and erroneous priesthood of Nichiren Shoshu that is today trying to destroy kosen-rufu.

By rigorously denouncing slander of the Law, a genuine revolution in the realm of Buddhism can be achieved. If we undertake such a struggle, we are sure to be attacked and maligned by those seeking to block change. Our first and second presidents, Tsunesaburo Makiguchi and Josei Toda, however, regarded it as an honor to be criticized by such people.

As our eternal mentors, President Makiguchi and President Toda forever hold high the banner of Soka. Today, as we have just celebrated the Soka Gakkai's seventy-fifth anniversary [2005], countless noble ordinary people called forth by these great leaders of the Bodhisattvas of the Earth are illuminating the world with the brilliant light of compassion.

We who embrace Nichiren Buddhism are dedicated to igniting hope in the hearts of people mired in the depths of suffering and to constructing a peaceful society in which all people—most especially, mothers and children—can live in peace and security. Today, our movement has grown into a broad and deep river that flows throughout the world. I am confident that President Makiguchi and President Toda would rejoice at the valiant, compassionate actions of all our devoted members. And I have no doubt that Nichiren, too, would praise the unceasing acts of compassion our intrepid Bodhisattvas of the Earth perform daily in every land.

The Soka Gakkai organization embodies the Buddha's compassion. Taking pride in the fact that it is the legitimate heir to the virtues of sovereign, teacher and parent—with the mission to transform the world's destiny in these increasingly dark times—let us construct a century of Soka with our sights set on the Soka Gakkai's one hundredth anniversary in the year 2030.

18

The Sovereign, Teacher and Parent of the Buddhism of Sowing of the Latter Day of the Law, Part 2

I, Nichiren, am sovereign, teacher, and father and mother to all the people of Japan. (WND-1, 287)

In the previous chapter, we discussed the passage above—which forms the conclusion reached by Nichiren Daishonin in "The Opening of the Eyes"—and delved into the profound meaning of the three virtues—sovereign, teacher and parent—of the Buddhism of sowing of the Latter Day of the Law from the perspective of compassion. The main point of that discussion was that the three virtues reside in the compassionate action of the votary of the Lotus Sutra in the Latter Day.

In other words, the "virtue of parent" can be found in the efforts of the votary who, having empathy for people's suffering and cherishing their limitless potential, actively strives to propagate the Mystic Law while enduring intense opposition and persecution. The "virtue of teacher" can be found in the votary's struggle to bring an end to people's

slander of the Law arising from ignorance, to awaken them to faith in the Mystic Law and guide them toward enlightenment by revealing and propagating Nam-myoho-renge-kyo. Finally, the "virtue of sovereign" can be found in the votary's deep sense of responsibility for the peace and security of all people demonstrated in his wish for the widespread propagation of the Law throughout the entire world—that is, for worldwide kosen-rufu—and the establishment of the correct teaching for the peace of the land.

Nichiren's treatise "On Repaying Debts of Gratitude" contains a well-known passage that clearly expresses the three virtues embodied by the votary of the Lotus Sutra in the Latter Day—the three virtues embodied by Nichiren: "If Nichiren's compassion is truly great and encompassing, Nam-myoho-renge-kyo will spread for ten thousand years and more, for all eternity, for it has the beneficial power to open the blind eyes of every living being in the country of Japan, and it blocks off the road that leads to the hell of incessant suffering" (WND-1, 736).

To save the people of Japan in his day, who had succumbed to the grave illness of slander arising from ignorance, Nichiren propagated Nam-myoho-renge-kyo, the ultimate Law that has the power to awaken and bring forth the inherent Buddha nature of all humankind.

Whether it be in revealing the ultimate Law or in waging a selfless struggle to propagate it, Nichiren's dedicated efforts were all an expression of his "great and encompassing compassion" aimed at freeing people of the Latter Day from suffering on the most fundamental level.

"Great and encompassing compassion" corresponds to the "virtue of parent." "Opening the blind eyes of all living beings"—blind in terms of their slander of the Law arising from ignorance—corresponds to the "virtue of teacher." And "blocking off the road that leads to the hell of incessant suffering"—in other words, protecting not only the people of Japan of his day but all humankind throughout the Latter Day by propagating Nam-myoho-renge-kyo and cultivating people's Buddha nature—corresponds to the "virtue of sovereign."

Thus, the virtues of sovereign, teacher and parent embodied by Nichiren may be considered virtues endowed in the struggle to reveal and propagate Nam-myoho-renge-kyo as the seed of Buddhahood that activates the Buddha nature in the lives of all human beings. These are also referred to as the three virtues of the Buddhism of sowing.

In that sense, the passages in "The Opening of the Eyes" and "On Repaying Debts of Gratitude" where Nichiren declares that he possesses the three virtues may be viewed as referring to the establishment of the Buddhism

of sowing, which opens the path to enlightenment for all people into the eternal future of the Latter Day of the Law.

The Transformative Power of the Buddhism of Sowing

Taking up the challenge of leading humanity to enlightenment in the defiled age of the Latter Day of the Law, Nichiren urged people to cultivate their inherent Buddha nature. By doing so, he opened the way to fundamentally transforming the times and people's lives.

All suffering ultimately stems from not being aware of the Law or from a failure to believe in it even after encountering it—conditions that arise from fundamental ignorance and delusion. The enlightenment of the Buddha transforms this ignorance and delusion into wisdom. This does not mean eradicating earthly desires but rather conquering, by means of faith, the ignorance or fundamental darkness that is the source of earthly desires. As a result, wisdom shines forth and an inner transformation to the life state of Buddhahood is realized. This potential to instantly transform ignorance into wisdom, just like the Buddha, is our Buddha nature. All life inherently possesses this nature.

Nichiren named the Buddha nature inherent in all life Nam-myoho-renge-kyo. And he established the means whereby all people can attain Buddhahood in this lifetime through believing in and chanting Nam-myoho-renge-kyo—a process whereby we can change darkness into light, earthly desires into enlightenment, and achieve an unsurpassed state of life overflowing with benefit. That is the foundation of Nichiren Buddhism.

After declaring the establishment of his teaching, Nichiren made the practice of chanting Nam-myoho-renge-kyo the basis for the enlightenment of people in the Latter Day and gave his life to pursuing the great path of propagating the Mystic Law of Nam-myoho-renge-kyo.

Something that we must not overlook is that manifesting the world of Buddhahood in our lives entails an inner struggle to defeat, by means of faith, our fundamental ignorance of Buddhahood's universality. That is why Nichiren, in emphasizing the importance of chanting Nam-myoho-renge-kyo, also strictly warns that if we think Nam-myoho-renge-kyo exists outside ourselves, we are not embracing the Mystic Law (see "On Attaining Buddhahood in This Lifetime," WND-1, 3).

This inner transformation from ignorance to faith in the depths of our lives is the very heart of Nichiren Buddhism. As we develop unshakable conviction in the Mystic Law, our inherent Buddha nature is activated and the life state of the Buddha powerfully manifests. On the other hand, when we lack confidence and give in to disbelief, our Buddha nature falls dormant, and our lives, at that moment, become shrouded in darkness.

"Sowing the seed of Buddhahood" is a figurative expression for activating the Buddha nature. In "The Essentials for Attaining Buddhahood," Nichiren explains this very simply, saying, "The Lotus Sutra is like the seed, the Buddha like the sower, and the people like the field" (WND-1, 748). After the seed has been planted by the sower, people can then bring forth great fruit in the field of their heart— they themselves gain the fruit of Buddhahood.

It is wrong, however, to interpret this to mean that the seed of Buddhahood does not exist in people's lives unless it is first planted there by the Buddha. The truth is that the Buddha nature already and eternally exists in people's lives. But since it is activated and nurtured into the life state of Buddhahood through the teaching of the Buddha, it seems as if the seed of Buddhahood is planted by the Buddha. Accordingly, "the seed of Buddhahood" in some cases refers to the Buddha nature inherent in people's lives, and in others indicates the teaching of the Buddha, which has the power to activate the Buddha nature.

Nichiren cites the Lotus Sutra passage, "The seeds of Buddhahood sprout as a result of conditions, and for this reason they [the Buddhas] preach the single vehicle" ("The Properties of Rice," WND-1, 1117; see LSOC, 75). The lives of all people are originally endowed with the Buddha nature—the "cause" for attaining Buddhahood. The condition that activates the Buddha nature is the "single vehicle"—the Lotus Sutra, or, in the Latter Day of the Law, Nam-myoho-renge-kyo.

Opening the Way to the Enlightenment of All People in the Latter Day

What "sowing the seeds of Buddhahood" actually means is to teach people to embrace faith in the Mystic Law, conquering ignorance and illuminating their lives with the light of wisdom. The profound inner transformation that results in the depths of people's lives activates their Buddha nature, bringing forth their potential for Buddhahood from within.

In "On Attaining Buddhahood in This Lifetime," Nichiren writes: "If the minds of living beings are impure, their land is also impure, but if their minds are pure, so is their land. There are not two lands, pure or impure in themselves. The difference lies solely in the good or evil of our minds. It is the same with a Buddha and an ordinary being. When deluded, one is called an ordinary being, but when enlightened, one is called a Buddha" (WND-1, 4).

When the seeds of Buddhahood are planted in this way, people's hearts can be instantly transformed from delusion to enlightenment. To illustrate, as long as heavy clouds block the sunlight, the land will be dark, but once the clouds clear and the sun shines through, the land will be instantly illuminated. The land itself has not changed. Rather, a place that had been submerged in deep darkness is transformed into a bright land of hope.

As Nichiren indicates when he speaks of "a lantern lighting up a place that has been dark for a hundred, a thousand, or ten thousand years" ("The One Essential Phrase," WND-1, 923), even a cave that has been pitch dark for incalculable eons can be suddenly illuminated. This is analogous to the power of sowing the seeds of Buddhahood of the Mystic Law.

When we light a lamp amid the darkness of ignorance, the darkness immediately disappears. It is instantly transformed. This is Nichiren Buddhism—the Buddhism of sowing. Nichiren is the "lord of teachings," the Buddha who chants Nam-myoho-renge-kyo, the core doctrine of this Buddhism. We therefore regard him as possessing the three virtues of the Buddhism of sowing in the Latter Day—in other words, we regard him as the Buddha of the Latter Day of the Law. The Buddhism of sowing is the sole teaching that enables ordinary people of the Latter Day to attain Buddhahood.

The Eternity and Universality of the Three Virtues of the Buddhism of Sowing

If Nichiren's compassion is truly great and encompassing, Nam-myoho-renge-kyo will spread for ten thousand years and more, for all eternity, for it has the beneficial power to open the blind eyes of every living being in the country of Japan, and it blocks off the road that leads to the hell of incessant suffering. ("On Repaying Debts of Gratitude," WND-1, 736)

The passage above from "On Repaying Debts of Gratitude," which I also cited earlier, suggests that the three virtues embodied by Nichiren Daishonin will shine on in the eternal transmission of Nam-myoho-renge-kyo.

The eternity of the three virtues derives from the universality of Nam-myoho-renge-kyo, but the universality of the Law alone does not assure its eternal perpetuation. Another indispensable element is people who strive to propagate the Law. Through people's tenacious, committed efforts, the universality of the Law shines and the Law itself spreads. This is as Nichiren indicates when he says: "The Law does not spread by itself; because people propagate it, both the people and the Law are worthy of respect" (GZ, 856).

Nichiren's conduct naturally shines with the three virtues because he waged a great struggle, based on his profound compassion for all humankind, to ensure that the Law would be transmitted on into the eternal future.

In the age after Nichiren's passing, the teaching that "both the people and the Law are worthy of respect" is given true meaning when disciples propagate the Law with the spirit of faith of "not begrudging one's life" exactly as Nichiren instructs. When disciples in a defiled age devote themselves to spreading the Law with the spirit of the oneness of mentor and disciple, Nichiren's three virtues will also shine forth in their lives. At the same time, Nam-myoho-renge-kyo, the Law that they spread, manifests its original power to activate the Buddha nature in others' lives. As a result, those who embrace faith in the Mystic Law gain the immeasurable benefit of attaining Buddhahood in this lifetime.

Further, when the river of kosen-rufu broadly expands in tandem with this propagation in which "both the people and the Law are worthy of respect," the power of Nam-myoho-renge-kyo that activates the Buddha nature will come to fill the land and spread throughout the world, becoming a force that can change the times. In other words, when the true Law of Nam-myoho-renge-kyo is combined with the dedicated efforts of practitioners who uphold steadfast faith, then Nichiren's virtues of sovereign, teacher and parent will bring rich benefit to flow throughout the ten thousand years and more of the Latter Day.

The Three Virtues of Nichiren Live On in the SGI

November 2005 marked the auspicious seventy-fifth anniversary of the Soka Gakkai's founding. From the time of the first president, Tsunesaburo Makiguchi, the Soka Gakkai has cherished deep conviction in the potential of the Buddhism of sowing, translating it into action and widely sharing it with others. This is nothing short of extraordinary, given that many of the established Buddhist schools in Japan have devolved into purveyors of "funeral Buddhism" and are largely preoccupied with abstract theory unrelated to daily life, a trend that only highlights their limitations and ineffectiveness.

President Makiguchi called on Soka Gakkai members to joyfully practice the correct teaching of Buddhism as a guide to daily life, as a principle of value creation. And he encouraged them to share it with others. He insightfully captured the essence of the Buddhism of sowing in these words: "The greatest [sense of purpose] is one where, while remaining conscious of our own selves, we strive to base our lives on faith in the Law of the universe that spans infinite time and space and to live in harmony with that Law. A life of the highest value that is guided by this supreme sense of purpose—in other words, a life of unsurpassed happiness—is so lived that one may bask in benefit that is shared by all humankind . . . It would be impossible to have this supreme sense of purpose without encountering the Lotus Sutra. That is perhaps what is meant by 'opening the eyes' in Buddhism."[1]

President Makiguchi asserted that the purpose of the Lotus Sutra teachings is for us to lead lives of the highest value creation by fusing our lives with the Mystic Law, the fundamental law of the universe.

The second Soka Gakkai president, Josei Toda, while in prison for his opposition to Japanese militarism during World War II, had an experience in which he realized that "the Buddha is life itself" and awakened to his identity as a Bodhisattva of the Earth. Advocating the idea of "human revolution," Mr. Toda stood up to wage a fierce struggle for kosen-rufu, vowing to expand the Soka Gakkai's membership to 750,000 households. President Toda also had a profound understanding of the essence of the Buddhism of sowing.

Nichiren Buddhism is a teaching of ultimate humanism. I am ever more convinced that this humanism—rooted in a belief in people's fundamental capacity for change, which lies at the heart of the Buddhism of sowing—is exactly the kind of humanism the world now needs. It is not going too far to say that the movement for peace, culture and education that we are promoting is an expression of this Buddhist humanism.

Some thirty years have passed since I began to earnestly engage the world's leading intellectuals in dialogue across civilizations. In these discussions, it has always been my aim to transcend differences of culture, religion and ideology and to focus instead on the basic common denominator of the human being. I have sought to deepen mutual understanding by expressing the humanistic ideals of Nichiren Buddhism through the concept of human revolution.

Everything depends on human beings. When people change for the better, thereby inspiring fresh hope, the world will also change for the better. That is the cornerstone of the Buddhism of sowing. I have been sharing this message through the philosophy of human revolution—which is based on the conviction that "a great human revolution in just a single individual will help achieve a change in the destiny of a nation and further, will enable a change in the destiny of all humankind."[2]

Many eminent scholars I have spoken with, such as the British historian Arnold J. Toynbee, the French art historian René Huyghe, and Austrian thinker and proponent of European unification Count Richard Coudenhove-Kalergi, have expressed deep concord with the idea of human revolution.

Also, through our discussions, Aurélio Peccei, co-founder of the global think tank Club of Rome and fighter in the Italian antifascist underground during World War II, came to rephrase what he had previously termed *humanistic revolution* as *human revolution*. He said that this revolution in the hearts and minds of human beings "alone can help us understand that . . . we must now shoulder, for the first time, long-term global responsibilities and strive to leave to coming generations a more livable planet and a more governable society."[3]

The age has arrived when people throughout the world yearn for Nichiren's humanistic Buddhist teachings. Indeed, the time has come for each of us to demonstrate the illuminating power of the three virtues of the Buddhism of sowing that can activate the Buddha nature of all humankind. Our network for kosen-rufu now encompasses the entire globe, and people everywhere will be watching our spirited efforts in this endeavor, as we set our sights toward our next brilliant milestone, the Soka Gakkai's one hundredth anniversary in 2030.

Enjoying Infinite Benefit Throughout Eternity—The Boundless Joy of a Life of Unceasing Challenge Based on the Mystic Law

What is the true benefit of faith? It is to advance on the path of indestructible happiness across the three existences—past, present and future. It is to construct in this lifetime the correct path of life that will guide us into eternity throughout the unending cycle of birth and death. This path is also the sure road to victory in the battle against negativity, both within and without. Unless we actively challenge negative forces, we cannot realize lives of eternal happiness. If we run away from this struggle, we will end up wandering forever in the darkness of ignorance and illusion. If we give in to fear, obstacles and hindrances will only increase. If we are cowardly, the workings of negative and destructive forces will eat away at our lives.

It is vital that our fighting spirit is fueled by strong faith—or confidence—in our practice of the Mystic Law so that we can break through ignorance and illusion and defeat obstacles and devilish functions. Not only is this the driving force for changing poison into medicine in our present existence but

also for radically changing the orientation of our lives across the three existences—from transmigration grounded in ignorance (fundamental darkness) to transmigration grounded in the Dharma nature (enlightenment). Consequently, when we firmly solidify our fighting spirit, the great hardships we encounter become a source of great joy.

This chapter will examine the final section of "The Opening of the Eyes." In the following passage, which constitutes the closing lines, Nichiren Daishonin reveals his state of infinite joy to his followers, who were themselves undergoing bitter obstacles: "For what I have done, I have been condemned to exile, but it is a small suffering to undergo in this present life and not one worth lamenting. In future lives I will enjoy immense happiness, a thought that gives me great joy" (WND-1, 287).

Nichiren indicates that the spiritual state he has attained through battling unrelenting persecutions as the votary of the Lotus Sutra is one of great joy transcending the bounds of life and death. In this passage, we can sense his fervent wish to convey this profound, everlasting benefit to his embattled followers in Kamakura.

We of the SGI have taken faith in Nichiren Buddhism in order to become happy and lead better lives, and we have learned about the importance of kosen-rufu as the way to realize happiness and peace for ourselves and others. Nichiren teaches that the ultimate goal of faith lies in attaining the same kind of immense and eternally indestructible happiness that he himself has secured through overcoming enormous hardships and obstacles.

Those Lacking a Desire for the Way Become Mired in the Sufferings of Birth and Death

I, Nichiren, am sovereign, teacher, and father and mother to all the people of Japan. But the men of the Tendai school [who do not refute misleading teachings] are all great enemies of the people. [As Chang-an has noted,] "One who rids the offender of evil is acting as his parent."

One who has not conceived a desire for the way can never free oneself from the sufferings of birth and death. Shakyamuni Buddha, the lord of teachings, was cursed by all the followers of non-Buddhist teachings and labeled as a man of great evil. The Great Teacher T'ien-t'ai was regarded with intense enmity by the three schools of the south and seven schools of the north, and Tokuitsu [of the Dharma Characteristics school] of Japan criticized him for using his three-inch tongue to try to destroy the five-foot body of the Buddha. The Great Teacher Dengyo was disparaged by the priests of Nara, who said, "Saicho has never been to the capital of T'ang China!" But all of these abuses were incurred because of the Lotus Sutra, and they are therefore no shame to the men who suffered them. To be praised by fools—that is the greatest shame. Now that I, Nichiren, have incurred the wrath of the authorities, the priests of the Tendai and True Word schools are no doubt delighted. They are strange and shameless men.

Shakyamuni Buddha appeared in the saha world, Kumarajiva journeyed to the Ch'in dynasty in China, and Dengyo likewise went to China [all for the sake of the Lotus Sutra]. Aryadeva and Aryasimha sacrificed their bodies. Bodhisattva Medicine King burned his arms as an offering, and Prince Jogu stripped off the skin on his hand [and copied the sutra on it]. Shakyamuni, when he was a bodhisattva, sold his flesh to make offerings, and another time, when he was a bodhisattva named the ascetic Aspiration for the Law, he used one of his bones as a pen [to write down the Buddha's teaching].

T'ien-t'ai has said that "the method chosen should be that which accords with the time." The propagation of the Buddhist teachings should follow the time. For what I have done, I have been condemned to exile, but it is a small suffering to undergo in this present life and not one worth lamenting. In future lives I will enjoy immense happiness, a thought that gives me great joy. (WND-1, 287)

Many people questioned and criticized Nichiren Daishonin's insistence on practicing *shakubuku*—the method of propagation through rebuking slander of the Law, a great affront to Buddhism—saying to the effect: "Doesn't shakubuku only lead to harsh persecution, without bringing any advantage?" In response, in "The Opening of the Eyes," Nichiren explains that compassion is what motivates the votary of the Lotus Sutra in his efforts to denounce evil and refute the error of slander, citing the words of the Great Teacher Chang-an of China, "One who rids the offender of evil is acting as his parent" (WND-1, 287). Based on this spirit of compassion, Nichiren declares himself to be the sovereign, teacher and parent of the Buddhism of sowing of the Latter Day of the Law.

Nichiren castigates the priests of the Tendai school of his day who, in stark contrast to his own lofty commitment to protect the Law, allowed slander of the Lotus Sutra to go unchallenged, even while supposedly basing themselves on that teaching. He pronounces that those who have not conceived a desire for the Buddha way cannot hope to free themselves from the sufferings of birth and death (see WND-1, 287). In other words, the priests of the Tendai school had forgotten the spirit to fight against evil. When the time came to take a stand, they failed to do so. Those who call themselves practitioners but have no seeking spirit toward Buddhism are nothing but imposters and frauds; they are pseudo-Buddhists.

The Tendai school, in whose halls of learning Nichiren had also studied in his youth, could be described as the leading Buddhist school in Japan at the time. Yet, no matter how magnificent its temples or how actively it engaged in scholarship, religious ceremonies or prayers, it could not be said to uphold the correct teaching of Buddhism if it failed to inspire ordinary people to embrace faith that would lead to genuine enlightenment.

Furthermore, even though they professed belief in the teachings of the Lotus Sutra—the underlying spirit of which is to enable all people to attain Buddhahood—the practitioners of the Tendai school not only failed to denounce misleading teachings that obstructed people from attaining enlightenment, but some among their ranks also joined in ridiculing and attacking Nichiren, who was doing his utmost to propagate the Lotus Sutra. This is why Nichiren sternly rebukes them, going so far as to call them "great enemies" of all the people of Japan. He declares that such individuals, bereft of any desire to seek the Buddha way, cannot possibly free themselves from the sufferings of birth and death.

In contrast, Nichiren is dedicated to actively refuting slander of the Law. He declares that the momentous persecutions he is now undergoing as a result of those efforts are merely a minor suffering to be borne in this life, and that he feels tremendous joy in the knowledge that he will experience immense happiness throughout countless future lifetimes.

When we come to savor this great joy in the depths of our beings, the four sufferings—birth, aging, sickness and death—are imbued with the fragrance of the four noble virtues—eternity, happiness, true self and purity.

Nichiren also writes: "I do not regret meeting with such great persecutions as the votary of the Lotus Sutra. However many times I were to repeat the cycle of birth and death, no life could be as fortunate as this. [If not for these troubles,] I might have remained in the three or four evil paths. But now, to my great joy, I am sure to sever the cycle of the sufferings of birth and death, and attain the fruit of Buddhahood" ("Earthly Desires Are Enlightenment," WND-1, 317).

Buddhahood: A Life State in Which Struggles Themselves Are a Source of Joy

Genuine, wholehearted struggles in the realm of faith abound with joy. Those who battle tenaciously against obstacles and negative functions can polish themselves and attain an expansive state of life. The Nirvana Sutra says that those who continually exert themselves for the sake of Buddhism can attain a "diamond-like body."

Josei Toda, the second Soka Gakkai president, once described the state of life of the Buddha of the Latter Day demonstrated by Nichiren Daishonin as follows: "Buddhahood is a state of absolute happiness. A state of being that at each moment is like a translucent ocean or a cloudless sky, utterly invincible and fearless—this is how I perceive the Daishonin's state of life during his exile on Sado."[1]

When we are in this state of absolute happiness, all struggles are pervaded with joy, just as the sutra indicates when it says, "living beings enjoy themselves at ease" (LSOC, 272). In fact, when we read the various letters Nichiren composed while on Sado, we find that even when faced with such extreme circumstances that he is prompted to say, "The chances are one in ten thousand that I will survive" ("On the Buddha's Prophecy," WND-1, 402), he repeatedly expresses his joy at having read the sutra with his life and having gained the fruit of Buddhahood.

He writes for example: "When our prayers for Buddhahood are answered and we are dwelling in the true land of Tranquil Light . . . we will experience the boundless joy of the Law" ("On Practicing the Buddha's Teachings," WND-1, 395); "What fortune is mine . . .! How delighted I am . . .!" ("On the Buddha's Prophecy," WND-1, 402); "It is indeed a matter of joy that my situation perfectly fits the sutra passage that reads, 'Again and again we will be banished.' How delightful! How gratifying!" ("The Joy of Fulfilling the Sutra Teachings," WND-2, 463); "We have cause to be joyful in both body and mind!" ("Reply to Sairen-bo," WND-1, 312); "There can be none who overflow with joy as we do" ("Reply to Sairen-bo," WND-1, 313); and "I feel immeasurable delight" ("The True Aspect of All Phenomena," WND-1, 386).

These joyous exclamations underscore just how great is the benefit of "having attained the fruit of Buddhahood, the eternally inherent three bodies [of the Buddha]"[2] ("Letter to Gijo-bo," WND-1, 390).

Buddhism teaches that life is eternal, extending throughout the three existences—past, present and future. While it may be possible to attain a certain degree of happiness and fulfillment in this life merely as a result of one's fortune or good circumstances, this alone is not enough to free one from the sufferings of birth and death. Only a religious philosophy that truly has the power to lead people to enlightenment can serve as the means for achieving peace and security eternally throughout the three existences.

Our lives are endowed with both ignorance (fundamental darkness) and the Dharma nature (enlightenment) from the beginningless past. When our lives are dominated by ignorance, we are destined to wander from darkness into darkness in lifetime after lifetime, ultimately falling into the three evil paths. The greatest significance of encountering Nichiren Buddhism in this lifetime is that it enables us to break free of the accursed chains of this negative cycle.

Chanting Nam-myoho-renge-kyo is an activity whereby, through faith, we align our lives with Myoho-renge-kyo—the essential nature of phenomena, or Dharma nature; it is a struggle to dispel the darkness of ignorance and illusion and bring forth our enlightened nature. Our efforts each day to chant Nam-myoho-renge-kyo and advance kosen-rufu solidify within us the fundamental struggle to defeat negative functions and imbue our lives with the Mystic Law; they are the means by which we forge and polish ourselves at the deepest level.

This is clear from the following well-known passage in Nichiren's writing "On Attaining Buddhahood in This Lifetime": "A mind now clouded by the illusions of the innate darkness of life is like a tarnished mirror, but when polished, it is sure to become like a clear mirror, reflecting the essential nature of phenomena and the true aspect of reality. Arouse deep faith, and diligently polish your mirror day and night. How should you polish it? Only by chanting Nam-myoho-renge-kyo" (WND-1, 4).

Any position, honor or wealth we may gain we will possess only during our present existence. But the unshakable state of life we develop through faith in the Mystic Law represents our greatest spiritual treasure and manifests the eternity of Myoho-renge-kyo. Through faith, we can establish an invincible state of being that enables us to fight on undaunted whenever or whatever the occasion.

Those who have forged such an imperturbable spirit to fight continually can live confidently, recognizing that birth and death are an innate part of life. This awareness that our lives are eternal over the three existences doesn't mean, however, we can somehow see, with telescopic vision, specific scenes or events from our past or future existences. Those who continue making efforts for the sake of Buddhism are awakened in the depths of their beings to the eternal and indestructible nature of their lives. Those who have valiantly carried out the struggle of compassion to refute error and proclaim the true in this lifetime know that they can rejoin that great struggle once more in their next existence.

There is absolutely no doubt that Soka Gakkai members who have devoted long years to the noble struggle for the happiness of their friends and fellow members and the peace and security of society have already solidified, deep inside, their inherently enlightened state of life. They apprehend the eternity of their lives intuitively through their own experience, even if they cannot explain it in words. That is, through chanting Nam-myoho-renge-kyo come what may, they gain a powerful sense of self-reliance, a resolute stand-alone spirit. With the Gohonzon as their anchor, they are undeterred in the face of problems and summon forth the courage and wisdom to challenge their situations. With a deep sense of appreciation toward all with whom they have a connection, they excel in imparting assurance and peace of mind. Calmly surmounting the sufferings of sickness, aging and death, and with a vow to be reborn in the beautiful realm of the Soka Gakkai in their next existence to work once more for kosen-rufu, they can conclude their lives of mission in this world with great joy. I do not think I am alone in seeing the Buddha's eternal spirit of unflagging challenge in our fellow members who bring their lives to such a magnificent close.

These courageous Bodhisattvas of the Earth, champions of kosen-rufu, have established a state of absolute freedom across past, present and future, based on the Mystic Law that permeates the life of the universe, as described by the passage, "Passing through the round of births and deaths, one makes one's way on the land of the Dharma nature, or enlightenment, that is inherent within oneself" (OTT, 52). This describes the truly eternal life span of the Buddha. The Japanese term for life span is *juryo*, which the Daishonin explains literally means "an overall reckoning" (OTT, 123)—in other words, an overall reckoning of the immeasurable benefit

that Buddhas possess. Ultimately, without an indomitable fighting spirit, it is not possible to gain this immense benefit of eternally indestructible joy.

The Soka Gakkai's brilliant seventy-five-year history has been one of enabling countless ordinary people to attain Buddhahood in their present form. This triumphant legacy will shine forever in the annals of Buddhism.

To Be Praised by Fools Is the Greatest Shame

At the end of "The Opening of the Eyes," Nichiren Daishonin, from the vantage of his towering state of life, reassures his followers that there is no reason to be troubled by the defamatory attacks of adherents of other schools. Those who practice the Lotus Sutra as it teaches will invariably be cursed and spoken ill of (see LSOC, 232). But this is in fact the highest possible honor. "To be praised by fools—that is the greatest shame" (WND-1, 287), declares Nichiren. Accordingly, there is no worse disgrace than being lauded by ignorant people who follow every whim of public opinion. This was a conviction shared by Tsunesaburo Makiguchi and Josei Toda, the Soka Gakkai's first and second presidents, and it is also one that I have embraced, as their successor and third president.

As Buddhists, what matters most is not how we are judged by society, but whether we are actively waging a struggle to spread the correct teaching of Buddhism in a manner that accords with the time.

In the passage from "The Opening of the Eyes" that we are studying, Nichiren explains the way various practitioners devoted themselves to Buddhism at different times: Shakyamuni, who began expounding the Law in this strife-filled saha world; Kumarajiva,[3] who traveled from Central Asia to China to translate Buddhist sutras; the Great Teacher Dengyo of Japan, who went to China in pursuit of the correct teaching; Bodhisattva Aryadeva and the Venerable Aryasimha, who sacrificed their lives to protect Buddhism; Bodhisattva Medicine King,[4] who burned his arms as an offering; Prince Jogu (also known as Prince Shotoku),[5] who stripped off the skin of his hand to copy the sutra on it; Shakyamuni in a previous existence as a bodhisattva,[6] who sold his own flesh to make offerings to the sutra; and Aspiration for the Law,[7] another incarnation of Shakyamuni, who used one of his bones as a pen to write down the teaching (see WND-1, 287).

While the form of practice in each of these cases is different, they are all actions that accord with the respective times in terms of selfless dedication to Buddhism. Their actions arise from a spiritual struggle committed to steadfastly protecting and perpetuating the correct teaching. When these Buddhist practitioners win in this spiritual struggle and act to spread the teaching in a way most suited to the times, boundless joy wells forth in their lives.

Therefore, Nichiren says that the persecutions he has encountered as a result of confronting the devilish nature inherent in life are no more than "a small suffering to undergo in this present life" (WND-1, 287). He also clarifies that the eternally indestructible happiness he has attained through practicing in accord with the time in the Latter Day of the Law is the great benefit he

has derived from his struggle as the votary of the Lotus Sutra.

A Movement "Opening the Eyes" of People Around the Globe

It is evident that Nichiren Daishonin was trying to convey to his followers, who were then facing various persecutions in Kamakura, the vast and towering state of life he had attained. By describing his own imperturbable spirit, he undoubtedly sought to encourage them from the depths of his being, reassuring them to the effect: "You don't have anything to worry about! We can become eternal victors. My disciples, follow my example!" Here we find the true meaning of "opening the eyes," through which Nichiren sought to free all of his followers from the darkness of ignorance and awaken them from delusion.

The fighting spirit of one person who takes up the challenge to battle negative forces can inspire a stand-alone spirit in the heart of another and then another in an unending chain reaction. As the number of such courageous individuals steadily spreads, people throughout the land will come "to open their eyes." Today, Nichiren Buddhism is "opening the eyes" of multitudes around the globe. There is no greater act of compassion than conveying this spirit of unceasing challenge to others.

Nichiren writes, "Though we may suffer for a while, ultimately delight awaits us" ("Protecting the Atsuhara Believers," WND-2, 882). He felt it imperative at this juncture to teach his followers the fighting spirit in which struggles themselves are viewed as a source of great joy. Hence we find Nichiren closing "The Opening of the Eyes" with the cry to his followers that now, when they are facing harsh persecution, is the very time that they can make the cause for attaining Buddhahood.

While deeply engraving Nichiren's spirit in my life, I likewise call to all our members throughout the world, who have together celebrated the milestone of the Soka Gakkai's seventy-fifth anniversary, to do the same. At this time, which represents the pioneering phase of worldwide kosen-rufu, we have forged, through profound life-to-life ties, a global network of countless courageous Bodhisattvas of the Earth possessing an invincible spirit of challenge. This network of people who have awakened to the fighting spirit epitomized in Nichiren's own struggle truly embodies the essence of "The Opening of the Eyes." I hope that with this great conviction, each of you will become a sun-like presence in the place of your mission while solidly accumulating in your life infinite benefit that is indestructible throughout past, present and future.

The time for us to challenge ourselves is now.

Notes

Introduction:

1. This is noted by Nichiken of the Minobu school in a list detailing a collection of Nichiren Daishonin's writings. A list by another Minobu priest, Nichii, refers to the same text as a draft, so it is possible that it was not the final version of the treatise. The document in question was lost with other important writings in a fire at Minobu in 1875.

2. Ignorance: Also, illusion or darkness. In Buddhism, ignorance about the true nature of existence. It is deemed the fundamental cause of suffering and delusion. It prevents people from recognizing the true nature of their lives and taking faith in the Mystic Law, which enables all people to attain enlightenment.

3. The punishments meted out at the time, in order of increasing severity, were as follows: whipping, caning, imprisonment, exile and execution. However, sentences of execution were avoided in the case of monks and nuns, so from a practical standpoint exile was the highest punishment imposed on such persons.

4. The world of animals: This means a state in which one is ignorant of the principle of causality and is completely absorbed in immediate events; it is the base state of those who live according to the law of the jungle. In "Letter from Sado," the Daishonin writes: "It is the nature of beasts to threaten the weak and fear the strong. Our contemporary scholars of the various schools are just like them. They despise a wise man without power, but fear evil rulers" (WND-1, 302).

5. Tsukahara Debate: In January 1272, several hundred priests of the Pure Land, True Word and other schools from both Sado and Japan's mainland gathered in the snow in front of Nichiren's dwelling at Tsukahara on Sado, the Sammai-do, and challenged him to a debate. Nichiren refuted all their arguments, pointing out the contradictory assertions and scriptural incompatibilities contained in their doctrines. Several of these priests, along with their lay followers, renounced their former beliefs on the spot and converted to Nichiren's teachings.

6. The lunisolar calendar was used in 13th–century Japan and differs from the current Gregorian calendar commonly used in the West.

7. Eight cold hells: Hells said to lie under the continent of Jambudvipa next to the eight hot hells. Those who reside there are tormented by unbearable cold.

8. Translated from Japanese. Josei Toda, *Toda Josei zenshu* (Collected Writings of Josei Toda) (Tokyo: Seikyo Shimbunsha, 1983), vol. 3, pp. 240–41.

9. Dharma nature: The unchanging nature inherent in all things and phenomena. In Buddhism, the term *dharma* means both phenomena and the truth underlying them. A Buddha is defined as one who is enlightened to the essential nature of phenomena, and an ordinary person as one who is ignorant of this nature. Hence both enlightenment and ignorance, or darkness, originate from one source, the essential nature of phenomena.

10. *Nayutas*: Extremely large numerical units used in ancient India.

11. Devadatta: A cousin of Shakyamuni, who after Shakyamuni's enlightenment, first followed him as a disciple but later became his enemy. He was behind various schemes to persecute and even kill Shakyamuni.

12. When Buddhism was introduced to Japan, Mononobe no Moriya, a powerful minister, opposed it. Prince Shotoku and another minister named Soga no Umako supported the new religion. The two sides fought and Prince Shotoku and the Soga faction won, setting the stage for the rise of Buddhism in Japan.

13. In the lotus, the blossom (flower) and calyx (fruit or receptacle) are formed at the same time. This is an important characteristic that distinguishes the lotus from other flowering plants.

14. This simile, which appears in "King Wonderful Adornment," the 27th chapter of the Lotus Sutra, indicates that it is as rare for a person to encounter the Mystic Law as it is for a one-eyed turtle to find a floating sandalwood log with a hollow that is just the right size to hold him.

15. Fundamental darkness: Also, fundamental ignorance or primal ignorance. The most deeply rooted illusion inherent in life, said to give rise to all other illusions. Fundamental darkness means the inability to see or recognize the truth, particularly the true nature of one's life. Nichiren interprets fundamental darkness as ignorance of the ultimate Law, or ignorance of the fact that one's life is essentially a manifestation of the Law, which he identifies as Nam-myoho-renge-kyo.

16. An expression used in the Great Collection Sutra.

17. Fivefold comparison: Five successive levels of comparison set forth by Nichiren in "The Opening of the Eyes" to demonstrate the superiority of his teaching of Nam-myoho-renge-kyo over all other teachings. They are (1) Buddhism is superior to non-Buddhist teachings; (2) Mahayana Buddhism is superior to Hinayana Buddhism; (3) true Mahayana is superior to provisional Mahayana; (4) the essential teaching of the Lotus Sutra is superior to the theoretical teaching of the Lotus Sutra; and (5) the Buddhism of sowing is superior to the Buddhism of the harvest. In this way, Nichiren explains that the doctrine of the "actual three thousand realms in a single moment of life" found in the depths of "Life Span," the 16th chapter of the Lotus Sutra, or Nam-myoho-renge-kyo, is the fundamental teaching that people should believe and practice.

18. T'ien-t'ai (538–97): Also known as Chih-i. The founder of the T'ien-t'ai school in China. Commonly referred to as the Great Teacher T'ien-t'ai. His lectures were compiled in such works as *The Profound Meaning of the Lotus Sutra*, *The Words and Phrases of the Lotus Sutra*, and *Great Concentration and Insight*. T'ien-t'ai refuted all the other Buddhist schools in China and spread the Lotus Sutra.

Dengyo (767–822): Also known as Saicho. The founder of the Tendai (T'ien-t'ai) school in Japan. In 804, he traveled to China to study T'ien-t'ai doctrine and Buddhism generally. On his return and the founding of his school, he strove actively to refute the doctrines of the older established schools in Japan.

19. Translated from Japanese. Josei Toda, *Toda Josei zenshu* (Collected Writings of Josei Toda) (Tokyo: Seikyo Shimbunsha, 1981), vol. 1, p. 306.

20. A reference to the Buddhist concept of "doubt-free faith." Volume 10 of T'ien-t'ai's *The Words and Phrases of the Lotus Sutra* contains the passage, "Having no doubt means faith."

21. Translated from Japanese. Josei Toda, *Toda Josei zenshu* (Collected Writings of Josei Toda) (Tokyo: Seikyo Shimbunsha, 1981), vol. 3, p. 179.

Chapter 1:

1. Mystery: In preceding passages in "The Opening of the Eyes," the Daishonin asserts that the writings of China's four sages do not go beyond the three mysteries. These he defines as: (1) the mystery of Being, (2) the mystery of Non-Being and (3) the mystery of Both Being and Non-Being. He also adds, "Mystery denotes darkness" (WND-1, 220). The shortcoming of theories limited to the three mysteries, he declares, is that they fail to take into account either the past or the future, and thus the causality of life.

2. This is found in *Lieh Tzu*, an early Taoist text.

3. Propriety and music were regarded as instrumental in enhancing people's sense of morality and in maintaining social order.

4. Precepts, meditation and wisdom: These refer to the three types of learning a practitioner of Buddhism should master. They are said to encompass all aspects of Buddhist doctrine and practice.

5. Six non-Buddhist teachers: Influential thinkers in India during Shakyamuni's lifetime who openly broke with the old Vedic tradition and challenged Brahman authority in the Indian social order.

6. *Kalpa*: (Skt) In ancient Indian cosmology, an extremely long period of time. Sutras and treatises differ in their definitions, but kalpas fall into two major categories, those of measurable and immeasurable duration. There are three kinds of measurable kalpas: small, medium and major. One explanation sets the length of a small kalpa at approximately 16 million years.

7. Ninety-five non-Buddhist schools: Schools said to have existed in Shakyamuni's time. Their names and particular doctrines are unknown. Another view holds that there were ninety-six schools.

8. Four sages: Four sages of ancient China. Yin Shou, the teacher of Emperor Yao; Wu Ch'eng, the teacher of Emperor Shun; T'ai-kung Wang, the teacher of King Wen; and Lao Tzu, the teacher of Confucius (see WND-1, 220).

9. Three ascetics: Kapila, Uluka and Rishabha, religious teachers who appeared before the time of Shakyamuni. Kapila, founder of the Samkhya school, taught that causes produce effects. Uluka, the founder of the Vaesheshika school, taught that causes do not produce effects. And Rishabha, founder of Jainism, taught that causes both do and do not produce effects.

10. Three categories of illusion. A classification established by T'ien-t'ai. They are: (1) illusions of thought and desire (the former are distorted perceptions of the truth, while the latter refer to base inclinations such as greed and anger); (2) illusions innumerable as particles of dust and sand, which arise when bodhisattvas try to master innumerable teachings in order to save others; and (3) illusions about the true nature of existence.

11. Six paths: Also, the six paths of existence. The realms or worlds in which unenlightened beings transmigrate. They are the realms of hell, hungry spirits, animals, *asuras*, human beings and heavenly beings.

12. Transmigration with change and advance: This refers to the transmigration of voice-hearers, cause-awakened ones and bodhisattvas. In this transmigration, they change, or emancipate, from the body subject to "transmigration of delusion with differences and limitations," while gradually removing illusions leading to sufferings.

13. Transmigration with differences and limitations: This refers to the transmigration of unenlightened beings through the six paths. In this repeating cycle of rebirth through the six lower deluded worlds, living beings are born with limited spans of life and in different forms in accordance with their karma.

14. Three virtues: The virtues or benevolent functions of sovereign, teacher and parent that a Buddha is said to possess. The virtue of sovereign is the power to protect all living beings, the virtue of teacher is the wisdom to instruct them and lead them to enlightenment, and the virtue of parent is the compassion to nurture and support them.

15. Saha world: This world, which is full of suffering. In the Chinese version of Buddhist scriptures, the Sanskrit *saha* is translated as "endurance." The term *saha world* suggests that the people who live in this world must endure suffering. It is also identified as an impure land, in contrast to a pure land.

16. Threefold world: The world of unenlightened beings who transmigrate within the six paths (from hell through the realm of heavenly beings). The threefold world consists of, in ascending order, the world of desire, the world of form and the world of formlessness.

17. See LSOC, 94.

18. The doctrine of original cause and original effect: Fundamental cause for attaining Buddhahood, and the actual state of life of Buddhahood attained thereby.

19. Six difficult and nine easy acts: Comparisons expounded in "Treasure Tower," the 11th chapter of the Lotus Sutra, to explain how difficult it will be to embrace and propagate the sutra in the Latter Day of the Law. The six difficult acts are: (1) to propagate the Lotus Sutra widely, (2) to copy it or cause someone else to copy it, (3) to recite it even for a short while, (4) to teach it to even one person, (5) to hear of and accept it and inquire about its meaning and (6) to maintain faith in it.

The nine easy acts are: (1) to teach innumerable sutras other than the Lotus Sutra, (2) to take up Mount Sumeru and hurl it across countless Buddha lands, (3) to kick a major world system into a different quarter with one's toe, (4) to stand in the Summit of Being Heaven and preach innumerable sutras other than the Lotus Sutra, (5) to grasp the sky with one's hand and travel around with it, (6) to place the earth on one's toenail and ascend to the Brahma Heaven, (7) to carry dry grass on one's back into the great fires occurring at the end of the kalpa without being burned, (8) to preach eighty-four thousand teachings and enable one's listeners to obtain the six transcendental powers and (9) to enable innumerable people to reach the stage of arhat and acquire the six transcendental powers.

20. Three powerful enemies: Types of powerful enemies who will persecute those who spread the Lotus Sutra in the evil age after Shakyamuni's passing. Based on the twenty-line verse section of "Encouraging Devotion," the 13th chapter of the Lotus Sutra, the Great Teacher Miao-lo of China identifies them as arrogant lay people, arrogant priests and arrogant false sages.

21. Lessening one's karmic retribution: This term, translated literally, meaning "transforming the heavy and receiving it lightly," appears in the Nirvana Sutra. "Heavy" indicates negative karma accumulated over countless lifetimes in the past. The principle of lessening karmic retribution means that by overcoming relatively light karmic retribution in this lifetime, we can expiate heavy karma that ordinarily would adversely affect us not only in this lifetime, but over many lifetimes to come.

22. In *The Record of the Orally Transmitted Teachings*, the Daishonin cites the Nirvana Sutra passage, "The varied sufferings that all living beings undergo—all these are the Thus Come One's own sufferings," and says, "the varied sufferings that all living beings undergo—all these are Nichiren's own sufferings" (OTT, 138).

In "Remonstration with Bodhisattva Hachiman," citing the same sutra passage, he writes: "Nichiren declares that the sufferings that all living beings undergo, all springing from this one cause—all these are Nichiren's

own sufferings" ("On Reprimanding Hachiman," WND-2, 934).

"Different sufferings" means the varied and diverse sufferings that people individually experience. "Shared suffering" refers to the suffering experienced by society as a whole, the fundamental cause of which is slander of the Law unconsciously committed by vast numbers of people. The Daishonin is saying that he takes both of these on as his own suffering and seeks to overcome them.

23. *Daimoku* of faith and practice: The daimoku of faith and the daimoku of practice are two aspects of the daimoku of the essential teaching (Nam-myoho-renge-kyo). In "Letter to Horen," the Daishonin writes, "If you try to practice the teachings of the sutra [the Lotus Sutra] without faith, it would be like trying to enter a jeweled mountain without hands [to pick up its treasures], or like trying to make a thousand-mile journey without feet" (WND-1, 511). Thus the daimoku of the essential teaching requires both faith and practice.

24. Translated from Japanese. Tsunesaburo Makiguchi, *Makiguchi Tsunesaburo zenshu* (Collected Writings of Tsunesaburo Makiguchi) (Tokyo: Daisanbunmei-sha, 1984), vol. 8, pp. 52–53.

25. Ibid., 53–54.

26. Ibid., 43.

27. Ibid., 407–08.

28. Ibid., 408.

Chapter 2:

1. This refers to the two aspects of the doctrine of "three thousand realms in a single moment of life." That is, the "theoretical

three thousand realms in a single moment of life" and the "actual three thousand realms in a single moment of life." The theoretical principle is based on the theoretical teaching (first half) of the Lotus Sutra, while its actual embodiment is revealed in the essential teaching (latter half) of the sutra.

2. Three thousand: The number three thousand here comes from the following calculation: 10 (Ten Worlds) x 10 (Ten Worlds) [mutual possession] x 10 (ten factors) x 3 (three realms of existence). Life at each moment manifests one of the Ten Worlds. Each of these worlds possesses the potential for each of the other nine within itself, and this "mutual possession" of the Ten Worlds is represented as one hundred possible worlds. Each of these one hundred worlds possesses the ten factors, making one thousand factors or potentials, and these operate within each of the three realms of existence (the realm of the five components, the realm of living beings and the realm of the environment), thus making three thousand realms.

3. Earthly desires, karma and suffering (the three paths): These are called "paths" because one leads to the other. Earthly desires include greed, anger, foolishness, arrogance and doubt. Karma refers to evil actions of a mental, verbal or physical nature that arise due to earthly desires. The effect of this karma manifests as suffering. Suffering aggravates earthly desires, leading to further misguided action, which in turn brings on more evil karma and suffering. The three paths function to prevent a person from attaining Buddhahood.

4. Changing poison into medicine: The principle that earthly desires and suffering can be transformed into benefit and enlightenment by virtue of the power of the Law. The phrase appears in a passage in Nagarjuna's *Treatise on the Great Perfection of Wisdom* that states, "[The Lotus Sutra is] like a great physician who can change poison into medicine" (WND-1, 146). In *The Profound Meaning of the Lotus Sutra,* the Great Teacher T'ien-t'ai expands on this quote, saying, "That persons of the two vehicles were given the prophecy of their enlightenment in this sutra means that it can change poison into medicine" (WND-1, 631).

5. Purification of the six sense organs: Also, purification of the six senses. The six sense organs or faculties of awareness are the eyes, ears, nose, tongue, body and mind. Their purification means that they function correctly and become pure, free of influence of earthly desires.

6. Text, principle and intent: Text indicates the literal meaning of the words of the sutra. Principle means the teaching or doctrine conveyed by the literal meaning. And intent refers to the fundamental or ultimate meaning, the true purpose behind the principle.

7. "As an expedient means I appear to enter nirvana" (LSOC, 271): This means that the Buddha enters nirvana as an expedient means to arouse in people a seeking mind for the Buddha and the Law.

8. Opening the near and revealing the distant: A revelation made in the essential teaching of the Lotus Sutra that discards the assumption that Shakyamuni attained enlightenment for the first time in India and reveals that he originally gained enlightenment in the immeasurably distant past.

9. Original effect: The original enlightenment that Shakyamuni attained countless aeons before his enlightenment in India.

10. Original cause: The practice that became the cause for Shakyamuni to attain enlightenment in the remote past. The fundamental practice for attaining the Buddha way.

11. Some quotes on the religious spirit by SGI President Ikeda:

    "The religious spirit is a kind of mental capacity that turns nihilism into a bright future and despair into hope. A cynic sees everything as empty or worthless, and the soul of such a person will not create anything of value . . . Is it not philosophy or what I call 'the religious spirit' that will brighten our inner world?" Daisaku Ikeda and Majid Tehranian, *Global Civilization: A Buddhist-Islamic Dialogue* (London: British Academic Press, 2003), pp. 52–53.

    "Dewey does not identify a specific external power. For him 'the religious' is a generalized term for that which supports and encourages people in the active pursuit of the good and the valuable. 'The religious,' as he defines it, helps those who help themselves." Daisaku Ikeda, "Mahayana Buddhism and Twenty-First-Century Civilization," *A New Humanism: The University Addresses of Daisaku Ikeda* (New York: I.B. Tauris & Co. Ltd., 2010), p. 172.

12. Translated from Japanese. Josei Toda, *Toda Josei zenshu* (Collected Writings of Josei Toda) (Tokyo: Seikyo Shimbunsha, 1981), vol. 1, p. 306.

Chapter 3:

1. The content of the two flaws stated here is summarized from the writing of the Great Teacher Miao-lo of China. In *The Annotations on "The Profound Meaning of the Lotus Sutra,"* Miao-lo writes: "Because the Ten Worlds are separate from one another in these [pre-Lotus Sutra] teachings, they fail to move beyond the provisional," and "Because they teach that Shakyamuni first attained enlightenment in this world, they fail to discard the Buddha's provisional status" ("The Essence of the 'Life Span' Chapter," WND-1, 182).

2. *Kalpa*: An immensely long period of time described in "Parable of the Phantom City," the 7th chapter of the Lotus Sutra, to indicate how much time has passed since Shakyamuni preached the sutra to his voice-hearer disciples as the sixteenth son of the Buddha Great Universal Wisdom Excellence.

3. True aspect of all phenomena: The ultimate truth or reality that permeates all phenomena and is in no way separate from them. "Expedient Means," the 2nd chapter of the Lotus Sutra, clarifies that all people are inherently endowed with the potential to become Buddhas, and the truth that they can tap and manifest this potential.

4. First stage of security: The first of the ten stages of security, which corresponds to the eleventh of the fifty-two stages of bodhisattva practice. At this stage, one arouses the aspiration for Buddhahood. It is regarded as the point at which bodhisattvas no longer regress in practice.

5. Four universal vows: Also, four great vows, or simply four vows. Vows that every bodhisattva makes upon initially resolving to embark on Buddhist practice. They are (1) to save innumerable living beings, (2) to eradicate countless earthly desires, (3) to master immeasurable Buddhist teachings and (4) to attain supreme enlightenment.

6. The Mystic Law of hearing the name and words of the truth in the remote past:

The fundamental Mystic Law that the Buddha of beginningless time embraced and attained enlightenment as an ordinary person at the stage of hearing the name and words of the truth of the original cause.

7. Actual three thousand realms in a single moment of life: The doctrine of three thousand realms in a single moment of life, which is the fundamental teaching for attaining enlightenment, is classified into: the theoretical principle and the actual embodiment of this principle. These are respectively termed "theoretical three thousand realms in a single moment of life" and "actual three thousand realms in a single moment of life." The theoretical principle is based on the theoretical teaching of the Lotus Sutra, while the actual principle is revealed in the essential teaching of the Lotus Sutra. In the Latter Day of the Law, however, these are both theoretical; and Nam-myoho-renge-kyo of the Three Great Secret Laws that Nichiren Daishonin revealed is the actual three thousand realms doctrine.

8. This letter was written at Ichinosawa on Sado Island in May 1273 to Gijo-bo, who had been one of Nichiren's teachers at Seicho-ji, a temple in Awa Province (present-day Chiba Prefecture). Nichiren declares in this letter that, in his capacity as the Buddha of the Latter Day of the Law, he realized and embodied Nam-myoho-renge-kyo of the Three Great Secret Laws that is hidden in the depths of the "Life Span" chapter.

Chapter 4:

1. Five major principles—name, essence, quality, function and teaching: The five viewpoints from which T'ien-t'ai interprets the Lotus Sutra in his treatise, *The Profound Meaning of the Lotus Sutra*. "Name" signifies the meaning of the title of a sutra. "Essence" signifies the ultimate principle of a sutra. "Quality" indicates the principal doctrines of a sutra. "Function" indicates the benefit and power of a sutra. And "teaching" refers to the position and influence of a sutra with respect to other sutras.

2. In *The Profound Meaning of the Lotus Sutra* (vol. 1), T'ien-t'ai says, "Quality refers to the key point. It is represented by the causality arising from the Buddha's own practice."

3. From T'ien-t'ai's *The Profound Meaning of the Lotus Sutra*, vols. 8 and 9.

4. For example, Confucius, founder of Confucianism, said such things as, "You do not yet know life, how could you know death?" [*The Analects of Confucius*, translated by Simon Leys (New York: W. W. Norton & Company, 1997), p. 50].

5. Brahmanism: A system of thought that developed before Buddhism, based on the Vedas and commentaries on them.

6. Six schools of philosophy: The six leading schools of Brahman philosophy in ancient India. They are the Sanmkhya, Yoga, Nyana, Vaisheshika, Mimamsa and Vedanta schools.

7. In "The Opening of the Eyes," Nichiren, in explaining the differences between the Lotus Sutra and all other sutras, says: "In the case of the Great Collection Sutra, the Larger Wisdom Sutra, the Golden Light Sutra, and the Amida Sutra, the Buddha, in order to censure the ideal of the two vehicles demonstrated in the various Hinayana sutras, described the pure lands of the ten directions, and thereby inspired ordinary people and bodhisattvas to aspire to attain

them. Thus he caused the persons of the two vehicles to feel confounded and vexed" (WND-1, 231).

8. The "Expedient Means" chapter of the Lotus Sutra explains that all Buddhas appear in the world (1) "to open the door of Buddha wisdom to all living beings," (2) "to show the Buddha wisdom to living beings," (3) "to cause living beings to awaken to the Buddha wisdom" and (4) "to induce living beings to enter the path of Buddha wisdom" (LSOC, 64). These are referred to as the four aspects of Buddha wisdom.

9. In "On the Mystic Principle of the True Cause," Nichiren writes: "The four types of teaching are as follows. The first is a teaching of cause and effect of disparate nature. These are expedient and provisional teachings. The second is a teaching of cause and effect of identical nature. This is the theoretical teaching. The third is a teaching of cause and effect of eternal coexistence. This is the essential teaching. The fourth is a teaching of cause and effect in a single moment of life. Volume five of [T'ien-t'ai's] *Great Concentration and Insight* states: 'If there is the slightest bit of life, it contains all the three thousand realms.' This is none other than the transfer of the essence of the Lotus Sutra, the Mystic Law, the pure and perfect teaching of the Latter Day of the Law" (GZ, 871).

Chapter 5:

1. The Former Day of the Law is an age after the Buddha's passing when people correctly transmit and practice the Buddha's teaching. The Middle Day is a time when the teaching grows formalized and rigid. The ensuing period, known as the Latter Day, is a time when people lose sight of the correct teaching, and when society is rife with confusion and conflict.

2. Amida is a Buddha described in the Pure Land sutras as dwelling in the Pure Land of Perfect Bliss in the west. He is revered by the followers of the Pure Land, or Nembutsu, school. Mahavairochana (Jpn Dainichi) is described in the Mahavairochana Sutra, which is prized by the True World school; this Buddha is regarded as the source from which the universe springs. Both Amida and Mahavairochana are transcendent beings who were expounded as expedient means for people's instruction.

3. "Encouraging Devotion," the 13th chapter of the Lotus Sutra, states, "Evil demons will take possession of others" (LSOC, 233). This passage describes how demons and devils will enter the lives of various people, causing them to deride and disparage those who uphold the correct teaching and to obstruct their Buddhist practice.

4. Three pronouncements: Exhortations by Shakyamuni Buddha in "Treasure Tower," the 11th chapter of the Lotus Sutra, urging the assembly at the Ceremony in the Air three times to propagate the Lotus Sutra after his passing. In the third pronouncement, the Buddha expounds the difficulty of propagating the sutra after his death by employing the teaching of the six difficult and nine easy acts. This pronouncement reads in part: "Many Treasures Thus Come One, I myself, / and these emanation Buddhas who have gathered here, / surely know this is our aim . . . / [E]ach of you must consider carefully! / This is a difficult matter—it is proper you should make a great vow . . . / After I have entered extinction, / who can guard and uphold, / read and recite this sutra? / Now

in the presence of the Buddha / let him come forward and speak his vow!" (LSOC, 217–20).

5. A bodhisattva described in "Never Disparaging," the 20th chapter of the Lotus Sutra. Never Disparaging represents Shakyamuni in a past life engaged in bodhisattva practice. His practice consisted of addressing all he met in the following manner, irrespective of the persecution he encountered: "I have profound reverence for you, I would never dare treat you with disparagement or arrogance. Why? Because you will all practice the bodhisattva way and will then be able to attain Buddhahood" (LSOC, 308). The sutra explains that through this practice Never Disparaging made the cause to attain Buddhahood.

6. Shariputra: One of Shakyamuni's ten major disciples, who was known as foremost in wisdom for his understanding of the true intent of the Buddha's preaching.

7. Eye-begging Brahman: A Brahman who begged for Shariputra's eye when the latter was practicing austerities in a previous existence. The story is found in *The Treatise on the Great Perfection of Wisdom*. In the distant past, Shariputra, practicing the bodhisattva way, engaged in the offering of alms. When he had practiced almsgiving for sixty kalpas, a Brahman came to him and asked him for his eye. Shariputra gouged out one of his own eyes and gave it to him. But the Brahman was so revolted by the smell of the eye that he spat on it, dropped it on the ground and trampled on it. Seeing this, Shariputra thought it too difficult to lead such persons to salvation and decided to seek only his own liberation from the sufferings of birth and death; he withdrew from bodhisattva practice, retreating into the Hinayana teachings, or the way of voice-hearers.

Chapter 6:

1. In *The Words and Phrases of the Lotus Sutra*, T'ien-t'ai writes, "It will be much worse in the future because the principles [of the Lotus Sutra] are so hard to teach" (WND-1, 240). In his annotations on that work, Miao-lo explains, "'Hatred' refers to those who have not yet freed themselves from impediments, and 'jealousy,' to those who take no delight in listening to the doctrine'" (WND-1, 240). The Daishonin also cites passages from Dengyo's treatises, *A Clarification of the Precepts* and *The Outstanding Principles of the Lotus Sutra*, and lines from the Chinese T'ien-t'ai school priest Chih-tu's *Supplement to the Meanings of the Commentaries on the Lotus Sutra*.

2. The fundamental darkness is said to usually erupt in the lives of those who have overcome the first two of the three categories of illusion, that is, illusions of thought and desire and illusions innumerable as particles of dust and sand. In this case, however, the Daishonin points out that quite unusually, the fundamental darkness has erupted in the lives of ordinary people caught in the first of the illusions.

3. Ajatashatru: A king of Magadha in India in the time of Shakyamuni. Incited by Devadatta, he gained the throne by killing his father, King Bimbisara, a follower of Shakyamuni. He also made attempts on the lives of the Buddha and his disciples by releasing a drunken elephant upon them. Under Ajatashatru's reign, Magadha became the most powerful kingdom in India. Later he converted to Buddhism out of remorse for his evil acts and supported the First Buddhist Council in its compilation of Shakyamuni's

teachings undertaken the year following Shakyamuni's death.

4. Voluntarily assuming the appropriate karma: This refers to bodhisattvas who, though qualified to receive the pure rewards of Buddhist practice, relinquish them and vowing to be reborn in an impure world in order to save living beings. They spread the Mystic Law, while undergoing the same suffering as those born in the evil world due to karma. This term derives from Miao-lo's interpretation of relevant passages in "The Teacher of the Law," the 10th chapter of the Lotus Sutra.

Chapter 7:

1. Four great voice-hearers: Four outstanding voice-hearers who, in the Lotus Sutra, express their joy at being able to take faith in the Mystic Law. They are Mahakashyapa, Maudgalyayana, Katyayana and Subhuti.

2. The fifth five-hundred-year period refers to the "age of conflict," when Shakyamuni's teachings become obscured and lost; it corresponds to the beginning of the Latter Day of the Law.

3. "Expedient Means," the 2nd chapter of the Lotus Sutra, clarifies that all living beings are endowed with and can manifest the world of Buddhahood. This indicates that the lower nine worlds, which are states of life of illusion, and the world of Buddhahood, which is the state of life of enlightenment, each contain the other. This is termed the principle of "the mutual possession of the Ten Worlds."

4. The first of the four great vows that bodhisattvas take upon commencing their Buddhist practice. Shakyamuni

accomplished this vow by expounding the Lotus Sutra, which reveals that all people can attain Buddhahood.

5. Two places and three assemblies: The settings in which Shakyamuni preached the Lotus Sutra, as described in the sutra.

6. The fundamental nature of enlightenment: The original nature of the Buddha's ultimate enlightenment with which life is originally endowed. Corresponds to the world of Buddhahood or the Buddha nature. In his writing "The Treatment of Illness," the Daishonin says, "The fundamental nature of enlightenment manifests itself as [the Buddhist gods] Brahma and Shakra" (WND-1, 1113).

Chapter 8:

1. According to Nichiren, the founders of the various schools respected the Lotus Sutra, which T'ien-t'ai and Dengyo taught them. Therefore, even though they were outwardly at odds with T'ien-t'ai and Dengyo, they actually gave allegiance to these two (see WND-1, 225–26 and 260).

2. The Lotus Sutra, which is the true Mahayana teaching expounded by Shakyamuni, is the true teaching; and the preceding Mahayana and Hinayana teachings, expounded as expedient means to introduce the Lotus Sutra, are the provisional teachings. The various schools that base themselves on these provisional teachings set forth erroneous doctrines attacking the true teaching. In response, Nichiren Daishonin waged a verbal offensive to refute these various schools.

3. The work of the Thus Come One (the Buddha) to lead people to enlightenment.

"Teacher of the Law," the 10th chapter of the Lotus Sutra reads: "He or she is the envoy of the Thus Come One. He has been dispatched by the Thus Come One and carries out the Thus Come One's work" (LSOC, 200).

4. *The Outstanding Principles of the Lotus Sutra:* A work, composed in 821, in which the Great Teacher Dengyo explains ten respects in which the Lotus Sutra is superior to other sutras, and refutes the erroneous teachings of the Dharma Characteristics, Three Treatises, Flower Garland, True Word and other schools.

5. Trainer of people (Jpn *jogo jobu*): One of the Buddha's ten honorable titles. Refers to someone who, like an outstanding trainer, skillfully instructs and guides people. The term *jobu* in Japanese also has the meaning of "a person of courage."

6. In "The Essence of the Lotus Sutra," Nichiren notes that while every sutra claims to be foremost, "It is important that we should clearly understand what is being compared when we try to decide which sutras are superior and which inferior" ("Choosing the Heart of the Lotus Sutra," WND-2, 483).

7. For example, the Golden Light Sutra says, "This teaching is the king among sutras" (WND-1, 264). The Secret Solemnity Sutra says, "[This] is the greatest of all sutras" (WND-1, 264). The Flower Garland Sutra says, "To believe in the doctrines of this sutra is difficult in the extreme" (WND-1, 266). These claims simply indicate that they are the most outstanding teachings among a set of teachings expounded for a particular audience or during a particular period.

8. In "Teacher of the Law," the 10th chapter of the Lotus Sutra, Shakyamuni says: "The sutras I have preached number immeasurable thousands, ten thousands, millions. Among the sutras I have preached, now preach, and will preach, this Lotus Sutra is the most difficult to believe and the most difficult to understand. Medicine King, this sutra is the storehouse of the secret crux of the Buddhas" (LSOC, 203).

9. Ch'eng-kuan and others of the Flower Garland school maintained: "Both the Flower Garland Sutra and the Lotus Sutra belong to the 'six difficult acts' category. Though in name they are different sutras, they are identical in their teachings and principles" (WND-1, 263). Chia-hsiang and others of the Three Treatises school asserted, "The Wisdom Sutra and the Lotus Sutra are different names for a single entity, two sutras that preach one teaching" (WND-1, 263). Tz'u-en and others of the Dharma Characteristics school state: "The Profound Secrets Sutra and the Lotus Sutra both expound the Consciousness-Only doctrine. They date from the third period of the Buddha's teaching and belong to the 'six difficult acts' category" (WND-1, 263). Kobo of the Japanese True Word school said: "The Mahavairochana Sutra belongs neither to the 'six difficult [acts]' nor to the 'nine easy [acts]' category. The Mahavairochana Sutra . . . stands apart from all the sutras preached by Shakyamuni Buddha, since it was preached by the Thus Come One Mahavairochana, a Buddha of the Dharma body" (WND-1, 263).

10. Mount Sumeru: In ancient Indian cosmology, the mountain that stands at the center of the world.

Chapter 9:

1. In the "Treasure Tower" chapter, which marks the start of the Ceremony in the Air, Shakyamuni three times exhorts the assembly to propagate the Lotus Sutra after his passing.

2. Transmission section: Also, transmission. One of the three sections or divisions of a sutra employed to interpret the sutra's teachings, the other two being the preparation section and the revelation section. The transmission section is the concluding section, which explains the benefit of the sutra and urges that the core teaching in the revelation section be transmitted to the future.

3. *Icchantika* (Skt): A person of incorrigible disbelief. *Icchantika* means one who is filled with desires or cravings. Originally icchantika meant a hedonist or one who cherishes only secular values. In Buddhism, the term came to mean those who neither believe in Buddhism nor aspire for enlightenment and therefore have no prospect of attaining Buddhahood.

4. Sunakshatra: One of Shakyamuni's disciples, regarded as one of his sons from before becoming a monk. According to the Mahaparinirvana Sutra, Sunakshatra joined the Buddhist Order, freed himself from all ties with the world of desire and mastered the four stages of meditation. Influenced by evil teachers, however, he lost his mastery of the four stages of meditation and became attached to the mistaken view that there is no Buddha, no Law and no attainment of nirvana. The same sutra also states: "At that time the Thus Come One and [Bodhisattva] Kashyapa went to where Sunakshatra was. The monk Sunakshatra saw them coming from afar and immediately evil thoughts arose in his mind. And because of this evil in his mind, he fell alive into the Avichi hell."

5. Five cardinal sins: The five most serious offenses in Buddhism. Explanations vary according to the sutras and treatises. The most common is (1) killing one's father, (2) killing one's mother, (3) killing an *arhat*, (4) injuring a Buddha and (5) causing disunity in the Buddhist Order. It is said that those who commit any of the five cardinal sins invariably fall into the hell of incessant suffering. The last three offenses are collectively referred to as the three cardinal sins. Devadatta is well known for committing these three.

6. Seven cardinal sins: Killing a monk of high virtue and killing a teacher, in addition to the five cardinal sins (see above footnote).

7. "Sweet dew" refers to *amrita*, a legendary, ambrosia-like liquid. In ancient India, it was regarded as the sweet-tasting beverage of the gods. In China, it was thought to rain down from heaven when the world became peaceful. *Amrita* is said to remove sufferings and give immortality. The word *amrita* means immortality and is often translated as sweet dew.

8. Quote from Miao-lo's commentary, *The Annotations on "The Words and Phrases of the Lotus Sutra."*

9. Dragon king's daughter: Also, known as the dragon girl. The eight-year-old daughter of Sagara, one of the eight great dragon kings said to dwell in a palace at the bottom of the sea. She conceives the desire for enlightenment upon hearing Bodhisattva Manjushri preach the Lotus Sutra. She then appears in front of the assembly of the Lotus Sutra and instantaneously attains Buddhahood in her present form.

10. Immediate attainment of Buddhahood based on the doctrine of three thousand realms in a single moment of life: This refers to beings in the nine words bringing forth their inherent Buddhahood and attaining enlightenment. The term is used in contrast to attaining Buddhahood through transformation, that is, through devoting oneself ceaselessly to arduous Buddhist practice over countless lifetimes until one gradually ascends to the highest stage of supreme enlightenment.

11. True aspect of the ten factors: The "Expedient Means" chapter of the Lotus Sutra explains the Buddha's ultimate enlightenment in terms of the "true aspect of all phenomena." This true aspect is described as consisting of the ten factors: appearance, nature, entity, power, influence, internal cause, relation, latent effect, manifest effect and their consistency from beginning to end.

12. The Nirvana Sutra states: "I always proclaim that all living beings possess the Buddha nature, and I likewise say that even icchantikas possess the Buddha nature. Icchantikas do not embrace the good Dharma, but because they possess the potential for Buddhahood and goodness in the future, icchantikas, too, all possess the Buddha nature."

13. In "The Daimoku of the Lotus Sutra," the Daishonin explains that *to open* means "to reveal the Buddha's enlightenment" (see WND-1, 145), that *to be fully endowed* means "to encompass all teachings" (see WND-1, 146) and that *to revive* means "to return to life" (see WND-1, 149).

14. Nagarjuna: A Mahayana scholar of southern India thought to have lived between the years 150 and 250. His many writings, which include *The Treatise on the Middle Way*

and *The Treatise on the Great Perfection of Wisdom,* elevated Mahayana Buddhism and had a major impact on Buddhism in China and Japan.

15. A letter composed on February 28, 1278, while Nichiren was living at Minobu.

16. Ten evil acts: Evils enumerated in the Buddhist scriptures. They are the three physical evils of killing, stealing and sexual misconduct; the four verbal evils of lying, flattery or indiscriminate and irresponsible speech, defamation and duplicity; and the three mental evils of greed, anger and foolishness or the holding of mistaken views.

17. Four grave prohibitions: Prohibitions against the four major offenses, which were proscribed by monastic discipline for monks and nuns and carried the penalty of automatic expulsion from the Buddhist Order, i.e., the offenses of (1) killing a human being, (2) stealing, (3) having sexual relations and (4) lying (particularly, lying about one's level of insight or spiritual attainment).

18. The four sufferings and the eight sufferings: The four sufferings are the four universal sufferings of birth, aging, sickness and death. The eight sufferings are eight kinds of universal suffering. They comprise the four fundamental sufferings, plus the sufferings of having to part from those whom one loves, the suffering of having to meet with those whom one hates, the suffering of being unable to obtain what one desires and the suffering arising from the five components that constitute one's body and mind.

19. Translated from Japanese. Tsunesaburo Makiguchi, *Selected Quotes of Tsunesaburo Makiguchi,* edited by Takehisa Tsuji (Tokyo: Daisanbunmei-sha, 1979), pp. 196–97.

20. Both Toki Jonin and his mother were followers of Nichiren. While she was still alive and despite her advanced age, the mother had made a handwoven summer robe as a gift for Nichiren. After she became ill, she was nursed by Toki's wife, who also embraced faith in Nichiren's teaching. Toki's mother was more than ninety years old when she passed away in February 1276. The following month, Toki himself visited Nichiren at Minobu, taking with him a small urn of his mother's ashes so that Nichiren might conduct a memorial service for her.

Chapter 10:

1. On September 12, 1271, powerful figures in the government unjustly arrested Nichiren and led him off in the middle of the night to a place called Tatsunokuchi on the outskirts of Kamakura, the capital, where they tried to execute him under cover of darkness. The execution attempt failed, and approximately one month later Nichiren was exiled to Sado Island. At the time, exile to Sado was tantamount to a death sentence.

2. The twenty-line verse section: The concluding verse section of "Encouraging Devotion," the 13th chapter of the Lotus Sutra, in which countless multitudes of bodhisattvas vow to Shakyamuni to propagate the sutra in the evil age after his passing. The Chinese translation of this verse section consists of twenty lines and begins with the passage: "We beg you not to worry. / After the Buddha has passed into extinction, / in an age of fear and evil / we will preach far and wide" (LSOC, 232). It enumerates the persecutions that will occur in the evil age designated in the sutra. Based on this section, Miao-lo classified those who persecute practitioners of the Lotus Sutra into three types of enemies—arrogant lay people, arrogant priests and arrogant false sages.

3. An arhat is one who has attained the highest of the four stages that voice-hearers aim to achieve through the practice of Hinayana teachings, that is, the highest stage of Hinayana enlightenment. The term *arhat* means one worthy of respect. The six transcendental powers are powers that Buddhas, bodhisattvas and arhats are said to possess. They are: (1) the power to be anywhere at will, (2) the power to see anything anywhere, (3) the power to hear any sound anywhere, (4) the power to know the thoughts of all other minds, (5) the power to know past lives and (6) the power to eradicate illusions and earthly desires.

4. Honen: (1133–1212): Also known as Genku. Founder of the Pure Land school of Buddhism in Japan. He advocated the exclusive practice of Nembutsu, or the chanting of Amida Buddha's name. In his work *Nembutsu Chosen above All*, Honen urges that people "discard, close, ignore and abandon" the sutras, including the Lotus Sutra, and instead embrace the Pure Land faith. In "On Establishing the Correct Teaching for the Peace of the Land," the Daishonin strictly denounces the Nembutsu as the "one evil" that is the cause of the various disasters befalling the country.

5. Shoichi (1202–80): Also known as Enni or Bennen. A priest of the Rinzai school of Zen Buddhism in Japan. He studied Zen in China and, after returning to Japan in 1241, propagated its teachings at court and obtained the patronage of the nobility, becoming the first chief priest of Tofuku-ji, a temple in Kyoto.

6. Ryokan (1217–1303): Also known as Ninsho. A priest of the True Word Precepts school in Japan. In 1267, Ryokan became chief priest of Gokuraku-ji, a temple in Kamakura that had been established by a high-ranking military government official. It became Ryokan's permanent abode. He undertook a number of social welfare projects, building hospitals, roads, etc. The people of Kamakura revered him, and he enjoyed great influence. At the government's command, Ryokan often conducted esoteric prayer rituals to bring about rain and to ward off invasion by the Mongols. During the great drought of 1271, Ryokan vied with the Daishonin in praying for rain and failed. After that, he contrived to have accusations brought against the Daishonin, which eventually led to the Tatsunokuchi Persecution.

7. Nen'a (1199–1287): Another name for Ryochu or Nen'amidabutsu, the third patriarch of the Japanese Pure Land school, after Honen and Bencho. He won the support of Hojo Tsunetoki, the fourth regent of the Kamakura shogunate, and other members of the Hojo clan and founded Goshin-ji (later renamed Renge-ji and then Komyo-ji) in Kamakura in 1243. He made this temple the center of propagation of the Pure Land teaching and went on to win support from other shogunate authorities.

8. Hei no Saemon (d. 1293): A leading official of the Hojo regency, the de facto ruling body of Japan during the Kamakura period (1185–1333). He served two successive regents, Hojo Tokimune and Hojo Sadatoki, and wielded tremendous influence as deputy chief of the Office of Military and Police Affairs (the chief being the regent himself). He collaborated with Ryokan of Gokuraku-ji temple of the True Word Precepts school and other leading priests to persecute the Daishonin and his followers.

Chapter 11:

1. *Tung-ch'un*: Another title for *The Supplement to the Meanings of the Commentaries on the Lotus Sutra*, by Chih-tu, a T'ien-t'ai priest of Tang-dynasty China. The work was called *Tung-ch'un* after the place where the author lived.

2. Gomyo (750–834) and Shuen (771–835): Both priests of the Dharma Characteristics school in Japan. Gyomo served as administrator of priests, while Shuen lived at Kofuku-ji and was famed as its most learned priest. Both men protested Dengyo's request to construct a Mahayana ordination platform on Mount Hiei.

3. Six schools of Nara: Six schools of Buddhism that flourished in Nara, the capital of Japan, during the Nara period (710–94). They are the Dharma Analysis Treasury (Kusha), Establishment of Truth (Jojitsu), Three Treatises (Sanron), Precepts (Ritsu), Dharma Characteristics (Hosso) and Flower Garland (Kegon) schools.

4. Eizon (1201–90): Also known as Eison and Shien. A restorer of the Precepts school in Japan. Eizon engaged in the practice of both the precepts and the True Word teachings. He is regarded as the founder of the True Word Precepts school. Visited Kamakura at the request of Hojo Sanetoki, presenting the precepts to Hojo Tokiyori and other key figures in the government, among whom he wielded much influence.

5. Also known respectively as Doa Dokyo and Nen'a Ryochu.

6. "Eleven letters of remonstration": In 1268, following the arrival of the Mongol emissaries and with threat of foreign invasion looming, Nichiren composed a series of letters in which he strove to clarify the errors of various schools and implored people to take faith in the correct teaching of the Lotus Sutra. The eleven recipients included central figures in government and at influential temples.

7. In "Response to the Petition from Gyobin," Nichiren writes: "The petition in which the Sage Ryokan, the foremost upholder of the precepts in present-day Japan, and sages such as Nen'amidabutsu and Doamidabutsu [Nen'a and Doa], second-generation disciples of the Honorable Honen, bring action against Nichiren, says: 'We wish to have Nichiren summoned immediately and to demolish his erroneous views so that the correct doctrines can flourish.' I say that if erroneous views were demolished so that the correct doctrines could flourish, it would be as if a one-eyed turtle had fit perfectly into a hole in a floating log. It would be a matter of the utmost delight" (WND-2, 385).

Chapter 12:

1. "Peaceful Practices," the 14th chapter of the Lotus Sutra, LSOC, 249.

2. Ibid.

3. "The Parable of the Medicinal Herbs," the 5th chapter of the Lotus Sutra, LSOC, 134.

4. Arjaka: A tree that grows in India and other tropical areas. It is said that when a branch of this tree falls to the ground, it splits into seven pieces.

5. "Dharani" chapter, LSOC, 348.

6. "Encouragements of the Bodhisattva Universal Worthy" chapter, LSOC, 360.

7. Ibid.

8. Three proofs: The three proofs are documentary proof, theoretical proof and actual proof. Three standards set forth by Nichiren Daishonin for judging the validity of a given Buddhist teaching. Documentary proof means that the doctrine of a particular Buddhist school is based upon or in accord with the sutras. Theoretical proof means that a doctrine is compatible with reason and logic. Actual proof means that the content of a doctrine is borne out by actual result when put into practice (see WND-1, 599).

9. Nine great ordeals: Also, nine great persecutions. The major hardships that Shakyamuni underwent. They are listed in *The Treatise on the Great Perfection of Wisdom* by Nagarjuna and in other Buddhist works, but differ slightly according to the source. They include such incidents as an assassination attempt by Devadatta, who pushed a boulder from a cliff hoping to crush Shakyamuni but succeeded only in injuring the latter's toe; and a group of Brahmans instigating a beautiful woman named Sundari to spread scandalous rumors about Shakyamuni in order to besmirch his reputation.

10. Bodhisattva Never Disparaging: A bodhisattva described in "Never Disparaging," the 20th chapter of the Lotus Sutra. This bodhisattva—Shakyamuni in a previous lifetime—would bow to everyone he met and say: "I have profound reverence for you, I would never dare treat you with disparagement or arrogance. Why? Because you will all practice the bodhisattva way and will then be able to attain Buddhahood"

(LSOC, 308). However, he was attacked by arrogant people, who beat him with sticks and staves and threw stones at him. The sutra explains his practice of respect for others became the cause for Bodhisattva Never Disparaging to attain Buddhahood.

11. Maudgalyayana: One of Shakyamuni ten major disciples, known as foremost in transcendental powers. Maudgalyayana died before Shakyamuni, killed by a hostile Brahman while begging for alms in Rajagriha.

12. Aryadeva (n.d.): Also known as Bodhisattva Aryadeva. A scholar of the Madhyamika school in southern India during the third century and the successor of Nagarjuna. After he defeated non-Buddhist teachers in a religious debate, he was killed by one of their disciples. According to one biography, Aryadeva displayed compassion even during his last moments, telling his assailant about the Buddhist teaching in order to lead him to enlightenment.

13. Aryasimha (n.d.): Also known as the Venerable Aryasimha. The last of Shakyamuni Buddha's twenty-three or twenty-four successors, who lived in central India during the sixth century. When Aryasimha was propagating Buddhism in Kashmir, he was among the monks executed by King Mirakutsu, who was hostile to Buddhism. Legend has it that when he was decapitated milk flowed forth instead of blood—symbolic of his selfless devotion to the pure Law.

14. Garudas are gigantic birds in Indian mythology that are said to feed on dragons. Anavatapta, or Heat-Free Lake, located north of the Snow Mountains, contains cool, clear water that removes all sufferings. The lake is said to be inhabited by a dragon king of the same name.

15. In another letter, Nichiren writes: "When an asura demon tried to shoot at the god Shakra, his arrow rebounded and pierced him in the eye. And when the garuda birds attempted to attack the dragon king Anavatapta, flames erupted from their own bodies and consumed them" ("Rebuking Slander of the Law," WND-1, 442).

16. From T'ien-t'ai's *The Profound Meaning of the Lotus Sutra.*

17. LSOC, 312.

18. The Lotus Sutra states: "[When I, Shakyamuni, as Bodhisattva Never Disparaging in a past life, attained supreme enlightenment,] the four kinds of believers, the monks, nuns, laymen, and laywomen, because anger arose in their minds and they treated me with disparagement and contempt, were for two hundred million kalpas never able to encounter a Buddha, to hear the Law, or to see the community of monks. For a thousand kalpas they underwent great suffering in the Avichi hell [the hell of incessant suffering]. After they had finished paying for their offenses, they once more encountered the bodhisattva Never Disparaging, who instructed them in supreme perfect enlightenment" (LSOC, 310–11).

19. This passage means that Bodhisattva Never Disparaging expiated his past offense of slandering the Law by being subjected to persecutions on account of the Law. When his offenses were wiped out and his life was drawing to a close, he could then hear the Lotus Sutra. As a result, his six sense organs were purified and his life span extended. He also widely preached the Lotus Sutra for others, and ultimately attained Buddhahood.

20. Inconspicuous punishment is karmic retribution not immediately recognizable or

visibly manifested. This is in contrast to conspicuous punishment, which is retribution in a clearly recognizable form.

21. This was a common concept found in such sutras as the Golden Light Sutra, the Great Collection Sutra, the Benevolent Kings Sutra and the Medicine Master Sutra. In "The Rationale for Writing 'On Establishing the Correct Teaching for the Peace of the Land,'" the Daishonin also asserts: "As a result [of people's pervasive slander of the Law], the Sun Goddess, Great Bodhisattva Hachiman, and the gods of the seven shrines of Sanno, who guard and protect Mount Hiei, as well as the other great benevolent deities who protect the different parts of the nation, could no longer taste the flavor of the Law. Their power and brilliance waned, and they abandoned the country. Thus the demons gained access to the nation and brought about disasters and calamities" (WND-1, 163).

22. Flavor of the Law: Refers to the exquisite flavor of the correct teaching. It is said to be the only source of nourishment for the protective forces of the universe—the various Buddhas, bodhisattvas and heavenly deities throughout the ten directions—increasing their majesty and strength. Likened to ghee (the finest clarified butter), the highest of the five flavors, the Lotus Sutra is regarded as the supreme flavor of the Law. In the Latter Day, the sole flavor of the Law that can strengthen the protective forces is Nam-myoho-renge-kyo of Nichiren Buddhism of sowing.

Chapter 13:

1. This story appears in *The Treatise on the Great Perfection of Wisdom* and elsewhere.

In a past existence, Shariputra was practicing bodhisattva austerities, engaged in the offering of alms. When he had practiced almsgiving for sixty kalpas, a Brahman came to him and begged for his eye. Shariputra gouged out one of his own eyes and gave it to him, but the Brahman was so revolted by its smell that he spat on it, threw it on the ground and trampled on it. Seeing this, Shariputra thought it too difficult to lead such persons to salvation and decided to seek only his own liberation from the sufferings of birth and death; he withdrew from bodhisattva practice, backsliding into the Hinayana teachings, or the way of voice-hearers.

2. The two groups respectively refer to people who initially heard and embraced but failed to continue to practice the teaching of the Lotus Sutra taught by (1) Shakyamuni who attained enlightenment in the incalculably distant past of numberless major world system dust particle kalpas ago and (2) Shakyamuni in his existence as the sixteenth son of the Buddha Great Universal Wisdom Excellence at a time major world system dust particle kalpas ago. (Buddha Great Universal Wisdom Excellence is described in the "Parable of the Phantom City" chapter of the Lotus Sutra.) The two groups in turn respectively fell into the hell of incessant suffering for periods of numberless major world system dust particle kalpas and major world system dust particle kalpas. "The Opening of the Eyes" attributes "evil companions" as the cause of their abandoning the way.

3. This world, which is full of suffering. Often translated as the world of endurance. *Saha* means the earth; it derives from a root meaning "to bear" or "to endure." For this reason, in the Chinese versions of Buddhist

scriptures, *saha* is rendered as endurance. In this context, the saha world indicates a world in which people must endure suffering. In some Buddhist scriptures, including the Lotus and Vimalakirti sutras, it is held that the saha world, this world full of distress and suffering, is in itself a pure land, the Land of Eternally Tranquil Light. In "Life Span," the 16th chapter of the Lotus Sutra, Shakyamuni states, "Ever since then I have been constantly in this saha world, preaching the Law, teaching and converting," indicating that the place where the Buddha dwells, the Buddha land, is in fact the saha world.

4. Also, Avichi hell. The eighth and most horrible of the eight hot hells. It is so called because its inhabitants are said to suffer without a moment's respite. The hell of incessant suffering is situated at the lowest level of the world of desire. Those who commit even one of the five cardinal sins or slander the correct teaching are said to fall into this hell.

5. The four major persecutions: (1) the Matsubagayatsu Persecution of 1260; (2) the Izu Exile of 1261; (3) the Komatsubara Persecution of 1264; and (4) the Tatsunokuchi Persecution and subsequent Sado Exile of 1271.

6. According to a commentary on "The Opening of the Eyes" by Nichikan, the twenty-sixth high priest of the Nikko lineage, the "pillar, eyes and great ship of Japan" can be interpreted as referring to the virtue of the teacher alone or to all three virtues—sovereign, teacher and parent. When the latter interpretation is applied, the "pillar" refers to the virtue of the sovereign, the "eyes" to the virtue of the teacher and the "great ship" to the virtue of the parent.

7. Also, devil king or heavenly devil. The king of devils, who dwells in the highest or the sixth heaven of the world of desire. He is also named Freely Enjoying Things Conjured by Others, the king who makes free use of the fruits of others' efforts for his own pleasure. Served by innumerable minions, he obstructs Buddhist practice and delights in sapping the life force of other beings. One of the four devils.

Chapter 14:

1. In "The Opening of the Eyes," Nichiren cites the Nirvana Sutra, which describes a poor woman and her profound concern for her child: "She thinks of nothing but her child, which is similar to Buddhist compassion. That must be why, although she created no other causes to bring it about, she was reborn in the Brahma heaven" (WND-1, 283). Nichiren also writes, "Although I and my disciples may encounter various difficulties, if we do not harbor doubts in our hearts, we will as a matter of course attain Buddhahood" (WND-1, 283). In this way, he indicates that those who selflessly practice the Lotus Sutra can attain Buddhahood without fail.

2. Health and illness here refers to the ten objects of meditation formulated by the Great Teacher T'ien-t'ai of China in his *Great Concentration and Insight*. Through meditations on these ten objects, one aims to realize the limitations of the lower nine worlds.

3. Parinirvana Sutra: Also known as the Mahaparinirvana Sutra. A Chinese version of the Nirvana Sutra in six volumes, translated by Fa-hsien and Buddhabhadra around 417.

4. These are also known as the "eight kinds of sufferings."

5. There are two levels to the principle of causality. The first is that of simple karmic retribution—receiving reward or punishment in accord with one's actions. This way of thinking teaches that making good causes leads to happiness, joy and ease, while making bad causes leads to suffering, pain and misery. The second level goes beyond this former idea to reveal a still more fundamental principle of causality governing all life. Buddhism teaches that when we reveal the supreme world of Buddhahood inherent in our lives, we actualize the highest good and can thereby instantly establish a state of unshakable happiness. In other words, it is possible for us—as living beings of the nine worlds, bound by the causality of the three paths (earthly desires, karma and suffering)—to bring forth the effect or fruit of enlightenment by revealing our innate Buddhahood or Buddha nature.

    This deeper level of causality taught in Buddhism differs from ordinary temporal cause and effect, or "general causality." At work here is the principle of the "simultaneity of cause and effect," which teaches that through a change in the depths of our own hearts or minds, we can bring forth our inherent Buddhahood, right here and now.

6. A letter Nichiren addressed to three followers, Ota Saemon-no-jo, the lay priest Soya Kyoshin and Dharma Bridge Kimbara in Shimosa Province (present-day Chiba Prefecture) from Echi (present-day Atsugi City, Kanagawa Prefecture) on October 5, 1271, immediately after the Tatsunokuchi Persecution.

7. Refers to bodhisattvas who, though qualified to receive the pure rewards of Buddhist practice, relinquish them and make a vow to be reborn in an impure world in order to save living beings. They spread the Mystic Law, while undergoing the same sufferings as those born in the evil world due to karma. This term derives from Miao-lo's interpretation of relevant passages from "The Teacher of the Law," the 10th chapter of the Lotus Sutra.

Chapter 15:

1. "Expedient Means," the 2nd chapter of the Lotus Sutra, states: "The Buddhas, the World-Honored Ones, wish to open the door of Buddha wisdom to all living beings, to allow them to attain purity. That is why they appear in the world. They wish to show the Buddha wisdom to living beings, and therefore they appear in the world. They wish to cause living beings to awaken to the Buddha wisdom, and therefore they appear in the world. They wish to induce living beings to enter the path of Buddha wisdom, and therefore they appear in the world. Shariputra, this is the one great reason for which the Buddhas appear in the world" (LSOC, 64).

2. Soka Kyoiku Gakkai (Value-Creating Education Society): An association founded by Tsunesaburo Makiguchi and Josei Toda in 1930 for educators sympathetic to Mr. Makiguchi's theories of value-creating education. It gradually developed into an organization dedicated to promoting the practice and spread of Nichiren Buddhism. During World War II, the Japanese militarist authorities cracked down on the organization as part of efforts to strengthen their ideological control over the population. Twenty-one leaders of the Soka Kyoiku Gakkai, including Mr. Makiguchi

and Mr. Toda, were arrested in 1943. While the others all eventually bowed to the government's demands, Mr. Makiguchi and Mr. Toda refused to compromise their beliefs. Mr. Makiguchi died in prison in November 1944. Mr. Toda was released in July 1945, and dedicated the rest of his life to reconstructing the organization, which he renamed the Soka Gakkai (Value Creation Society).

3. Gaining Buddhahood without seeking it: This comes from a passage in the "Belief and Understanding," the 4th chapter of the Lotus Sutra. The chapter describes how Mahakashyapa and the other great voice-hearers, after hearing Shakyamuni expound the replacement of the three vehicles with the one vehicle, understand that they can in fact attain Buddhahood, even though they had previously been deemed incapable of doing so. Joyfully they exclaim, "This cluster of unsurpassed jewels / has come to us unsought" (LSOC, 124).

4. "Belief means to be without doubt": This is a passage from T'ien-t'ai's *The Words and Phrases of the Lotus Sutra*. Describing the mind of someone at the first stage of faith—that is, the stage of believing in and understanding the Lotus Sutra even for a moment—it says: "Belief means to be without doubt. Clear comprehension is called understanding."

5. Nirvana Sutra: Any of the sutras either recording the teachings that Shakyamuni Buddha expounded immediately before his death or describing the events surrounding his death, or entry into nirvana. There are both Mahayana and Hinayana Nirvana sutras in Chinese translation. The parable of the poor woman that the Daishonin cites in "The Opening of the Eyes" is found in the Mahayana text, the Mahaparinirvana Sutra.

6. Brahma heaven: Buddhist texts describe the existence of many different heavens, into which people were thought to be reborn depending on the good fortune they had created. The Brahma heaven is the first and lowest of the four meditation heavens in the world of form above Mount Sumeru.

7. In *The Record of the Orally Transmitted Teachings*, the Daishonin states: "If in a single moment of life we exhaust the pains and trials of millions of kalpas, then instant after instant there will arise in us the three Buddha bodies with which we are eternally endowed. Nam-myoho-renge-kyo is just such a 'diligent' practice" (OTT, 214). The three bodies of the Buddha refer to the Dharma body, the reward body and the manifested body. The Dharma body is the fundamental truth, or Law, to which a Buddha is enlightened. The reward body is the wisdom to perceive the Law. And the manifested body is the compassionate actions the Buddha carries out to lead people to happiness.

8. Yellow stones: This means either literally yellow-colored stones, or it may refer to calcite. In either case, it indicates something of lesser value than gold or precious gems.

9. Reducing the body to ashes and annihilating consciousness: A reference to the Hinayana doctrine asserting that one can attain nirvana, escaping from the sufferings of endless cycle of birth and death, only upon extinguishing his or her body and mind, which are deemed to be the sources of earthly desires, illusions and sufferings.

Chapter 16:

1. Seed of Buddhahood of three thousand realms in a single moment of life: The

Mystic Law of three thousand realms in a single moment of life, which is revealed in the Lotus Sutra, is the fundamental cause for all people to attain Buddhahood. It is, therefore, called the seed of Buddhahood.

2. Object of devotion of sowing: Enabling people to believe in and embrace the Mystic Law, which is the fundamental cause for attaining Buddhahood, is metaphorically referred to as "planting the seed." It is, therefore, called the benefit of sowing. Because the Gohonzon, or object of devotion, that Nichiren Daishonin revealed actualizes this benefit, it is called "the object of devotion of sowing."

3. *The Outstanding Principles of the Lotus Sutra.*

4. The realm [world] of *asuras*. The fourth of the Ten Worlds. Also called the world of animosity or the world of anger. In Indian mythology, asuras are arrogant and belligerent demons. This condition is called the world of animosity because it is characterized by persistent, though not necessarily overt, aggressiveness. "The Object of Devotion for Observing the Mind" states, "Perversity is the world of asuras" (WND-1, 358).

5. "Peaceful Practices" chapter of the Lotus Sutra: In this chapter, Shakyamuni expounds four rules or peaceful practices to be observed by his followers in spreading the correct teaching in the evil age after his passing. The Great Teacher T'ien-t'ai of China summarized the chapter's lengthy descriptions into the four peaceful practices of action, word, thought and vow.

6. Nirvana: A Sanskrit term indicating a state of peace and tranquillity in which all illusions and desires are extinguished.

7. *Shoju*: A method of expounding Buddhism in which one gradually leads people to the correct teaching according to their capacity and without refuting their attachment to mistaken views.

8. Evil people without wisdom: This means people who are ignorant of Buddhism because they have never encountered it before, and who consequently commit evil acts without realizing it. They do not actively oppose or slander the correct teaching.

9. People of perverse views who slander the Law: This indicates people who, though aware of the correct teaching, are driven by illusions and desires and as a result cling to erroneous teachings. They try to justify and spread these teachings, while slandering and attacking what is correct.

10. The "twenty-four-character Lotus Sutra" refers to the sutra passage in which Bodhisattva Never Disparaging says: "I have profound reverence for you, I would never dare treat you with disparagement or arrogance. Why? Because you will all practice the bodhisattva way and will then be able to attain Buddhahood" (LSOC, 308). It is known as the twenty-four-character Lotus Sutra, because it is composed of twenty-four Chinese characters in the Kumarajiva translation.

11. True teaching refers to the Lotus Sutra, which explains the truth to which the Buddha became enlightened, and provisional teachings are those that Shakyamuni expounded as expedient means to help people understand the true teaching.

12. Unification of the teachings: Refers to the unification of the provisional or expedient teachings within the highest teaching, the Lotus Sutra. When unified in this way, all the pre-Lotus Sutra teachings are put in their proper place and gain their true significance.

13. The Nirvana Sutra states: "The Buddha replied: 'Kashyapa, it is because I was a defender of the correct teaching that I have been able to attain this diamond-like body. Kashyapa, because [in the past] I devoted myself to the correct teaching, I have been able to achieve this diamond-like body that abides forever and is never destroyed" (WND-1, 285).

Chapter 17:

1. Loving-kindness: (Skt *karuna*) Altruistic action that seeks to relieve living beings from their sufferings and give ease and delight to them. A Buddha is revered as one who shares in the torments of all living beings and strives to release all beings from suffering and bring them happiness.

2. *The Group of Discourses (Sutta-nipata)*, translated by K. R. Norman (Oxford: The Pali Text Society, 1995), vol. 2, p. 16. Bracketed portions of the text are based on the Japanese translation: *Budda no Kotoba—Suttanipata* (Words of the Buddha—Sutta-nipata), translated by Hajime Nakamura (Tokyo: Iwanami Shoten, 1994), p. 37.

3. Ibid., 17. See *Budda no Kotoba—Sutta-nipata*, 37.

4. Nichiren writes: "All the Buddhas and bodhisattvas are our compassionate fathers and mothers. And you should understand that the greatest expression of compassion with which they teach and convert living beings is to be found in the Lotus Sutra alone" ("On Reciting the Daimoku of the Lotus Sutra," WND-2, 223).

5. The Buddha who actually attained enlightenment in the remote past: "Life Span," the 16th chapter of the Lotus Sutra, explains that Shakyamuni is the eternal Buddha, having originally attained the Way at a time in the infinite past known as "numberless major world system dust particle kalpas" (see LSOC, 265–73).

6. *Jigage* verse section: This refers to the verse section of the "Life Span" chapter of the Lotus Sutra, which is recited in the second part of *gongyo*, or the SGI liturgy. It begins with the line, *Ji ga toku burrai* (Since I attained Buddhahood), and ends with the passage, *Mai ji sa ze nen, i ga ryo shujo, toku nyu mujo do, soku joju busshin* (At all times I think to myself: / How can I cause living beings / to gain entry into the unsurpassed way / and quickly acquire the body of a Buddha?) (LSOC, 273).

7. Westward transmission of Buddhism: Nichiren predicted that his Buddhism of the sun would flow from Japan toward the west, returning to the countries through which Buddhism had originally been transmitted and spreading throughout the entire world. In "On the Buddha's Prophecy," he writes: "The moon appears in the west and sheds its light eastward, but the sun rises in the east and casts its rays to the west. The same is true of Buddhism. It spread from west to east in the Former and Middle Days of the Law, but will travel from east to west in the Latter Day" (WND-1, 401).

8. Translated from Japanese. Josei Toda, *Toda Josei zenshu* (Collected Writings of Josei Toda) (Tokyo: Seikyo Shimbunsha, 1983), vol. 3, pp. 47–48.

9. People of perverse views who slander the Law: This indicates people who, though they are aware of the correct teaching, are driven by illusions and desires and as a result cling to erroneous teachings. They try to justify and spread these teachings,

while slandering and attacking the correct teaching.

10. Tendai school: The Japanese counterpart of the Chinese T'ien-t'ai (Jpn Tendai) school, founded in the early ninth century by Dengyo, also known as Saicho. However, because of a tolerant attitude toward the erroneous teachings of other schools, including the True Word, Pure Land and Zen, by the time of Nichiren Daishonin, it had lost the stance of strictly basing itself on the Lotus Sutra.

Chapter 18:

1. Translated from Japanese. Tsunesaburo Makiguchi, *Makiguchi Tsunesaburo zenshu* (Complete Writings of Tsunesaburo Makiguchi) (Tokyo: Daisanbunmei-sha, 1984), vol. 8, p. 45.

2. Daisaku Ikeda, *The Human Revolution*, abridged edition in two volumes (Santa Monica, CA: World Tribune Press, 2004), vol. 1, p. viii.

3. Aurélio Peccei and Daisaku Ikeda, *Before It Is Too Late*, ed. Richard L. Gage (Tokyo: Kodansha International, 1984), pp. 121–22.

Chapter 19:

1. Translated from Japanese. Josei Toda, *Toda Josei zenshu* (Collected Writings of Josei Toda) (Tokyo: Seikyo Shimbunsha, 1983), vol. 3, pp. 240–41.

2. The three bodies of the Buddha refer to the Dharma body, the reward body and the manifested body. The Dharma body is the fundamental truth, or Law, to which a Buddha is enlightened. The reward body is the wisdom to perceive the Law. And the manifested body is the compassionate actions the Buddha carries out to lead people to happiness.

3. Kumarajiva (344–413): A Buddhist scholar and translator of Buddhist scriptures into Chinese. He studied Buddhism from a young age, and later actively spread the Mahayana teachings. In 401, at the invitation of Yao Hsing, ruler of the Later Ch'in dynasty of ancient China, Kumarajiva made his way to the capital Ch'ang-an, where he immersed himself in the translation of Buddhist scriptures. His prodigious body of translated works includes the Lotus Sutra.

4. Bodhisattva Medicine King: A bodhisattva appearing in the Lotus Sutra. In a previous lifetime as a bodhisattva named Gladly Seen by All Living Beings, he burned his arms as an offering to the Buddha.

5. Prince Jogu (574–622): Also called Prince Shotoku. The second son of Japan's thirty-first emperor, Yomei and the regent under the Empress Suiko. He had devout faith in Buddhism and contributed to its establishment in Japan. According to legend, he peeled off the skin of his arms to copy down a portion of the Lotus Sutra.

6. According to one source, this is thought to refer to Shakyamuni in a previous lifetime as a wheel-turning king who sold his flesh to make an offering of light.

7. Aspiration for the Law: The name of Shakyamuni in a past existence when he practiced bodhisattva austerities. A devil disguised as a Brahman appeared to him and said that he would teach him one verse of a Buddhist teaching if he was ready to transcribe it using his skin as paper, one of his bones as a pen and his blood as ink. So great was his seeking mind for Buddhism that he gladly complied.

Index